The Complete

Plant–Based

Cookbook

For Beginners

1500 Days Easy , Delicious and Nutritious Plant-Based Recipes for a More Sustainable and Healthier Lifestyle Incl. 30-Day Meal Plan

Patrick F. Lemieux

Table of Contents

INTRODUCTION

Welcome to the world of plant-based eating! In recent years, there has been a growing interest in plant-based diets as people around the globe are recognizing the numerous benefits of incorporating more plants into their meals. Plant-based diets have a rich history and have evolved over time, with roots in various cultures and traditions. Today, they are gaining popularity for their potential health benefits, sustainability, and ethical considerations.

The history and development of plant-based diets can be traced back to ancient civilizations, where plant-based foods were prominently featured in traditional cuisines. In more recent times, plant-based diets have gained attention as a response to health concerns, environmental issues, and animal welfare. With advancements in nutrition science, we now have a better understanding of the potential benefits of plant-based diets, including reduced risk of chronic diseases such as heart disease, diabetes, and certain types of cancers, improved digestion, increased energy levels, and better weight management.

Embracing a plant-based diet is not only about what you exclude from your meals, but also about the abundance of nutritious foods you can include. A well-planned plant-based diet can provide all the essential nutrients your body needs, including protein, healthy fats, fiber, vitamins, and minerals. However, it's important to pay attention to key aspects to ensure a nutritionally balanced and healthy plant-based diet.

Plant-Based Diet: More Than a Healthy Way to Eat

A plant-based diet is a way of eating that focuses primarily on plant-derived foods and minimizes or eliminates animal-derived foods. It's important to note that a well-planned plant-based diet should ensure adequate intake of all essential nutrients, including protein, vitamin B12, iron, calcium, omega-3 fatty acids, and others, through a balanced and diverse selection of plant-based foods or supplements as needed. Consulting with a healthcare professional or a registered dietitian can help ensure that a plant-based diet is nutritionally adequate and meets individual dietary needs. Here are some of the benefits it offers:

▶ **Improved Health:** Plant-based diets can be rich in essential nutrients, such as fiber, vitamins, minerals, and antioxidants, which are important for overall health and well-being. Plant-based diets have been associated with a reduced risk of chronic diseases, including heart disease, type 2 diabetes, certain cancers, and obesity. They can also support weight management, lower cholesterol and blood pressure, and improve digestive health.

▶ **Increased Fiber Intake:** Plant-based diets tend to be high in dietary fiber, which is important for digestive health, weight management, and disease prevention. Fiber can help regulate bowel movements, lower cholesterol levels, and promote satiety, helping to control appetite and manage weight.

▶ **Higher Antioxidant Intake:** Plant-based diets are typically rich in antioxidants, which are compounds that help neutralize harmful molecules called free radicals and protect against cellular damage. Antioxidants have been associated with a reduced risk of chronic diseases, including cancer, heart disease, and neurodegenerative diseases.

▶ **Environmental Sustainability:** Plant-based diets have a lower environmental impact compared to animal-based diets. Animal agriculture is associated with deforestation, greenhouse gas emissions, water usage, and pollution, while plant-based agriculture generally requires fewer resources and has a lower carbon footprint. Choosing a plant-based diet can contribute to reducing environmental degradation and promoting sustainability.

▶ **Animal Welfare:** Many people choose a plant-based diet due to ethical concerns about the treatment of animals in food production. By choosing plant-based foods, individuals can reduce their support for the use of animals in food production and promote more compassionate and ethical food choices.

▶ **Diversity and Creativity in Cooking:** Plant-based diets offer a wide variety of plant-derived foods, such as fruits, vegetables, whole grains, legumes, nuts, seeds, and plant-based protein sources, which can promote culinary creativity and diversity in cooking. Experimenting with plant-based recipes can lead to the discovery of new flavors, textures, and cuisines, and can be a fun and enjoyable way to expand culinary horizons.

▶ **Long-term Sustainability:** Plant-based diets can be sustainable in the long term as they are generally based on whole, minimally processed foods that are widely available, affordable, and can be grown and produced in a sustainable manner. This makes plant-based diets a viable option for long-term healthy eating and sustainable food choices.

Key Aspects to Maintain a Healthy Plant Diet

When adopting a plant-based diet, it's important to pay attention to a few key aspects to ensure that the diet is nutritionally balanced and meets your dietary needs. Here are some tips for a healthy plant-based diet:

▶ **Variety of Foods:** Aim for a diverse selection of plant-based foods to ensure you're getting a wide range of nutrients. Include a variety of fruits, vegetables, whole grains, legumes, nuts, seeds, and plant-based protein sources in your meals and snacks.

▶ **Protein Sources:** Pay attention to protein sources in your plant-based diet. Include a variety of plant-based protein sources such as beans, lentils, chickpeas, tofu, tempeh, seitan, nuts, seeds, and whole grains. Combining different protein sources can help ensure that you're getting all the essential amino acids your body needs.

▶ **Essential Nutrients:** Make sure you're getting enough essential nutrients, such as vitamin B12, iron, calcium, omega-3 fatty acids, and vitamin D, which can be more challenging to obtain in a plant-based diet. Consider incorporating fortified foods or supplements as needed and consult with a healthcare professional or a registered dietitian for personalized guidance.

▶ **Balanced Meals:** Create balanced meals that include a variety of food groups to ensure you're getting a good mix of nutrients. Aim for meals that include carbohydrates (from whole grains, fruits, and vegetables), protein (from plant-based sources), healthy fats (from nuts, seeds, avocados, and plant oils), and a good amount of fiber.

▶ **Minimize Processed Foods:** While there are many plant-based processed foods available in the market, it's important to prioritize whole, minimally processed foods as the foundation of your plant-based diet. Processed foods can be high in added sugars, unhealthy fats, and sodium, and may be low in essential nutrients. Focus on whole foods in their natural state as much as possible.

▶ **Mindful Eating:** Pay attention to your hunger cues and practice mindful eating. Listen to your body and eat when you're hungry, paying attention to portion sizes and eating slowly. Mindful eating can help you develop a healthy relationship with food and prevent overeating.

▶ **Food Safety:** Just like with any other diet, practice food safety measures when preparing and storing plant-based foods. Wash fruits and vegetables thoroughly, handle and store foods properly to prevent contamination, and follow food safety guidelines to ensure food safety.

▶ **Sustainability:** Consider the sustainability aspect of your plant-based diet by choosing locally sourced, organic, and seasonal plant-based foods when possible. This can help reduce the environmental impact of your food choices and support sustainable food production practices.

▶ **Personalization:** Remember that a plant-based diet can be personalized to meet individual needs and preferences. It's important to find what works best for you and your body, and consider any specific dietary restrictions or health conditions you may have.

Get Ready to Dive In!

In this cookbook, we will guide you on your plant-based journey by providing delicious and nourishing recipes that celebrate the goodness of plants. We will cover a wide range of plant-based foods, including fruits, vegetables, whole grains, legumes, nuts, seeds, and plant-based protein sources, and show you how to create satisfying and flavorful meals that are packed with nutrients.

We will also share tips and strategies to help you make the most of your plant-based diet, including ways to obtain essential nutrients, create balanced meals, minimize processed foods, practice mindful

eating, consider sustainability, and personalize your plant-based diet to suit your individual needs and preferences. Our goal is to inspire you to explore the world of plant-based cooking, experiment with new flavors and ingredients, and experience the many benefits that a plant-based diet can offer.

So, let's embark on this exciting plant-based culinary adventure together and discover the joys of nourishing your body and soul with wholesome, plant-powered meals!

30 Days Plant-Based Diet Meal Plan

DAYS	BREAKFAST	LUNCH	DINNER	SNACK/DESSERT
1	Southwestern-Style Breakfast Burritos	Pineapple Chutney	Sweet Potato, Kale, and Red Cabbage Salad	Poached Pears
2	Toasty French Toast Bake	Chickpea Pâté	Israeli Quinoa Salad	Mango-Peach Sorbet
3	Blueberry Banana Muffins	Southwest Stuffed Peppers	Chickpea and Avocado Salad	Cherry Chocolate Bark
4	Eggplant Bacon	Plant-Based Fish Sauce	Succotash Salad	Chocolate Tahini Muffins
5	Mango Choco Protein Pudding	Fried Rice with Tofu Scramble	Creamy Chickpea and Avocado Salad	Pear Chia Pudding
6	Sunshine Muffins	Black and White Bean Chili	Smoky Potato Salad over Greens	Stone Fruit Compote
7	Almond Explosion	Creamy Avocado-Lime Dressing	Classic French Vinaigrette	Chocolate's Best Friends Brownies
8	Peaches and Cream Overnight Oats	Red Lentil Dahl	Garden Salad with Sumac Vinaigrette	Stone Fruit Pecan Crumble
9	Avocado Toast with Tomato and Hemp Hearts	Cabbage and Millet Pilaf	Farro Salad with Italian Vinaigrette	Basic Vanilla Chia Pudding
10	Vanilla Coconut Coffee Creamer	Hemp Mylk	Orange, Fennel and White Bean Salad	Protein Chocolate Chip Cookies
11	Five-Ingredient Peanut Butter Bites	Kasha Varnishkes	Strawberry-Pistachio Salad	Two-Ingredient Peanut Butter Fudge
12	Tofu, Mushroom, and Spinach Scramble	Wild Rice, Cabbage and Chickpea Pilaf	Ancient Grains Salad	Molasses-Ginger Oat Cookie Balls
13	Crazy Quinoa Protein Muffins	Lemon-Thyme Dressing	Roasted Root Vegetable Salad Bowl	"Here Comes Autumn" Apple Crisp
14	Simple Tofu Scramble	Chickpea Caponata	Mango Lentil Salad	Stone Fruit Chia Pudding
15	Sunrise Smoothie Bowl	Chickpea Tortilla Fajita Stack	Thai-ish Cabbage Salad	Caramelized Banana with Yogurt and Toasted Coconut
16	Tofu Scramble	Herbed Millet Pizza Crust	Cabbage Salad and Peanut Butter Vinaigrette	Vanilla Corn Cake with Roasted Strawberries
17	Paradise Island Overnight Oatmeal	Barley and Sweet Potato Pilaf	Taco Tempeh Salad	Chocolate Dirt Yogurt Cup
18	Baked Flaxseed-Battered French Toast	Green Chile Rice with Black Beans	Quinoa, Corn and Black Bean Salad	Seasonal Fruit Crumble
19	Buckwheat Porridge	Tomato Sauce	Bulgur, Cucumber and Tomato Salad	Berry Chia Pudding
20	Banana-Date Shake with Oats	Tahini Green Beans	Detox Salad	Poppy's Carrot Cake
21	Grain-Free Chia Bircher Bowl	Spinach, Mushroom and Quinoa Pilaf	Fiery Couscous Salad	Two-Minute Turtles

DAYS	BREAKFAST	LUNCH	DINNER	SNACK/DESSERT
22	Cherry Pecan Granola Bars	Tahini Dressing	Zingy Melon and Mango Salad	Black Sesame–Ginger Quick Bread
23	Breakfast Tofu	Oil-Free Rice-and-Vegetable Stir-Fry	Crunchy Curry Salad	Salted Chocolate Truffles
24	Gluten-Free Blueberry Blender Pancakes	Barley Bowl with Cranberries and Walnuts	Green Mix Salad	Berry Compote
25	Peanut Butter Banana Breakfast Cookies	20-Minute Cashew Cheese Sauce	Tomato, Corn and Bean Salad	Coconut Chia Pudding
26	5-Minute Raw Granola	Lentil-Mushroom No-Meat Pasta	Winter Sunshine Salad	Apple Crisp
27	Homemade Granola Clusters	Chana Saag	Meyer Lemon Romanesco Glow Salad	Pumpkin Spice Bread
28	Maple, Apple, and Walnut Great Grains	Roasted Red Pepper Sauce	Bean and Corn Salad	Almond Anise Biscotti
29	Fresh and Juicy Fruit Salad	Red Curry "Fried" Rice	Lentil, Lemon and Mushroom Salad	Chocolate-Covered Strawberries
30	Sweet Potato and Apple Breakfast Bowl	Curried Chickpeas and Rice	Beet, Cabbage, and Black Bean Salad	Pecan Ranch Cheese Ball

Chapter 1   Breakfasts

Southwestern-Style Breakfast Burritos

Prep time: 10 minutes | Cook time: 2 to 3 hours | Serves 4 to 6

1 medium onion, diced
1 medium red bell pepper, diced
3 garlic cloves, minced
1 (10-ounce / 283-g) package frozen corn
1 (14-ounce / 397-g) can pinto beans, drained and rinsed
1 (14-ounce / 397-g) can no-salt-added diced tomatoes
2 handfuls chopped kale (about 2 heaping cups)
1 (14-ounce / 397-g) package extra-firm tofu
1 teaspoon ground turmeric
1 tablespoon chili powder
3 tablespoons nutritional yeast
Salt (optional)
Ground black pepper
6 to 8 (10-inch) whole-grain tortillas

1. Place the onion, bell pepper, and garlic in the slow cooker. Add the corn, beans, tomatoes, and kale. Crumble the tofu over the vegetables to look like scrambled eggs. Sprinkle the turmeric over the tofu and stir to coat, until the tofu is the color of scrambled eggs. Add the chili powder, nutritional yeast, salt (if using), and black pepper. Stir to combine. Cover and cook on High for 2 to 3 hours or on Low for 5 to 6 hours. 2. Using a slotted spoon to drain off excess liquid, scoop about ⅓ cup of burrito filling onto the center of each tortilla. Roll the bottom of the tortilla to cover the filling, fold one side over the filling, and continue rolling to close.
Per Serving:
calories: 632 | fat: 15g | protein: 32g | carbs: 98g | fiber: 18g

Toasty French Toast Bake

Prep time: 10 minutes | Cook time: 35 minutes | Serves 6

Virgin coconut oil, for greasing the pan (optional)
1½ cups unsweetened almond milk or coconut milk
¼ cup plus 1 tablespoon pure maple syrup, divided (optional)
2 teaspoons orange zest
3 tablespoons fresh orange juice
2 teaspoons pure vanilla extract
1 teaspoon ground cinnamon
2 tablespoons arrowroot powder
12 to 14 slices of stale, whole-grain bread
Serve:
Unsweetened coconut flakes
Sliced fresh fruit or whole berries
Pure maple syrup (optional)

1. Preheat the oven to 350ºF (180ºC). Lightly grease an 8-inch ovenproof dish with coconut oil, if using. 2. In a medium bowl, whisk together the almond milk, ¼ cup of maple syrup, orange zest, orange juice, vanilla, cinnamon, and arrowroot powder. Keep whisking until combined and there are no dry traces of arrowroot in the mix. 3. Arrange the bread slices in your dish. You can do two flat layers of bread or you can fan them out like a tian. You may have to cut your bread slices in half to accomplish this. Press the bread into the dish. 4. Pour about half the almond milk mixture over the bread. Push the bread down to absorb some of the liquid. Pour the remaining half of the almond milk mixture over the bread. Press down on the bread once more. Let the bread soak in the liquid for 10 minutes. 5. Slide the French toast bake into the oven, and bake until lightly browned on top and much of the liquid has been absorbed, about 30 minutes. Remove the bake from the oven and set the broiler to high. 6.Drizzle the 1 tablespoon of maple syrup over the top of the bake, and slide the dish back into the oven. Broil until the maple syrup caramelizes on the surface of the bread, about 30 seconds. Serve the French toast bake hot with coconut flakes, fruit, berries, and maple syrup.
Per Serving:
calories: 335 | fat: 17g | protein: 8g | carbs: 39g | fiber: 6g

Blueberry Banana Muffins

Prep time: 15 minutes | Cook time: 25 minutes | Makes 6 Muffins

1½ cups mashed ripe banana
⅓ cup canola oil, plus more for greasing (optional)
1 teaspoon baking powder
1 teaspoon baking soda
½ teaspoon salt (optional)
1½ cups whole wheat or all-purpose flour
1 cup fresh or frozen blueberries

1. Preheat the oven to 375ºF (190ºC), and lightly grease a muffin tin. 2. Place the mashed bananas in a large bowl. 3. Add the oil, baking powder, baking soda, salt (if desired), and flour, and gently mix together until well combined. 4. Fold the blueberries into the batter. 5. Spoon the batter into the muffin tin, filling each cup to the top. 6. Bake for 25 minutes or until the muffins are golden brown.
Per Serving: (1 muffin)
calories: 267 | fat: 14g | protein: 4g | carbs: 32g | fiber: 3g

Sunrise Smoothie Bowl

Prep time: 10 minutes | Cook time: 0 minutes | Serves 2

2 cups fresh spinach
½ cup water
1 orange, peeled and segmented
2 cups sliced peaches, preferably frozen
1 ripe banana, frozen
1 tablespoon fresh lemon juice
½ cup sliced strawberries
½ cup diced peaches
1 kiwifruit, diced
¼ cup raw cashews
4 fresh mint leaves, chopped

1. In a blender, purée the spinach, water, and orange until smooth. Add the sliced peaches and the banana and pulse a few times, then purée until the mixture is thick and smooth. You will need to stop the blender occasionally to scrape down the sides. Add a little extra water if needed. The texture should be thick and creamy like frozen yogurt. 2. Divide between 2 bowls and top each with half of the strawberries, diced peaches, kiwi, cashews, and mint. Serve immediately.
Per Serving:
calories: 307 | fat: 9g | protein: 7g | carbs: 56g | fiber: 9g

Sunshine Muffins

Prep time: 15 minutes | Cook time: 30 minutes | Makes 6 muffins

1 teaspoon coconut oil, for greasing muffin tins (optional)
2 tablespoons almond butter or sunflower seed butter
¼ cup nondairy milk
1 orange, peeled
1 carrot, coarsely chopped
2 tablespoons chopped dried apricots or other dried fruit
3 tablespoons molasses
2 tablespoons ground flaxseed
1 teaspoon apple cider vinegar
1 teaspoon pure vanilla extract
½ teaspoon ground cinnamon
½ teaspoon ground ginger (optional)
¼ teaspoon ground nutmeg (optional)
¼ teaspoon allspice (optional)
¾ cup rolled oats or whole-grain flour
1 teaspoon baking powder
½ teaspoon baking soda
Mix-Ins (optional):
½ cup rolled oats
2 tablespoons raisins or other chopped dried fruit
2 tablespoons sunflower seeds

1. Preheat the oven to 350°F (180°C). Prepare a 6-cup muffin tin by rubbing the insides of the cups with coconut oil (if using) or using silicone or paper muffin cups. 2. Purée the nut butter, milk, orange, carrot, apricots, molasses, flaxseed, vinegar, vanilla, cinnamon, ginger, nutmeg, and allspice in a food processor or blender until somewhat smooth. 3. Grind the oats in a clean coffee grinder until they're the consistency of flour (or use whole-grain flour). In a large bowl, mix the oats with the baking powder and baking soda. 4. Mix the wet ingredients into the dry ingredients until just combined. Fold in the mix-ins (if using). 5. Spoon about ¼ cup batter into each muffin cup and bake for 30 minutes, or until a toothpick inserted into the center comes out clean. The orange creates a very moist base, so the muffins may take longer than 30 minutes, depending on how heavy your muffin tin is.
Per Serving: (1 muffin)
calories: 226 | fat: 8g | protein: 7g | carbs: 34g | fiber: 6g

Baked Flaxseed-Battered French Toast

Prep time: 10 minutes | Cook time: 15 minutes | Serves 4

¼ cup ground flaxseeds
1½ cups unsweetened plant-based milk, divided
Olive oil cooking spray
1 tablespoon ground cinnamon
1 teaspoon vanilla extract
3 tablespoons maple syrup, plus more for serving (optional)
8 slices whole-grain bread

1. In a medium bowl, combine the flaxseeds and ½ cup of plant-based milk. Let the mixture stand for 10 minutes to give the flaxseeds time to absorb the liquid and thicken, which will give them an consistency. 2. Preheat the oven to 400°F (205°C). Spray a sheet pan with olive oil cooking spray. 3. Add the remaining 1 cup plant-based milk, the cinnamon, vanilla, and maple syrup (if using) to the flax mixture and mix until combined. Dip each slice of bread into the flax mixture, making sure to completely cover in the liquid. Let any excess drip back into the bowl and then put the slices on the sheet pan. 4. Bake for 10 minutes. Using a spatula, carefully flip the bread and bake for 5 minutes. Serve with maple syrup.
Per Serving:
calories: 272 | fat: 7g | protein: 11g | carbs: 42g | fiber: 7g

Almond Explosion

Prep time: 5 minutes | Cook time: 0 minutes | Serves 4

1½ cups unsweetened almond milk
½ cup dry oat meal
½ cup raisins
½ cup almonds
½ cup water
3 tablespoons peanut butter
3 scoops of vanilla flavor vegan protein powder
½ teaspoon cinnamon (optional)
2 ice cubes (optional)

1. Add all the required ingredients, including the optional cinnamon if desired, to a blender. Blend for 2 minutes. Transfer the shake to a large cup. Microwave the shake for a hot treat, or, add in the ice cubes and drink the shake with a straw.
Per Serving:
calories: 355 | fat: 15g | protein: 25g | carbs: 30g | fiber: 4g

Mango Choco Protein Pudding

Prep time: 5 minutes | Cook time: 0 minutes | Serves 2

2 cups fresh or frozen mango cubes
1 peeled banana
2 scoops soy protein isolate, chocolate flavor
¼ cup flaxseeds
3 cups water
Optional Toppings:
Blueberries
Cocoa powder
Kiwi slices

1. Add all the ingredients to a blender and blend until smooth. 2. Alternatively, blend the banana, soy isolate, 2 tablespoons of flaxseeds and the water first and divide half of the mixture between two glasses, bowls or Mason jars. 3. Scoop out the remaining banana mix into a glass or bowl and set it aside for now. 4. Blend the mango with the remaining flaxseeds. 5. Divide the mango purée between the two glasses, bowls or Mason jars, and top with the remaining banana mix. 6. Serve with the optional toppings and enjoy! 7. Store the pudding in an airtight container in the fridge, and consume within 2 days. Alternatively, store in the freezer for a maximum of 60 days and thaw at room temperature.
Per Serving:
calories: 343 | fat: 7g | protein: 31g | carbs: 39g | fiber: 8g

Banana-Date Shake with Oats

Prep time: 15 minutes | Cook time: 0 minutes | Serves 1

1 Medjool date
10 ounces (283 g) unsweetened vanilla almond milk
1 small banana (fresh or frozen)
2 tablespoons almond butter
¼ cup rolled oats, uncooked
3 ice cubes
Pinch ground cinnamon (optional)

1. Soak the date in hot water for 5 minutes to soften it. 2. Remove the date from the hot water, place it in a blender, and add the milk, banana, almond butter, oats, ice cubes, and cinnamon (if using). Blend until smooth. 3. Enjoy immediately.
Per Serving:
calories: 526 | fat: 22g | protein: 19g | carbs: 72g | fiber: 11g

Simple Tofu Scramble

Prep time: 5 minutes | Cook time: 15 minutes | Serves 2 to 4

2 tablespoons red miso paste
½ cup water
2 (14-ounce / 397-g) packages firm tofu, drained
2 tablespoons onion powder
2 tablespoons nutritional yeast
1 teaspoon dried parsley
½ teaspoon garlic powder
¼ teaspoon ground turmeric
¼ teaspoon freshly ground black pepper

1. In a sauté pan or skillet, dissolve the miso in the water. 2. Loosely crumble the tofu into the miso-water mixture. 3. Stir in the onion powder, nutritional yeast, parsley, garlic powder, turmeric, and pepper. Cook over medium heat, stirring occasionally, for 10 to 15 minutes, or until heated through and most of the liquid has been absorbed. Remove from the heat.
Per Serving:
calories: 84 | fat: 2g | protein: 7g | carbs: 9g | fiber: 0g

Avocado Toast with Tomato and Hemp Hearts

Prep time: 5 minutes | Cook time: 5 minutes | Serves 2

4 slices whole-wheat bread
1 avocado, peeled, pitted, cut into quarters, and thinly sliced
Pinch of salt (optional)
1 medium tomato, thinly sliced
Black pepper
Red pepper flakes
2 teaspoons extra-virgin olive oil (optional)
4 teaspoons hemp hearts

1. Toast the bread slices. 2. On each slice, arrange a quarter of the avocado slices, a pinch of salt (if using), a quarter of the tomato, a pinch of black pepper, and a pinch of red pepper flakes. Drizzle each with ½ teaspoon of olive oil and sprinkle with 1 teaspoon of hemp hearts.
Per Serving:
calories: 379 | fat: 22g | protein:12 g | carbs: 38g | fiber: 11g

Eggplant Bacon

Prep time: 10 minutes | Cook time: 35 minutes | Serves 4

1 large eggplant
1 tablespoon sea salt (optional)
1 tablespoon virgin olive oil (optional)
1 tablespoon pure maple syrup (optional)
1 tablespoon apple cider vinegar
1 teaspoon smoked paprika
½ teaspoon gluten-free tamari soy sauce
½ teaspoon mellow or light miso
Freshly ground black pepper, to taste

1. Preheat the oven to 400°F (205°C). Set a cooling rack on top of a parchment-lined baking sheet. 2. Cut off both ends of the eggplant. Then, with the cut bottom end flat on the cutting board, cut the eggplant down the middle. Lay each half, cut side down, on the board, and slice into ¼-inch strips. 3. In a large colander, layer the eggplant strips, sprinkling liberally with sea salt as you go. After you finish the layering, let the eggplant sit for 15 minutes. 4. Rinse the eggplant thoroughly. Towel-dry the pieces of eggplant, and arrange them on the rack-fitted baking sheet. 5. In a small bowl, whisk together the olive oil, maple syrup, if using, apple cider vinegar, smoked paprika, tamari, and miso. Brush half of this mixture onto the eggplant strips. Season the eggplant with black pepper. 6. Slide the baking sheet into the oven and roast for 20 minutes. Remove the eggplant and use tongs to carefully flip over all the strips. Brush the remaining half of the oil and maple syrup mixture onto the exposed side of the eggplant. Season the eggplant with black pepper once more. Roast the eggplant for another 15 minutes or until you start seeing some crisped edges. Serve eggplant bacon hot.
Per Serving:
calories: 81 | fat: 4g | protein: 2g | carbs: 12g | fiber: 5g

Peaches and Cream Overnight Oats

Prep time: 10 minutes | Cook time: 0 minutes | Serves 2

½ cup rolled oats
1 cup light unsweetened coconut milk
½ cup peaches, fresh or frozen, diced into 1-inch pieces
½ teaspoon vanilla extract
1 tablespoon maple syrup
(optional)
Pinch of salt (optional)
2 tablespoons slivered almonds, for serving
2 tablespoons plain plant-based yogurt, for serving

1. In a medium bowl, mix together the oats, coconut milk, peaches, vanilla, maple syrup, and salt (if using). Cover and refrigerate overnight. 2. To serve, top each serving with 1 tablespoon of slivered almonds and 1 tablespoon of plant-based yogurt.
Per Serving:
calories: 280 | fat: 17g | protein: 7g | carbs: 27g | fiber: 4g

Pan con Tomate

Prep time: 5 minutes | Cook time: 0 minutes | Makes 2 slices

2 large slices toast
1 garlic clove, halved
1 Roma tomato, halved
Salt (optional)
Nutritional yeast (optional)

1. Rub each slice of toast with a garlic clove half and half a Roma tomato. Sprinkle with salt and, if desired, nutritional yeast.
Per Serving: (1 slice)
calories: 90 | fat: 1g | protein: 3g | carbs: 17g | fiber: 2g

Almond and Protein Shake

Prep time: 5 minutes | Cook time: 0 minutes | Serves 2

1½ cups soy milk
3 tablespoons almonds
1 teaspoon maple syrup (optional)
1 tablespoon coconut oil (optional)
2 scoops of chocolate or vanilla flavor vegan protein powder
2 to 4 ice cubes
1 teaspoon cocoa powder (optional)

1. Add all the required ingredients, and if desired, the optional cocoa powder, to a blender. Blend for 2 minutes. Transfer the shake to a large cup or shaker. Serve and enjoy!
Per Serving:
calories: 340 | fat: 17g | protein: 32g | carbs: 15g | fiber: 2g

Vanilla Coconut Coffee Creamer

Prep time: 5 minutes | Cook time: 0 minutes | Makes 2 cups

6 Medjool dates, pitted
1 can (13½ ounces / 383 g) full-fat coconut milk
2 teaspoons pure vanilla extract
1 tablespoon coconut oil (optional)
Tiny pinch of fine sea salt (optional)

1. If your dates are very soft, proceed to the next step. If your dates are a little dry, place them in a small bowl and cover them in boiling water for 5 to 10 minutes. Thoroughly drain the dates. 2. In a blender, combine the pitted dates, coconut milk, vanilla, coconut oil, and sea salt, if using. Blend on high until you have a smooth and thick liquid with minimal chunks of date visible. 3. Over a medium bowl, strain the creamer with a fine-mesh strainer. Store the strained creamer in a jar with a tight-fitting lid. Keep the jar of creamer in the refrigerator. Shake to combine before using. The creamer will keep for roughly 1 week.

Per Serving:
calories: 297 | fat: 19g | protein: 1g | carbs: 32g | fiber: 5g

Five-Ingredient Peanut Butter Bites

Prep time: 5 minutes | Cook time: 20 minutes | Makes 10 bites

1 teaspoon canola oil, for greasing (optional)
½ cup raisins
1 cup hot water
2 ripe bananas
1 cup creamy or chunky peanut butter
⅔ cup old-fashioned rolled oats

1. Preheat the oven to 350°F (180°C), and lightly grease a muffin tin. 2. Put the raisins in the hot water for 2 minutes to soften, then drain the water. 3. In a food processor or high-powered blender, blend the softened raisins, bananas, peanut butter, and oats for 1 minute or until smooth. 4. Spoon the batter into the muffin tin, filling each cup halfway. 5. Bake for 18 to 20 minutes or until the bites are golden.

Per Serving: (1 bite)
calories: 196 | fat: 14g | protein: 8g | carbs: 14g | fiber: 4g

Tofu, Mushroom, and Spinach Scramble

Prep time: 10 minutes | Cook time: 20 minutes | Serves 4

1 tablespoon extra-virgin olive oil (optional)
1 (16-ounce / 454-g) package extra-firm tofu, drained and crumbled
½ teaspoon smoked paprika
½ teaspoon ground turmeric
8 ounces (227 g) white button
mushrooms, thinly sliced
2 medium tomatoes, cut into ½-inch dice
4 cups baby spinach
1 scallion, white and green parts, thinly sliced
1 tablespoon low-sodium soy sauce or gluten-free tamari

1. In a large sauté pan, heat the olive oil over medium heat. Add the tofu, smoked paprika, and turmeric and cook without stirring until the tofu is browned, about 5 minutes. 2. Stir the tofu and push it to one side of the pan. Add the mushrooms to the empty side and cook, stirring occasionally, for 5 minutes. Stir the tofu and mushrooms together. 3. Add the tomatoes and cook until they begin to release their juices, 2 to 3 minutes. Add the baby spinach, scallion, and soy sauce and cook, stirring well, until the spinach is wilted. Spoon into 4 bowls and serve. Refrigerate for up to 4 days.

Per Serving:
calories: 169 | fat: 10g | protein: 15g | carbs: 8g | fiber: 3g

Crazy Quinoa Protein Muffins

Prep time: 15 minutes | Cook time: 35 minutes | Serves 6

½ cup quinoa
2 tablespoons ground chia seeds
¼ cup almond flour
3 tablespoons vanilla protein powder
½ teaspoon salt (optional)
½ cup dates, chopped small
2 tablespoons coconut oil (optional)
3 tablespoons maple syrup (optional)
1 teaspoon vanilla extract
¼ cup unsweetened shredded coconut
½ cup raisins

1. Rinse the quinoa and place in a small saucepan with a lid. Cover with ½ cup water and bring to a boil over medium-high heat. Cover and turn down to low. Let cook for 20 minutes and then remove from the heat. Take off the lid and let cool. 2. Preheat the oven to 450°F (235°C). Line six muffin cups with paper liners. 3. Mix the ground chia seeds with ¼ cup plus 2 tablespoons water and set aside. 4. Add the almond flour, protein powder, and salt (if desired) to a small bowl. Mix well. Add the dates and mix to coat. Set aside. 5. Put the coconut oil (if desired) in a medium bowl. If it is not liquid already, put in the microwave and heat for 10 to 20 seconds or until melted. Remove from microwave and add the maple syrup, if desired. Stir well. When cool, add the chia seed mixture, vanilla extract, coconut, almond flour mixture, cooked quinoa, and raisins. Mix well. 6. Divide the batter between the six muffin cups and bake 12 to 15 minutes, until a toothpick inserted in the center comes out clean.

Per Serving: (1 muffin)
calories: 179 | fat: 6g | protein: 7g | carbs: 26g | fiber: 5g

Tofu Scramble

Prep time: 10 minutes | Cook time: 15 minutes | Serves 4

3 tablespoons water
½ cup diced green or red bell pepper
½ cup diced red, white, or yellow onion
1½ teaspoons minced garlic
1 (14-ounce / 397-g) block
extra-firm tofu, pressed
2 teaspoons turmeric
2 cups chopped fresh or frozen spinach or kale
Salt and pepper, to taste (optional)

1. In a large pan over medium heat, heat the water. Add the bell pepper, onion, and garlic, and sauté for 5 to 7 minutes or until the bell pepper and onion are tender. 2. Using your fingers, crumble the tofu into the pan. 3. Add the turmeric to the tofu and veggies and mix thoroughly. 4. Mix in the spinach (or kale). Cook for another 5 minutes, stirring occasionally. 5. Sprinkle with salt and pepper, if desired.

Per Serving:
calories: 146 | fat: 7g | protein: 14g | carbs: 11g | fiber: 3g

Paradise Island Overnight Oatmeal

Prep time: 5 minutes | Cook time: 0 minutes | Serves 2

2 cups rolled oats	chunks
2 cups plant-based milk	1 sliced banana
½ cup fresh or frozen mango, diced	1 tablespoon maple syrup (optional)
½ cup fresh or frozen pineapple	1 tablespoon chia seeds

1. In a large bowl, mix together the oats, milk, mango, pineapple, banana, maple syrup (if desired), and chia seeds. 2. Cover and refrigerate overnight or for a minimum of 4 hours before serving.

Per Serving:
calories: 510 | fat: 12g | protein: 14g | carbs: 93g | fiber: 15g

Grain-Free Chia Bircher Bowl

Prep time: 10 minutes | Cook time: 0 minutes | Makes 5 cups

½ cup raw pumpkin seeds, soaked overnight in 2 cups filtered water	soaked overnight in 2 cups filtered water
½ cup raw sunflower seeds, soaked overnight in 2 cups filtered water	3 cups filtered water
	2 tablespoons coconut flour
	1 tablespoon vanilla extract
¼ cup chia seeds	2 teaspoons ground cinnamon
¼ cup hemp seeds	Pinch of fine sea salt (optional)
2 tablespoons ground flaxseeds	½ cup unsweetened flaked dried coconut
½ cup whole raw almonds,	

1. Drain the pumpkin seeds and sunflower seeds in a strainer, rinse under cold water, and set the strainer over a bowl to drain thoroughly. 2. Combine the chia, hemp, and flaxseeds in a medium bowl; set aside. Drain and rinse the almonds and transfer them to an upright blender. Add the 3 cups water, coconut flour, vanilla, cinnamon, and salt, if using, and blend until completely smooth, then add the dried coconut and drained seeds and briefly blend or pulse until the seeds are roughly chopped. Pour into the chia mixture, stir well to combine, and set aside for 25 to 30 minutes, until thick and creamy. 3. The bowl can be eaten immediately, or stored in an airtight container in the fridge for up to 4 days. It will thicken further in the fridge.

Per Serving: (½ cup)
calories: 184 | fat: 15g | protein: 7g | carbs: 8g | fiber: 5g

Cherry Pecan Granola Bars

Prep time: 10 minutes | Cook time: 45 minutes | Makes 12 bars

2 cups rolled oats	1 cup fruit-sweetened dried cherries
½ cup dates, pitted and coarsely chopped	½ teaspoon ground cinnamon
½ cup orange juice	¼ teaspoon ground allspice
¼ cup chopped pecans	Pinch salt, or to taste (optional)

1. Preheat the oven to 325ºF (165ºC). 2. Spread the oats on a 13 × 18-inch baking sheet and bake for 10 minutes, or until they start to brown. Remove from the oven and place the oats in a large mixing bowl. 3. Combine the dates and orange juice in a small saucepan and cook over medium-low heat for about 15 minutes. Pour the mixture into a blender and process until smooth and creamy. 4. Add the date mixture to the bowl with the oats and add the pecans, dried cherries, cinnamon, allspice, and salt (if using). Mix well. 5. Press the mixture into a nonstick 8 × 8-inch baking pan and bake for 20 minutes, or until the top is lightly golden. Let cool before slicing into bars.

Per Serving: (1 bar)
calories: 92 | fat: 2g | protein: 3g | carbs: 20g | fiber: 3g

Breakfast Tofu

Prep time: 10 minutes | Cook time: 30 minutes | Makes 12 slices

2 (16-ounce / 454-g) packages sprouted or extra-firm tofu, drained	1 teaspoon ground cumin
	½ teaspoon garlic powder
	½ teaspoon ground turmeric
1 tablespoon reduced-sodium, gluten-free tamari	½ teaspoon yellow curry powder
¼ cup nutritional yeast	¼ teaspoon black pepper

1. Preheat the oven to 400ºF (205ºC). Line a baking sheet with parchment paper. 2. Slice each package of tofu into six pieces. Pat dry. Drizzle evenly with the tamari. 3. Combine the nutritional yeast, cumin, garlic powder, turmeric, curry powder, and black pepper in a large rectangular food storage container with a tight-fitting lid. Place the sliced tofu in the container and shake gently until all slices are covered. (You might need to open the container and rotate the slices a bit.) Let sit while the oven preheats. (The marinated tofu can be refrigerated for up to 1 day.) 4. Place tofu on the baking sheet. Spread any extra seasoning mix on top. Bake for 30 minutes, flipping halfway through. 5. Serve at room temperature or cold from the fridge.

Per Serving:
calories: 111 | fat: 6g | protein: 11g | carbs: 5g | fiber: 2g

Gluten-Free Blueberry Blender Pancakes

Prep time: 5 minutes | Cook time: 10 minutes | Serves 2

1 cup unsweetened plant-based milk	1 tablespoon baking powder
1 teaspoon apple cider vinegar	1 cup gluten-free flour
1 tablespoon extra-virgin olive oil (optional)	½ teaspoon salt (optional)
	1 tablespoon coconut oil (optional)
3 tablespoons maple syrup, plus more for serving (optional)	½ cup fresh or frozen blueberries
1 teaspoon vanilla extract	

1. In a blender, combine the plant-based milk and apple cider vinegar and let sit for 3 minutes to make a faux buttermilk. 2. Add the olive oil, maple syrup (if using), and vanilla to the "buttermilk" and blend until very smooth. 3. Add the baking powder, flour, and salt (if using) and pulse until just combined. Do not blend long. 4. In a griddle or a large skillet, melt the coconut oil over medium heat. When the griddle is hot, pour the pancake batter on the griddle to make 3-inch pancakes, leaving about 1 inch between them. Drop blueberries onto each pancake as they are cooking. Cook until the pancakes have bubbles in the middle, 3 to 5 minutes. Using a spatula, flip the pancakes and continue to cook until browned, another 3 to 5 minutes. Serve with maple syrup.

Per Serving:
calories: 565 | fat: 20g | protein: 16g | carbs: 87g | fiber: 9g

Peanut Butter Banana Breakfast Cookies

Prep time: 10 minutes | Cook time: 25 minutes | Serves 24

2 bananas, mashed
⅓ cup creamy peanut butter
⅔ cup unsweetened applesauce
¼ cup almond flour
2 tablespoons raw shelled

hempseed
1 teaspoon vanilla extract
1½ cups quick-cooking oats
½ cup pitted dates, chopped

1. Preheat the oven to 350ºF (180ºC). 2. Line a baking sheet with parchment paper and set aside. 3. Add the mashed banana and peanut butter to a large bowl and mix well. Add the applesauce, flour, hempseed, and vanilla. Mix well. Stir in the oatmeal and dates. 4. Drop cookie dough, 1 heaping tablespoon at a time and 2 inches apart, onto the prepared baking sheet. Flatten with the back of a fork. Bake cookies for 25 minutes. 5. Remove from the oven and let the cookies cool 5 minutes, then move to a cooling rack.
Per Serving: (3 cookies)
calories: 53 | fat: 3g | protein: 7g | carbs: 8g | fiber: 1g

5-Minute Raw Granola

Prep time: 2 minutes | Cook time: 0 minutes | Makes 2 cups

¼ cup raisins
¼ cup dried mulberries
1 cup unsweetened large
coconut flakes
¼ cup pumpkin seeds

¼ cup sesame seeds
½ teaspoon ground cinnamon
¼ teaspoon raw vanilla powder
Pinch of sea salt (optional)

1. Rinse and drain the raisins and mulberries. 2. In a blender or food processor, combine all the ingredients. Pulse on low speed until everything is combined. If using a blender, you may have to shake the blender a few times if it gets stuck. 3. Store in an airtight container in the fridge for up to 5 days.
Per Serving:
calories: 234 | fat: 15g | protein: 5g | carbs: 18g | fiber: 4g

Homemade Granola Clusters

Prep time: 15 minutes | Cook time: 1 minute | Makes 2 cups

1½ creamy or chunky cups
peanut butter
¼ cup agave or maple syrup
(optional)
1½ cups old-fashioned rolled
oats
¾ cup flaxseed meal

½ cup raisins
¾ cup raw sunflower seeds
Optional Toppings:
¼ cup coconut shreds
1 teaspoon cinnamon
Pinch of salt (optional)

1. Add the peanut butter and maple syrup (if desired) to a medium, microwave-safe bowl. Microwave on high for 30-second intervals, stirring between intervals until the mixture is creamy and well combined. 2. Add the oats, flaxseed meal, raisins, and sunflower seeds, and stir together with a spoon until thoroughly combined. 3. Transfer the mixture to a baking sheet. 4. Place in the freezer for at least 25 minutes. Store in the refrigerator in an airtight container for up to 7 days.

Per Serving: (¼ cup)
calories: 510 | fat: 29g | protein: 31g | carbs: 34g | fiber: 11g

Maple, Apple, and Walnut Great Grains

Prep time: 10 minutes | Cook time: 3 to 4 hours | Serves 4 to 6

2 large apples
½ cup quinoa, rinsed
½ cup steel-cut oats
½ cup wheat berries
½ cup pearl barley
½ cup bulgur wheat
1 tablespoon ground flaxseed
2 teaspoons ground cinnamon

½ teaspoon ground or grated
nutmeg
7 cups water
⅓ cup maple syrup (optional)
½ cup chopped walnuts
½ cup raisins
Unsweetened plant-based milk,
for serving (optional)

1. Peel, core, and chop the apples and place them in the slow cooker. Add the quinoa, oats, wheat berries, barley, bulgur wheat, flaxseed, cinnamon, nutmeg, water, and maple syrup (if using). Stir gently. Cover and cook on High for 3 to 4 hours or on Low for 7 to 8 hours. 2. Before serving, stir in the walnuts and raisins. Spoon into a bowl and add your favorite milk (if using).
Per Serving:
calories: 691 | fat: 13g | protein: 18g | carbs: 113g | fiber: 21g

Fresh and Juicy Fruit Salad

Prep time: 5 minutes | Cook time: 0 minutes | Serves 2

1 ripe mango, peeled, cored,
and cubed
1 kiwi, cubed
⅓ cup quartered strawberries
½ cup finely chopped fresh mint
leaves
¼ cup blueberries

¼ cup blackberries
¼ cup raspberries
⅓ cup halved seedless grapes
1 tablespoon freshly squeezed
lemon juice
1 tablespoon freshly squeezed
orange juice

1. In a large bowl, combine the mango, kiwi, strawberries, mint, blueberries, blackberries, raspberries, and grapes. 2. Drizzle the lemon juice over the fruit and gently mix; then drizzle in the orange juice. 3. Divide evenly between 2 bowls and serve.
Per Serving:
calories: 176 | fat: 1g | protein: 3g | carbs: 43g | fiber: 8g

Blueberry and Peanut Butter Parfait Bowls

Prep time: 10 minutes | Cook time: 0 minutes | Serves 2

2 cups plain plant-based yogurt
1 cup store-bought granola
2 tablespoons maple syrup
(optional)
½ cup fresh blueberries

2 tablespoons roughly chopped
walnuts
2 tablespoons natural peanut
butter

1. Divide the yogurt between 2 bowls. Top each with half the granola and drizzle with 1 tablespoon maple syrup (if using). 2. Top each bowl with half the blueberries, 1 tablespoon of walnuts, and 1 tablespoon peanut butter.
Per Serving:
calories: 567 | fat: 24g | protein: 17g | carbs: 75g | fiber: 13g

Vanilla Breakfast Smoothie

Prep time: 10 minutes | Cook time: 0 minutes | Serves 1

1 frozen banana, sliced	1 tablespoon flaxseed meal
1 cup vanilla almond milk	¼ teaspoon cinnamon
¼ cup old-fashioned oats	3 tablespoons vanilla protein
¼ cup raisins	powder

1. Add all the ingredients to a blender and blend until very smooth.
Per Serving:
calories: 399 | fat: 12g | protein: 26g | carbs: 48g | fiber: 12g

Overnight Pumpkin Spice Chia Pudding

Prep time: 10 minutes | Cook time: 0 minutes | Serves 4

¾ cup chia seeds	¼ cup maple syrup (optional)
2 cups unsweetened plant-based milk	1 tablespoon pumpkin pie spice blend
1 (15-ounce / 425-g) can unsweetened pumpkin purée	1 cup water
	½ cup pecans, for serving

1. In a large bowl, whisk together the chia seeds, plant-based milk, pumpkin purée, maple syrup (if using), pumpkin pie spice, and water. 2. Divide the mixture among 4 mason jars or containers with lids. Let sit for 10 minutes. Stir each container to break up any chia clumps. Cover and refrigerate overnight to firm up. To serve, garnish each with some of the pecans.
Per Serving:
calories: 421 | fat: 23g | protein: 12g | carbs: 47g | fiber: 20g

Sweet Potato and Apple Breakfast Bowl

Prep time: 5 minutes | Cook time: 15 minutes | Serves 2

2 tablespoons pure maple syrup	1½ cups diced (½-inch) Granny
2 tablespoons tahini	Smith apple
½ cup water	2 tablespoons unsweetened
½ teaspoon vanilla extract	raisins
1½ cups quartered sliced (½-inch) sweet potato	2 tablespoons walnut pieces
	⅛ teaspoon ground cinnamon

1. In a small bowl, whisk together the maple syrup and tahini into a sauce. 2. In a sauté pan or skillet, stir together the water and vanilla. 3. Add the sweet potato and apple. Cover and simmer over medium-low heat for 12 to 15 minutes, or until a knife slides easily into the sweet potato. Remove from the heat. 4. Stir in the raisins, walnuts, and cinnamon. 5. Serve the bowls drizzled with the maple-tahini sauce.
Per Serving:
calories: 443 | fat: 13g | protein: 8g | carbs: 79g | fiber: 11g

Blueberry, Cinnamon, and Pecan French Toast

Prep time: 10 minutes | Cook time: 2 to 3 hours | Serves 4 to 6

2 tablespoons ground flaxseed	whole-grain bread
5 tablespoons water	1 overripe banana, peeled
1 (16-ounce / 454-g) loaf crusty	1 (14½-ounce / 411-g) can full-
fat coconut milk	(optional)
1 cup unsweetened plant-based milk	2 cups fresh or frozen blueberries, divided
1 tablespoon chia seeds	¼ cup chopped pecans, for
1 teaspoon ground cinnamon	serving
1 tablespoon vanilla extract	Maple syrup, for serving
Nonstick cooking spray	(optional)

1. In a small bowl or ramekin, stir together the flaxseed and water to form flax eggs. Let rest while preparing the remaining ingredients. 2. Slice the bread into 1- to 2-inch chunks and place in a large casserole dish deep enough to have the bread submerged in the custard. 3. Place the banana, coconut milk, plant-based milk, chia seeds, cinnamon, vanilla, and flax eggs in a blender. Blend to combine and pour over the bread. Cover and refrigerate for at least 30 minutes to allow the bread to soak up the custard. 4. Coat the inside of the slow cooker with cooking spray (if using) or line it with a slow cooker liner. Remove the bread and custard mixture from refrigerator and place half in the bottom of the slow cooker. Add 1 cup of blueberries, then layer the remaining half of the bread and custard mixture. Top with the remaining 1 cup of blueberries. Cover and cook on High for 2 to 3 hours or on Low for 4 to 5 hours. 5. To serve, top each portion with a tablespoon of pecans and a drizzle of maple syrup (if using).
Per Serving:
calories: 644 | fat: 31g | protein: 5g | carbs: 81g | fiber: 18g

Green Banana Smoothie

Prep time: 5 minutes | Cook time: 0 minutes | Makes 2 glasses

2½ to 3 sliced frozen bananas	removed
1½ cups spinach or kale, stems	1½ cups plant-based milk

1. In a blender, blend all the ingredients on high until smooth.
Per Serving: (1 glass)
calories: 134 | fat: 4g | protein: 8g | carbs: 16g | fiber: 3g

Buckwheat Protein Bread

Prep time: 15 minutes | Cook time: 40 minutes | Serves 6

1 cup buckwheat flour	¼ cup raisins
½ cup pea protein	3-inch piece ginger, minced
¼ cup chia seeds	2 cups water

1. Preheat the oven to 375ºF (190ºC) and line a small loaf pan with parchment paper. 2. Add all the ingredients except the raisins to a food processor and blend into a smooth and sticky dough. Alternatively, add all ingredients to a large bowl and mix into a dough using a handheld mixer. 3. Add the raisins to the dough in the food processor container and stir to distribute them evenly, using a spatula. 4. Transfer the dough to the bread tin, spread it from edge to edge and smooth out the top with a tablespoon. 5. Transfer the bread tin to the oven and bake for 40 minutes. 6. Take the bread out of the oven and allow it to cool down completely. If you don't, the bread will fall apart when you cut a slice! 7. Store the bread in an airtight container and consume within 4 days. Alternatively, store in the freezer for a maximum of 90 days and thaw at room temperature.
Per Serving:
calories: 376 | fat: 30g | protein: 16g | carbs: 11g | fiber: 9g

Cookies for Breakfast

Prep time: 10 minutes | Cook time: 20 minutes | Makes 12 cookies

1¼ cups certified gluten-free rolled oats
1 teaspoon ground cinnamon
½ teaspoon baking soda
½ teaspoon fine sea salt (optional)
½ cup almond flour
¼ cup brown rice flour
½ cup mashed ripe banana

½ cup smooth almond butter, stirred
3 tablespoons pure maple syrup (optional)
2 tablespoons ground flaxseed
3 tablespoons liquid virgin coconut oil (optional)
1 teaspoon pure vanilla extract

1. Preheat the oven to 350°F (180°C). Line a baking sheet with parchment paper and set aside. 2. In a large bowl, stir together the rolled oats, cinnamon, baking soda, sea salt, if using, almond flour, and brown rice flour until combined. 3. In the bowl of a food processor, combine the mashed banana, almond butter, maple syrup, if using, ground flaxseed, coconut oi, if using, and vanilla. Process on high until the mixture is smooth. 4. Scrape the almond butter mixture into the large bowl with the oats and flour mixture. Stir the mixture with a spatula until you have a unified and very stiff cookie dough. 5. Drop 2 tablespoons of dough per cookie onto the prepared baking sheet. Flatten each mound of dough with the palm of your hand. Slide the baking sheet into the oven and bake until lightly golden brown, about 15 to 17 minutes. Cool cookies completely before storing in an airtight container. These will last on the counter for 5 days. You can also wrap each cookie individually with plastic wrap and freeze them.
Per Serving:
calories: 160 | fat: 10g | protein: 5g | carbs: 17g | fiber: 4g

Whole-Wheat Blueberry Muffins

Prep time: 5 minutes | Cook time: 25 minutes | Makes 8 muffins

½ cup plant-based milk
½ cup unsweetened applesauce
½ cup maple syrup (optional)
1 teaspoon vanilla extract

2 cups whole-wheat flour
½ teaspoon baking soda
1 cup blueberries

1. Preheat the oven to 375°F (190°C). 2. In a large bowl, mix together the milk, applesauce, maple syrup (if desired), and vanilla. 3. Stir in the flour and baking soda until no dry flour is left and the batter is smooth. 4. Gently fold in the blueberries until they are evenly distributed throughout the batter. 5. In a muffin tin, fill 8 muffin cups three-quarters full of batter. 6. Bake for 25 minutes, or until you can stick a knife into the center of a muffin and it comes out clean. Allow to cool before serving.
Per Serving: (1 muffin)
calories: 200 | fat: 1g | protein: 4g | carbs: 45g | fiber: 2g

Breakfast Scramble

Prep time: 20 minutes | Cook time: 20 minutes | Serves 6

1 medium red onion, peeled and cut into ½-inch dice
1 medium green bell pepper, seeded and cut into ½-inch dice
2 cups sliced mushrooms (from about 8 ounces / 227 g whole mushrooms)
1 large head cauliflower, cut into florets, or 2 (19-ounce / 539-g) cans Jamaican ackee, drained and gently rinsed
Salt, to taste (optional)
½ teaspoon freshly ground

1 medium red bell pepper, seeded and cut into ½-inch dice
black pepper
1½ teaspoons turmeric
¼ teaspoon cayenne pepper, or to taste
3 cloves garlic, peeled and minced
1 to 2 tablespoons low-sodium soy sauce
¼ cup nutritional yeast (optional)

1. Place the onion, red and green peppers, and mushrooms in a medium skillet or saucepan and sauté over medium-high heat for 7 to 8 minutes, or until the onion is translucent. Add water 1 to 2 tablespoons at a time to keep the vegetables from sticking to the pan. 2. Add the cauliflower and cook for 5 to 6 minutes, or until the florets are tender. Add the salt (if using), black pepper, turmeric, cayenne pepper, garlic, soy sauce, and nutritional yeast (if using) to the pan and cook for 5 minutes more, or until hot and fragrant.
Per Serving:
calories: 65 | fat: 0g | protein: 5g | carbs: 11g | fiber: 4g

Buckwheat Porridge with Cherries and Almonds

Prep time: 5 minutes | Cook time: 25 minutes | Serves 2

½ cup buckwheat groats, rinsed
2 cups water
1 cup unsweetened vanilla almond milk
½ cup dried cherries, no added

sugar
½ cup sliced almonds, toasted
1 tablespoon maple syrup (optional)

1. In a small pot, combine the buckwheat and water. Bring to a boil; then reduce to a simmer. Cover and simmer for 15 minutes. 2. Turn off the heat. Keep covered and steam for another 5 minutes. 3. Pour the cooked buckwheat into two serving bowls, and divide the almond milk evenly between the bowls. 4. Top with the cherries and almonds, and drizzle with the maple syrup (if using).
Per Serving:
calories: 433 | fat: 14g | protein: 11g | carbs: 68g | fiber: 9g

Spelt Berry Hot Breakfast Cereal

Prep time: 5 minutes | Cook time: 55 minutes | Serves 2

1 cup spelt berries
¼ teaspoon salt (optional)
⅛ teaspoon ground cinnamon
⅛ teaspoon ground cloves
2 cups unsweetened almond

milk
¾ cup dates, pitted and chopped
¼ teaspoon orange zest

1. Bring 2½ cups of water to a boil in a medium saucepan. Add the spelt, salt (if using), cinnamon, and cloves. Cover the pot and bring the mixture to a boil. Reduce the heat to medium-low and cook for 45 to 50 minutes, or until the spelt is tender. Drain any excess water. 2. Add the almond milk, dates, and orange zest to the cooked spelt berries and simmer over medium-low heat for 10 to 12 minutes, or until heated through and creamy.
Per Serving:
calories: 423 | fat: 2g | protein: 18g | carbs: 88g | fiber: 13g

Zucchini Bread Oatmeal

Prep time: 5 minutes | Cook time: 20 minutes | Serves 4

2 cups rolled oats
1 medium zucchini, grated
4 cups water
½ cup unsweetened plant-based milk
1 tablespoon ground cinnamon
½ cup raisins

1 tablespoon maple syrup (optional)
Pinch of salt (optional)
2 medium bananas, sliced
4 tablespoons chopped walnuts (optional)

1. In a medium saucepan over medium-high, combine the oats, zucchini, and water and bring to a boil. Lower the heat to medium-low and simmer, stirring often, until the oats are soft and creamy, about 15 minutes. Remove from the heat, add the plant-based milk, cinnamon, raisins, maple syrup, and salt (if using) and stir well. 2. Divide the oatmeal among 4 bowls and top each portion with ½ sliced banana and 1 tablespoon of walnuts (if using).
Per Serving:
calories: 301 | fat: 4g | protein: 9g | carbs: 62g | fiber: 8g

Applesauce Crumble Muffins

Prep time: 10 minutes | Cook time: 15 to 20 minutes | Makes 12 muffins

1 teaspoon coconut oil, for greasing muffin tins (optional)
2 tablespoons nut butter or seed butter
1½ cups unsweetened applesauce
⅓ cup coconut sugar (optional)
½ cup nondairy milk
2 tablespoons ground flaxseed
1 teaspoon apple cider vinegar
1 teaspoon pure vanilla extract

2 cups whole-grain flour
1 teaspoon baking soda
½ teaspoon baking powder
1 teaspoon ground cinnamon
Pinch sea salt (optional)
½ cup walnuts, chopped
Toppings (optional):
¼ cup walnuts
¼ cup coconut sugar (optional)
½ teaspoon ground cinnamon

1. Preheat the oven to 350ºF (180ºC). Prepare two 6-cup muffin tins by rubbing the insides of the cups with coconut oil (if using), or using silicone or paper muffin cups. 2. In a large bowl, mix the nut butter, applesauce, coconut sugar (if using), milk, flaxseed, vinegar, and vanilla until thoroughly combined, or purée in a food processor or blender. 3. In another large bowl, sift together the flour, baking soda, baking powder, cinnamon, salt (if using), and chopped walnuts. 4. Mix the dry ingredients into the wet ingredients until just combined. 5. Spoon about ¼ cup batter into each muffin cup and sprinkle with the topping of your choice (if using). Bake for 15 to 20 minutes, or until a toothpick inserted into the center comes out clean. The applesauce creates a very moist base, so the muffins may take longer, depending on how heavy your muffin tins are.
Per Serving: (1 muffin)
calories: 178 | fat: 6g | protein: 4g | carbs: 28g | fiber: 3g

Banana French Toast with Raspberry Syrup

Prep time: 10 minutes | Cook time: 30 minutes | Makes 8 slices

French Toast:
1 banana

1 cup coconut milk
1 teaspoon pure vanilla extract

¼ teaspoon ground nutmeg
½ teaspoon ground cinnamon
1½ teaspoons arrowroot powder or flour
Pinch sea salt (optional)
8 slices whole-grain bread
Raspberry Syrup:

1 cup fresh or frozen raspberries, or other berries
2 tablespoons water or pure fruit juice
1 to 2 tablespoons maple syrup or coconut sugar (optional)

Make the French Toast: 1. Preheat the oven to 350ºF (180ºC). 2. In a shallow bowl, purée or mash the banana well. Mix in the coconut milk, vanilla, nutmeg, cinnamon, arrowroot, and salt (if using). 3. Dip the slices of bread in the banana mixture, and then lay them out in a 13-by-9-inch baking dish. They should cover the bottom of the dish and can overlap a bit but shouldn't be stacked on top of each other. Pour any leftover banana mixture over the bread, and put the dish in the oven. Bake about 30 minutes, or until the tops are lightly browned. 4. Serve topped with raspberry syrup. Make the Raspberry Syrup: 1. Heat the raspberries in a small pot with the water and the maple syrup (if using) on medium heat. 2. Leave to simmer, stirring occasionally and breaking up the berries, for 15 to 20 minutes, until the liquid has reduced.
Per Serving: (1 slice with syrup)
calories: 178 | fat: 8g | protein: 4g | carbs: 23g | fiber: 3g

Chocolate Chip Cookie Oatmeal

Prep time: 5 minutes | Cook time: 10 minutes | Serves 2

2 cups unsweetened soy milk
2 tablespoons pure maple syrup
1 teaspoon vanilla extract
1 cup rolled oats
1 tablespoon ground flaxseed

or flax meal
2 tablespoons mini vegan chocolate chips or shaved dark chocolate

1. In a small saucepan, combine the soy milk, maple syrup, and vanilla. Bring to a boil. 2. Reduce the heat to medium. Add the oats, and simmer for 5 to 7 minutes, or until the oatmeal has thickened. Remove from the heat. 3. Stir in the flaxseed, and let sit for 1 to 2 minutes. 4. Divide the oatmeal and chocolate chips between bowls.
Per Serving:
calories: 444 | fat: 13g | protein: 15g | carbs: 67g | fiber: 8g

Fruited Barley

Prep time: 10 minutes | Cook time: 55 minutes | Serves 2

1 to 1½ cups orange juice
1 cup pearled barley
2 tablespoons dried currants
3 to 4 dried unsulfured apricots,

chopped
1 small cinnamon stick
⅛ teaspoon ground cloves
Pinch salt, or to taste (optional)

1. Bring 1 cup of water and 1 cup of the orange juice to a boil in a medium saucepan over medium heat. Add the barley, currants, apricots, cinnamon stick, cloves, and salt, if using. Bring the mixture to a boil, cover, reduce the heat to medium-low, and cook for 45 minutes. If the barley is not tender after 45 minutes, add up to an additional ½ cup of orange juice and cook for another 10 minutes. 2. Remove the cinnamon stick before serving.
Per Serving:
calories: 420 | fat: 1g | protein: 10g | carbs: 93g | fiber: 16g

Chickpea Quiche

Prep time: 10 minutes | Cook time: 45 minutes | Serves 6

2 cups chickpea flour
¼ cup nutritional yeast
1 teaspoon gluten-free baking powder
½ teaspoon salt (optional)
¼ teaspoon ground turmeric

⅛ teaspoon black pepper
2 cups finely chopped greens
3 minced garlic cloves
2 cups water
1 tablespoon olive oil, plus extra for greasing the plates (optional)

1. Preheat the oven to 400ºF (205ºC). Coat two pie plates with olive oil, if desired. 2. Combine the flour, yeast, baking powder, salt (if desired), turmeric, and pepper in a large bowl. Stir in the greens and garlic, then whisk in the water. The batter should be the consistency of pancake batter. (The batter can be refrigerated overnight. You might need to add up to ¼ cup more water to thin it out the next morning.) 3. Pour in the batter and bake for 45 minutes, or until cooked through and a toothpick inserted in the middle comes out clean. Remove from the oven and let cool for 15 minutes. Slice into wedges and serve. (Leftovers can be stored, wrapped in parchment paper, for up to 3 days.)

Per Serving:
calories: 167 | fat: 4g | protein: 10g | carbs: 22g | fiber: 5g

Whole Oat Porridge

Prep time: 5 minutes | Cook time: 20 minutes | Makes 4 cups

1 cup whole oat groats, soaked overnight in 3 cups filtered water
4 cups filtered water

1 teaspoon ground cinnamon
Pinch of fine sea salt (optional)

1. Drain and rinse the oat groats and transfer them to an upright blender. Add the 4 cups water, cinnamon, and salt, if using, and pulse until the grains are coarsely ground. Pour into a medium pot and bring to a boil over high heat, whisking frequently. Cover the pot, reduce the heat to low, and simmer for about 20 minutes, stirring occasionally to prevent sticking, until the grains are soft and the porridge is creamy. 2. Serve hot. Pour leftover porridge into a widemouthed glass jar or other container and allow to cool, then cover tightly and store in the fridge for up to 5 days.

Per Serving: (1 cup)
calories: 153 | fat: 3g | protein: 7g | carbs: 26g | fiber: 5g

Chapter 2   Beans and Grains

Chickpea Pâté

Prep time: 10 minutes | Cook time: 0 minutes | Serves 4

1 cup whole raw nuts, toasted
2 tablespoons extra-virgin olive oil, plus more for drizzling (optional)
1 (15½-ounce / 439-g) can chickpeas, drained and rinsed well
½ cup filtered water
1 teaspoon fine sea salt, plus more to taste (optional)
½ teaspoon grated or pressed garlic
½ teaspoon raw apple cider vinegar

1. Put the nuts and oil in a food processor and blend until completely smooth, scraping down the sides as necessary. It will take a few minutes to reach a runny consistency. Add the chickpeas, water, salt, if using, garlic, and vinegar and blend until completely smooth. Add more cooking liquid or water if necessary to get the desired consistency; this will take a couple of minutes. Add more salt to taste and serve, drizzled with olive oil. Or store in an airtight container in the fridge for up to 4 days.
Per Serving:
calories: 321 | fat: 22g | protein: 11g | carbs: 23g | fiber: 7g

Southwest Stuffed Peppers

Prep time: 10 minutes | Cook time: 30 minutes | Serves 4

4 bell peppers
3 cups cooked brown rice
1 cup cooked black beans
1 cup fresh or frozen corn
1 cup vegetable broth
2 tablespoons tomato paste
2 tablespoons chili powder
1 teaspoon ground cumin

1. Preheat the oven to 375ºF (190ºC). 2. Cut the tops off the bell peppers, and remove any seeds or fibers that remain inside the core or inside the tops of the peppers. 3. In a large bowl, mix together the rice, beans, corn, broth, tomato paste, chili powder, and cumin until the tomato paste and spices have been thoroughly incorporated. 4. Spoon one-quarter of the rice mixture into each pepper. Set the peppers upright on a baking dish, and place the tops back onto the peppers. 5. Bake for 1 hour, or until the peppers are easily pierced with a fork, and serve.
Per Serving:
calories: 270 | fat: 3g | protein: 11g | carbs: 55g | fiber: 9g

Fried Rice with Tofu Scramble

Prep time: 15 minutes | Cook time: 35 minutes | Serves 2

4 cups cooked quick-cooking brown rice
1 cup cooked or canned green peas
1 (7-ounce / 198-g) pack extra-
firm tofu, scrambled
1 cup julienned carrots
¼ cup curry spices
1 cup water
Optional Toppings:

Lemon slices
Sauerkraut
Fresh cilantro

1. Cook 1½ cup of brown rice for about 25 minutes. 2. Put a large nonstick frying pan over medium heat and add ½ cup of water and the tofu scramble. 3. Add the curry spices and cook for about 5 minutes, stirring occasionally to prevent the tofu from sticking to the pan, until the tofu is well heated and most of the water has evaporated. 4. Add the carrots, rice, and green peas along with the remaining ½ cup water and stir-fry for another 5 minutes or until the water has evaporated. 5. Turn off the heat, divide the fried rice between 2 bowls, serve with the optional toppings and enjoy! 6. Store the fried rice in an airtight container in the fridge, and consume within 3 days. Alternatively, store in the freezer for a maximum of 30 days and thaw at room temperature. Reheat the fried rice in a nonstick frying pan or microwave.
Per Serving:
calories: 286 | fat: 10g | protein: 18g | carbs: 30g | fiber: 8g

Black and White Bean Chili

Prep time: 10 minutes | Cook time: 20 minutes | Serves 4

1 teaspoon extra-virgin olive oil (optional)
½ yellow onion, diced small
1 large carrot, peeled and diced small
1 red or yellow bell pepper, seeded and diced small
1 small zucchini, diced small
1 (15-ounce / 425-g) can cannellini beans, drained and rinsed
1 (15-ounce / 425-g) can black beans, drained and rinsed
1 (28-ounce / 794-g) can crushed tomatoes
1 cup frozen corn
1 teaspoon chili powder
½ teaspoon salt (optional)
½ teaspoon ground cumin
½ teaspoon garlic powder
1 cup water
2 tablespoons minced fresh cilantro, for garnish
Pinch red pepper flakes, for garnish
1 scallion, white and green parts, thinly sliced, for garnish
1 jalapeño pepper, cut into slices, for garnish (optional)
1 avocado, peeled, pitted, and diced, for garnish
1 lime, cut into wedges, for garnish

1. In a large pot, heat the olive oil over medium heat. Add the onion, carrot, bell pepper, and zucchini and cook, stirring often, until fragrant and the vegetables start to get tender, about 10 minutes. 2. Raise the heat to medium-high, add the cannellini beans, black beans, tomatoes, corn, chili powder, salt (if using), cumin, garlic powder, and water, stir well, and bring to a boil. Lower the heat to medium-low and simmer until heated through and the flavors meld, about 5 more minutes. 3. Spoon the chili into bowls and garnish with cilantro, red pepper flakes, scallion, jalapeño (if using), avocado, and a lime wedge.
Per Serving:
calories: 329 | fat: 3g | protein: 17g | carbs: 65g | fiber: 20g

Red Lentil Dahl

Prep time: 15 minutes | Cook time: 15 minutes | Serves 2

2 cups cooked or canned red lentils
1 cup canned or fresh tomato cubes
2 tablespoons curry spices
¼ cup shredded coconut

¼ cup water
Optional Toppings:
Lime juice
Cherry tomatoes
Nigella seeds

1. When using dry lentils, soak and cook ⅔ cup of dry lentils if necessary. 2. Put a large pot over medium heat, and add the tomato cubes, shredded coconut, and the water. 3. Cook for a few minutes, stirring occasionally, until everything is cooked, then add the curry spices and stir thoroughly. 4. Add the lentils, stir thoroughly making sure everything is well mixed. 5. Cook for a couple more minutes, stirring occasionally, until everything is cooked, then lower the heat to a simmer. 6. Let the dahl simmer for about 15 minutes while stirring occasionally. 7. Turn the heat off and let the dahl cool down for a minute. 8. Divide the lentil dahl between 2 bowls, garnish with the optional toppings, serve and enjoy! 9. Store the dahl in an airtight container in the fridge, and consume within 2 days. Alternatively, store in the freezer for a maximum of 30 days and thaw at room temperature. Reheat the dahl in the microwave or a saucepan.
Per Serving:
calories: 330 | fat: 7g | protein: 19g | carbs: 46g | fiber: 18g

Cabbage and Millet Pilaf

Prep time: 15 minutes | Cook time: 45 minutes | Serves 4

2¼ cups vegetable stock, or low-sodium vegetable broth
¾ cup millet
1 medium leek (white and light green parts), diced and rinsed
1 medium carrot, peeled and diced
1 celery stalk, diced

2 cloves garlic, peeled and minced
1 teaspoon minced thyme
1 tablespoon minced dill
3 cups chopped cabbage
Salt and freshly ground black pepper, to taste

1. In a medium saucepan, bring the vegetable stock to a boil over high heat. Add the millet and bring the pot back to a boil over high heat. Reduce the heat to medium and cook, covered, for 20 minutes, or until the millet is tender and all the vegetable stock is absorbed. 2. Place the leek, carrot, and celery in a large saucepan and sauté over medium heat for 7 to 8 minutes. Add water 1 to 2 tablespoons at a time to keep the vegetables from sticking to the pan. Add the garlic, thyme, dill, and cabbage and cook, stirring frequently, over medium heat until the cabbage is tender, about 10 minutes. Add the cooked millet and cook for another 5 minutes, stirring frequently. Season with salt and pepper.
Per Serving:
calories: 193 | fat: 2g | protein: 5g | carbs: 39g | fiber: 6g

Kasha Varnishkes (Buckwheat Groats with Bow-Tie Pasta)

Prep time: 20 minutes | Cook time: 35 minutes | Serves 4

2 cups vegetable stock, or low-sodium vegetable broth
1 cup buckwheat groats
1 large yellow onion, peeled and diced small
8 ounces (227 g) button mushrooms, sliced
½ pound (227 g) whole-grain

farfalle, cooked according to package directions, drained, and kept warm
2 tablespoons finely chopped dill
Salt and freshly ground black pepper, to taste

1. Place the vegetable stock in a medium saucepan and bring to a boil over high heat. Add the buckwheat groats and bring the pot back to a boil over high heat. Reduce the heat to medium and cook, uncovered, until the groats are tender, about 12 to 15 minutes. 2. Place the onion in a large saucepan and sauté over medium heat until well browned, about 15 minutes. Add water 1 to 2 tablespoons at a time to keep the onion from sticking, but use as little water as possible. Add the mushrooms and cook for another 5 minutes. Remove from the heat. Add the cooked pasta, buckwheat groats, and dill. Season with salt and pepper.
Per Serving:
calories: 240 | fat: 1g | protein: 8g | carbs: 51g | fiber: 6g

Wild Rice, Cabbage and Chickpea Pilaf

Prep time: 20 minutes | Cook time: 1 hour 20 minutes | Serves 4

½ cup wild rice
1 medium onion, peeled and diced small
1 medium carrot, peeled and grated
1 small red bell pepper, seeded and diced small
3 cloves garlic, peeled and minced

1 tablespoon grated ginger
1½ cups chopped green cabbage
1 cup cooked chickpeas
1 bunch green onions (white and green parts), thinly sliced
3 tablespoons chopped cilantro
Salt and freshly ground black pepper, to taste

1. Bring 2 cups of water to a boil in a large saucepan. Add the wild rice and bring the water back to a boil over high heat. Reduce the heat to medium and cook, covered, for 55 to 60 minutes. Drain off any excess water and set aside. 2. Heat a large skillet over medium heat. Add the onion, carrot, and red pepper and sauté the vegetables for 10 minutes. Add water 1 to 2 tablespoons at a time to keep the vegetables from sticking to the pan. Add the garlic and ginger and cook for another minute. Add the cabbage and cook for 10 to 12 minutes, or until the cabbage is tender. Add the chickpeas, green onions, and cilantro. Season with salt and pepper and cook for another minute to heat the chickpeas. Remove from the heat, add the cooked wild rice and mix well.
Per Serving:
calories: 171 | fat: 1g | protein: 7g | carbs: 33g | fiber: 6g

Chickpea Caponata

Prep time: 25 minutes | Cook time: 30 minutes | Serves 4

1 medium yellow onion, peeled and diced
2 celery stalks, chopped
1 medium eggplant, stemmed and diced
2 ripe Roma tomatoes, diced
2 cups cooked chickpeas, or 1 (15-ounce / 425-g) can, drained and rinsed
½ cup Kalamata olives, pitted
and coarsely chopped
3 tablespoons capers
3 tablespoons red wine vinegar
¼ cup golden raisins
¼ cup pine nuts, toasted (optional)
½ cup chopped basil
Salt and freshly ground black pepper, to taste

1. Place the onion and celery in a large saucepan and sauté over medium heat for 10 minutes. Add water 1 to 2 tablespoons at a time to keep the vegetables from sticking to the pan. 2. Add the eggplant, tomatoes, and chickpeas and cook, covered, for 15 minutes, or until the vegetables are tender. Stir in the olives, capers, red wine vinegar, raisins, and pine nuts (if using) and cook for 5 minutes more. Remove from the heat and add the basil. Season with salt and pepper.
Per Serving:
calories: 301 | fat: 10g | protein: 11g | carbs: 45g | fiber: 13g

Chickpea Tortilla Fajita Stack

Prep time: 20 minutes | Cook time: 0 minutes | Serves 4

Chickpea Tortillas:
1 tablespoon ground chia seeds
1 cup chickpea flour
¼ teaspoon sea salt (optional)
½ teaspoon ground cumin
2 tablespoons extra virgin olive oil (optional)
Filling:
1 tablespoon extra virgin olive oil (optional)
½ cup diced white onion
1 yellow bell pepper, diced
8 ounces (227 g) white
mushrooms, diced
½ cup diced tomatoes
2 teaspoons fajita seasoning
½ teaspoon salt (optional)
¼ teaspoon ground black pepper
1 (15 ounces / 425 g) can pinto beans, drained and rinsed
2 tablespoons raw shelled hempseed
Salsa, for garnish
Avocado, for garnish

Make Chickpea Tortillas: 1. Mix ground chia seeds with 3 tablespoons water. Set aside. 2. Add 1 cup water, the chickpea flour, chia seed mixture, salt (if desired), and cumin to a medium bowl. 3. Mix until just combined. 4. Add 2 tablespoons oil (if desired) to an 8-inch skillet and heat to medium high. 5. Add ¼ cup chickpea batter and tilt the pan in a circular tilt to let the batter flow to cover the bottom of the pan, as you would a crepe. 6. Cook until golden brown and flip. Cook for another minute and remove to a plate. Continue until all the batter is gone and the tortillas are made. Make Filling: 7. Add the oil (if desired) to a large skillet and heat to medium high. Add the onion, bell pepper, and mushrooms and sauté 10 to 15 minutes or until the onion is translucent. Add the tomatoes, fajita seasoning, salt (if desired), and pepper and cook for 5 minutes. Add the beans and hempseed. Heat through. Assemble: 8. Layer the chickpea tortilla stack starting with one tortilla on a plate. Spoon on about ½ cup filling. Add another tortilla and ½ cup filling and continue until the filling is all gone. Top with a tortilla, salsa, and avocado. Cut into quarters in a pie shape and serve.

Per Serving:
calories: 358 | fat: 12g | protein: 17g | carbs: 48g | fiber: 11g

Barley and Sweet Potato Pilaf

Prep time: 10 minutes | Cook time: 55 minutes | Serves 4

1 medium onion, peeled and chopped
2 cloves garlic, peeled and minced
3½ cups vegetable stock, or low-sodium vegetable broth
1½ cups pearled barley
1 large sweet potato (about ¾ pound / 340 g), peeled and diced small
¼ cup minced tarragon
Zest and juice of 1 lemon
Salt and freshly ground black pepper, to taste

1. Place the onion in a large saucepan and sauté over medium heat for 6 minutes. Add water 1 to 2 tablespoons at a time to keep the onion from sticking to the pan. Add the garlic and cook 3 minutes more. Add the vegetable stock and barley and bring the pot to a boil over high heat. 2. Reduce the heat to medium and cook, covered, for 30 minutes. Add the sweet potato and cook for 15 minutes longer, or until the potato and barley are tender. Remove from the heat, stir in the tarragon and lemon zest and juice, and season with salt and pepper.
Per Serving:
calories: 318 | fat: 0g | protein: 8g | carbs: 71g | fiber: 13g

Spinach, Mushroom and Quinoa Pilaf

Prep time: 30 minutes | Cook time: 35 minutes | Serves 4

⅓ ounce (9 g) porcini mushrooms, soaked for 30 minutes in 1 cup of water that has just been boiled, and roughly chopped
2 large leeks (white and light green parts), diced and rinsed
8 ounces (227 g) cremini mushrooms, thinly sliced
3 cloves garlic, peeled and minced
1 tablespoon thyme
2 cups vegetable stock, or low-sodium vegetable broth, plus more as needed
1½ cups quinoa
6 cups baby spinach, chopped
Salt and freshly ground black pepper, to taste
¼ cup pine nuts, toasted (optional)

1. Drain the porcini mushrooms, reserving the liquid. Finely chop the mushrooms and set aside. 2. Place the leeks and cremini mushrooms in a large saucepan and sauté over medium heat for 10 minutes. Add water 1 to 2 tablespoons at a time to keep the vegetables from sticking to the pan. Add the garlic and thyme and cook for 30 seconds. 3. Combine the porcini mushroom soaking liquid and vegetable stock. Add more vegetable stock as needed to make 3 cups. Add the liquid, quinoa, and chopped porcini mushrooms to the pan with the sautéed mushrooms and bring the pan to a boil over high heat. Reduce the heat to medium and cook the quinoa, covered, for 15 minutes, or until it is tender. Stir in the spinach and cook for another 5 minutes, or until the spinach is wilted. Season with salt and pepper and garnish with the pine nuts, if desired.
Per Serving:
calories: 358 | fat: 10g | protein: 14g | carbs: 55g | fiber: 7g

Green Chile Rice with Black Beans

Prep time: 20 minutes | Cook time: 1 hour | Serves 4

1 poblano chile pepper, seeded and diced small
1 (4-ounce / 113-g) can mild green chiles
1 cup coarsely chopped cilantro
½ cup spinach
4 cups vegetable stock, or low-sodium vegetable broth
1½ cups medium-grain brown rice

1 medium yellow onion, peeled and diced small
1 teaspoon ground cumin
1 jalapeño pepper, seeded and minced
2 cups cooked black beans, or 1 (15-ounce / 425-g) can, drained and rinsed
Zest of 1 lime
Salt, to taste (optional)

1. Add the poblano pepper, green chiles, cilantro, and spinach to a blender and purée. Add some of the vegetable stock, as needed, to achieve a smooth consistency. Add the mixture to a medium saucepan with the remaining vegetable stock. Add the brown rice and bring to a boil over high heat. Reduce the heat to medium and cook, covered, until the rice is tender, 45 to 50 minutes. 2. Place the onion in a large saucepan and sauté over medium heat for 7 to 8 minutes. Add water 1 to 2 tablespoons at a time to keep the onion from sticking to the pan. Add the cumin, jalapeño pepper, and black beans and cook for 5 minutes longer. Fold in the cooked rice and lime zest. Season with salt, if using.
Per Serving:
calories: 403 | fat: 2g | protein: 13g | carbs: 71g | fiber: 11g

Tahini Green Beans

Prep time: 10 minutes | Cook time: 10 minutes | Serves 4

1 pound (454 g) green beans, washed and trimmed
2 tablespoons gluten-free tahini
1 minced garlic clove
Grated zest and juice of 1

lemon
Salt and black pepper (optional)
1 teaspoon toasted black or white sesame seeds (optional)

1. Steam the beans in a medium saucepan fitted with a steamer insert over medium-high heat. Drain, reserving the cooking water. 2. Mix the tahini, garlic, lemon zest and juice, and salt (if desired) and pepper to taste. Use the reserved cooking water to thin the sauce as desired. 3. Toss the green beans with the sauce and serve warm or at room temperature. Garnish with the sesame seeds, if desired.
Per Serving:
calories: 73 | fat: 5g | protein: 3g | carbs: 8g | fiber: 3g

Oil-Free Rice-and-Vegetable Stir-Fry

Prep time: 5 minutes | Cook time: 15 minutes | Serves 4

2 cups fresh or frozen green peas
2 cups fresh or frozen green beans

¼ cup vegetable broth or water
1 teaspoon garlic powder
1 teaspoon onion powder
4 cups cooked brown rice

1. Heat a medium saucepan over medium heat. 2. Put the peas, green beans, broth, garlic powder, and onion powder in the pan, and stir. Cover and cook for 8 minutes, stirring every few minutes, or until crisp-tender. If any of the vegetables begin sticking, stir in a few

more tablespoons of vegetable broth or water. 3. Uncover, and stir in the cooked brown rice. Cook for an additional 5 minutes, stirring every other minute, and serve. (Add a tablespoon or two of water or broth if anything begins sticking to the bottom of the pan.)
Per Serving:
calories: 233 | fat: 2g | protein: 8g | carbs: 48g | fiber: 7g

Barley Bowl with Cranberries and Walnuts

Prep time: 5 minutes | Cook time: 30 minutes | Serves 4

1 cup pearl barley, uncooked
3 cups water
¼ cup poppy seeds

½ cup dried cranberries
½ cup chopped walnuts, toasted

1. In a medium pot, combine the barley and water and bring to a boil. Reduce the heat to medium and cook until the barley is tender, 25 to 30 minutes. Once done, drain off any excess water and let cool. 2. While the barley is cooking, place the poppy seeds and dried cranberries in a small bowl and soak them in hot water for 5 to 10 minutes; then drain the water and let cool. 3. In a large bowl, combine the cooked barley, cranberries, poppy seeds, and walnuts. Mix well, cover, and refrigerate for 30 minutes to 1 hour before serving cold.
Per Serving:
calories: 341 | fat: 14g | protein: 9g | carbs: 50g | fiber: 11g

Koshari (Lentils with Rice and Macaroni)

Prep time: 15 minutes | Cook time: 2 hours | Serves 6

1 cup green lentils, rinsed
Salt, to taste (optional)
1 cup medium-grain brown rice
1 large onion, peeled and minced
4 cloves garlic, peeled and minced
1 teaspoon ground cumin
1 teaspoon ground coriander
½ teaspoon ground allspice

½ teaspoon crushed red pepper flakes
2 tablespoons tomato paste
3 large tomatoes, diced small
1 cup whole-grain elbow macaroni, cooked according to package directions, drained, and kept warm
1 tablespoon brown rice vinegar

1. Add the lentils to a medium saucepan with 3 cups of water. Bring the pot to a boil over high heat, reduce the heat to medium, and cook, covered, for 40 to 45 minutes, or until the lentils are tender but not mushy. Drain any excess water from the lentils, season with salt (if using), and set aside. 2. Add the brown rice and 2 cups of water to a separate medium saucepan. Cover the pan with a tight-fitting lid and bring it to a boil over high heat. Reduce the heat to medium and cook for 45 minutes. 3. Heat a large skillet over high heat. Place the onion in the skillet and sauté over medium heat for 15 minutes, or until it is well browned. Add water 1 to 2 tablespoons at a time to keep the onion from sticking to the pan. Add the garlic and cook for 3 to 4 minutes more. Add the cumin, coriander, allspice, crushed red pepper flakes, and tomato paste and cook for 3 minutes longer. Add the fresh tomatoes and cook over medium heat for 15 minutes, or until the tomatoes start to break down. Season with salt, if using. 4. To serve, combine the lentils, rice, tomato mixture, cooked macaroni, and brown rice vinegar in a large bowl.
Per Serving:
calories: 298 | fat: 1g | protein: 13g | carbs: 59g | fiber: 6g

Lentil-Mushroom No-Meat Pasta (Bolognese)

Prep time: 15 minutes | Cook time: 45 minutes | Serves 4

¼ cup mushroom stock	1 cup brown lentils
1 large yellow onion, finely diced	1 (28-ounce / 794-g) can puréed or diced tomatoes with basil
1 (10-ounce / 283-g) package cremini mushrooms, trimmed and chopped fine	1 tablespoon balsamic vinegar
2 tablespoons tomato paste	Pasta
3 chopped garlic cloves	Salt and black pepper (optional)
1 teaspoon oregano	Chopped basil
2½ cups water	

1. Place a large stockpot over medium heat. Add the stock. Once the broth starts to simmer, add the onion and mushrooms. Cover and cook until both are soft, about 5 minutes. Add the tomato paste, garlic, and oregano and cook 2 minutes, stirring constantly. 2. Stir in the water and lentils. Bring to a boil, then reduce the heat to medium-low and cook for 5 minutes, covered. Add the tomatoes and vinegar. Replace the lid, reduce the heat to low and cook until the lentils are tender, about 30 minutes. 3. Meanwhile, cook the pasta according to the package instructions. 4. Remove the sauce from the heat and season with salt (if desired) and pepper to taste. Garnish with the basil and serve atop the pasta.

Per Serving:
calories: 181 | fat: 1g | protein: 9g | carbs: 40g | fiber: 7g

Chana Saag

Prep time: 20 minutes | Cook time: 30 minutes | Serves 4

1 medium yellow onion, peeled and diced small	1 teaspoon crushed red pepper flakes, or to taste
1 jalapeño pepper, minced (for less heat, remove the seeds)	1 large tomato, finely chopped
3 cloves garlic, peeled and minced	1 cup unsweetened plain almond milk
1 tablespoon grated ginger	2 pounds (907 g) fresh spinach, chopped (about 12 cups)
2 teaspoons ground cumin	2 cups cooked chickpeas, or 1 (15-ounce / 425-g) can, drained and rinsed
1 teaspoon ground coriander	
1 teaspoon turmeric	Salt, to taste (optional)
1 teaspoon fenugreek	

1. Place the onion in a large saucepan and sauté over medium-high heat for 8 to 10 minutes, or until it is browned. Add water 1 to 2 tablespoons at a time to keep the onion from sticking to the pan. 2. Reduce the heat to medium-low and add the jalapeño pepper, garlic, ginger, cumin, coriander, turmeric, fenugreek, and crushed red pepper flakes. Cook, stirring often, for 4 minutes, adding water only as needed. 3. Add the tomato and cook for another 5 minutes, then add the almond milk, spinach, and chickpeas. Cover the pot and reduce the heat to medium-low. Cook until the spinach is wilted, about 10 minutes. Season with salt, if using.

Per Serving:
calories: 235 | fat: 3g | protein: 16g | carbs: 39g | fiber: 12g

Red Curry "Fried" Rice

Prep time: 25 minutes | Cook time: 10 minutes | Serves 2

½ medium yellow onion, peeled and cut into ½-inch strips	4 teaspoons Thai red curry paste
2 large leeks (white and light green parts), thinly sliced and rinsed	¼ cup slivered almonds, toasted (optional)
	4 green onions (white and green parts), chopped
2 cups shiitake mushrooms, trimmed and thinly sliced	2 cups cooked brown rice, fully cooled
2 medium carrots, peeled and cut into matchsticks	Salt and freshly ground black pepper, to taste

1. Heat a large skillet over high heat. Add the onion, leeks, mushrooms, and carrots and cook, stirring frequently, for 5 to 6 minutes. Add water 1 to 2 tablespoons at a time to keep the vegetables from sticking to the pan. 2. Stir in the curry paste and cook for another 30 seconds. Add the almonds (if using), green onions, and rice and cook until heated through. Season with salt and pepper.

Per Serving:
calories: 415 | fat: 9g | protein: 12g | carbs: 74g | fiber: 12g

Curried Chickpeas and Rice

Prep time: 10 minutes | Cook time: 35 minutes | Serves 4

1 cup brown basmati rice	¼ teaspoons curry powder
¼ cup finely chopped green scallions	½ teaspoons salt, or to taste (optional)
¼ teaspoons cumin seeds, toasted	1½ cups cooked chickpeas
	½ tablespoon fresh lime juice

1. Rinse the rice and add it to a pot with 2½ cups of water. Bring to a boil over high heat and cook, uncovered, for 20 minutes. Reduce the heat to medium and simmer the rice, covered, for 10 minutes. 2. Add the scallions to a medium saucepan with 2 tablespoons of water and cook until soft. Add the cumin seeds, curry powder, salt (if using), and chickpeas and cook for a minute. Add the cooked rice, cook for another minute, and remove the pan from the heat. Add the lime juice and serve hot.

Per Serving:
calories: 275 | fat: 3g | protein: 9g | carbs: 53g | fiber: 6g

Marinated Beans

Prep time: 15 minutes | Cook time: 0 minutes | Serves 4

3 cups cooked beans, drained well	2 tablespoons raw apple cider vinegar, plus more to taste
3 tablespoons extra-virgin olive oil (optional)	½ teaspoon fine sea salt, plus more to taste (optional)

1. Put the beans in a medium bowl, add the olive oil, vinegar, and salt, and stir to combine. Adjust the seasoning to taste. Set aside for 30 minutes to marry the flavors if you have time, or serve immediately. Store the beans in a jar in the fridge for up to 4 days.

Per Serving:
calories: 116 | fat: 11g | protein: 1g | carbs: 5g | fiber: 2g

Mixed Beans Chili

Prep time: 20 minutes | Cook time: 1 hour | Serves 6

1 pound (454 g) beans, mixed varieties
1 tablespoon extra virgin olive oil (optional)
½ cup diced onion
4 cloves garlic, finely chopped
4 cups vegetable broth, more if needed
1 (28 ounces / 794 g) can crushed fire-roasted tomatoes
1 (8 ounces / 227 g) can tomato sauce
1 (6 ounces / 170 g) can tomato paste
2 tablespoons vegan Worcestershire sauce
2 tablespoons chili powder
2 teaspoons ground cumin
1½ teaspoons dried oregano
¼ teaspoon ground cloves
½ teaspoon cayenne pepper
1 teaspoon salt (optional)

1. Rinse the beans and place in a large stockpot. Cover with water by about 3 inches. The beans will swell. Let soak overnight. 2. Drain the beans and place back into the stockpot. 3. Heat the oil (if desired) in a large skillet over medium-high heat. Add the onion and sauté until translucent, about 10 to 15 minutes. Add the garlic and sauté another minute. Add this mixture to the beans in the stockpot. Add the vegetable broth, crushed tomatoes, tomato sauce, tomato paste, and Worcestershire sauce. The beans should be covered by a couple of inches of liquid. You can add more broth or water, if needed. Stir well. Add the remaining ingredients and stir well again. Cover and bring to a boil. 4. Remove the lid, turn down the heat, and simmer very low. So low you can barely see the liquid moving. Don't put the lid back on. It becomes much more flavorful with the lid off. If the liquid cooks down to where the beans are not submerged, then add some more broth or water. (If you add more liquid, you'll have to cover again, raise the heat to a boil, and then turn it down immediately and uncover.) Make sure your heat isn't too high. Cook for 45 minutes and check the beans. You will want them tender. If they are not done yet, then cook longer. You shouldn't need to cook longer than 1 hours.

Per Serving:
calories: 117 | fat: 4g | protein: 20g | carbs: 21g | fiber: 7g

Eggplant and Chickpea Rice Pilaf

Prep time: 20 minutes | Cook time: 1 hour 10 minutes | Serves 4

2 cups vegetable stock, or low-sodium vegetable broth
1 cup brown basmati rice
1 large yellow onion, peeled and diced small
6 cloves garlic, peeled and minced
2 jalapeño peppers, seeded and minced
1 tablespoon cumin seeds, toasted and ground
1 tablespoon ground coriander
1 teaspoon turmeric
1 large eggplant, stemmed and cut into ½-inch cubes
2 cups cooked chickpeas, or 1 (15-ounce / 425-g) can, drained and rinsed
¼ cup finely chopped mint
½ cup finely chopped basil
Salt, to taste (optional)
½ cup finely chopped cilantro

1. Bring the vegetable stock to a boil in a medium saucepan. Add the rice and bring the mixture back to a boil over high heat. Reduce the heat to medium and cook, covered, until the rice is tender, about 45 minutes. 2. Place the onion in a large saucepan and sauté over medium heat for 7 to 8 minutes. Add water 1 to 2 tablespoons at a time to keep the onion from sticking to the pan. Add the garlic, jalapeño peppers, cumin, coriander, turmeric, and eggplant and cook until the eggplant is tender, about 12 minutes. Add the cooked rice, chickpeas, mint, and basil. Season with salt (if using) and serve garnished with the cilantro.

Per Serving:
calories: 373 | fat: 4g | protein: 13g | carbs: 73g | fiber: 12g

BLAT (Bacon, Lettuce, Avocado and Tomato) Pitas

Prep time: 10 minutes | Cook time: 5 minutes | Makes 4 sandwiches

2 teaspoons coconut oil (optional)
½ cup dulse, picked through and separated
Few drops liquid smoke
Salt and black pepper (optional)
2 avocados, sliced
¼ cup chopped cilantro
2 sliced scallions
2 tablespoons lime juice
4 8-inch whole wheat pitas
4 cups greens
4 sliced plum tomatoes

1. Place a large cast-iron skillet over medium heat. Once it's warm, add the coconut oil (if desired), then the dulse and liquid smoke. Toss to combine. Cook, stirring often, until the dulse is crispy, about 5 minutes. Remove from the heat and season with pepper to taste. 2. Mash the avocado with the cilantro, scallions, and lime juice. Season with salt and pepper to taste, if desired. 3. Slice the pitas in half and toast lightly. Gently open them, and divide the avocado mixture evenly into all 8 halves. Divide the greens, tomatoes, and dulse evenly among the pitas and serve.

Per Serving: (1 sandwich)
calories: 381 | fat: 19g | protein: 10g | carbs: 50g | fiber: 14g

Black Pepper Tempeh Stir-Fry

Prep time: 15 minutes | Cook time: 20 minutes | Serves 4

1 (14-ounce / 397-g) pack tempeh, thinly sliced
¼ cup low-sodium soy sauce
2 medium onions, minced
3 cloves garlic, minced
2 tablespoons black pepper
½ cup water
Optional Toppings:
Sauerkraut
Roasted sesame seeds
Shredded coconut

1. Cut the tempeh into thin slices, put them into an airtight container and add the soy sauce. 2. Close the airtight container, shake well and put it in the fridge, allowing the tempeh to marinate for at least 1 hour, or up to 12 hours. 3. Put a nonstick deep frying pan over medium-high heat and add the minced onions, minced garlic and the water. 4. Stir continuously until everything is cooked, then add the tempeh slices. 5. Let it cook for about 20 minutes while stirring occasionally. 6. Turn the heat off, leave to cool down for a minute and drain the excess water if necessary. 7. Divide between 2 plates, garnish with the optional toppings and enjoy! 8. Store the tempeh stir-fry in an airtight container in the fridge, and consume within 3 days. Alternatively, store in the freezer for a maximum of 30 days and thaw at room temperature. The tempeh stir-fry can be eaten cold or reheated in a saucepan or a microwave.

Per Serving:
calories: 211 | fat: 10g | protein: 24g | carbs: 4g | fiber: 6g

Barley and White Bean Pilaf

Prep time: 15 minutes | Cook time: 55 minutes | Serves 4

1 medium yellow onion, peeled and finely diced
1 celery stalk, finely diced
1 medium carrot, peeled and finely diced
1½ cups pearled barley
2-inch piece orange peel

1 cinnamon stick
3 cups vegetable stock, or low-sodium vegetable broth
2 cups cooked navy or other white beans, or 1 (15-ounce / 425-g) can, drained and rinsed
¼ cup finely chopped dill

1. Place the onion, celery, and carrot in a large saucepan and sauté over medium heat for 7 to 8 minutes. Add water 1 to 2 tablespoons at a time to keep the vegetables from sticking to the pan. Add the barley, orange peel, cinnamon stick, and vegetable stock and bring the pan to a boil over high heat. 2. Reduce the heat to medium and cook for 35 minutes. Add the beans and cook for another 10 minutes, until the barley is tender. Remove from the heat and stir in the dill.
Per Serving:
calories: 418 | fat: 1g | protein: 15g | carbs: 78g | fiber: 18g

Quick Panfried Tempeh

Prep time: 5 minutes | Cook time: 10 minutes | Serves 2

2 tablespoons extra-virgin coconut oil, plus more as needed (optional)

½ pound (227 g) tempeh, cut into ¼-inch slices
Flaky or fine sea salt (optional)

1. Warm a large skillet over medium heat. Add the coconut oil and tilt the pan to coat. Add the sliced tempeh in a single layer and cook until golden, 3 to 4 minutes. Turn the tempeh over and cook the other side until golden and crisp, adding more oil if needed. Repeat with any remaining tempeh, adding more oil to the pan before adding the sliced tempeh. Transfer the tempeh to a serving plate and sprinkle with salt; serve warm.
Per Serving:
calories: 336 | fat: 25g | protein: 2g | carbs: 11g | fiber: 0g

Baked Brown Rice Risotto with Sunflower Seeds

Prep time: 10 minutes | Cook time: 1 hour | Serves 6

4 cups vegetable broth
1 cup short-grain brown rice
½ cup raw sunflower seeds
2 tablespoons dry sherry
1 shallot, minced

1 teaspoon dried tarragon
½ teaspoon dried dill
½ teaspoon salt (optional)
⅛ teaspoon black pepper
⅛ teaspoon ground turmeric

1. Preheat the oven to 400°F (205°C). Bring the broth to a boil in a medium saucepan. 2. Add the rice, sunflower seeds, sherry, shallot, tarragon, dill, salt (if desired), pepper, and turmeric to a medium baking dish. Pour the hot broth into the dish, cover, and carefully place in the oven. Bake for 30 minutes. The dish should still look soupy; if it begins to dry out, add 1 cup of water or broth. Continue to bake, covered, for another 30 minutes. Serve.
Per Serving:
calories: 196 | fat: 7g | protein: 5g | carbs: 29g | fiber: 2g

Nut-Crusted Tofu

Prep time: 10 minutes | Cook time: 20 minutes | Makes 8 slices

½ cup roasted, shelled pistachios
¼ cup whole wheat bread crumbs
1 shallot, minced
1 garlic clove, minced
1 teaspoon grated lemon zest
½ teaspoon dried tarragon

Salt and black pepper (optional)
1 (16-ounce / 454-g) package sprouted or extra-firm tofu, drained and sliced lengthwise into 8 pieces
1 tablespoon Dijon mustard
1 tablespoon lemon juice

1. Preheat the oven to 375°F (190°C) and line a baking sheet with parchment paper. 2. Using a food processor or a knife, chop the pistachios until they are about the size of the bread crumbs. In a pie plate, combine them with the bread crumbs, shallot, garlic, lemon zest, and tarragon. Season with salt (if desired) and pepper. 3. Season the tofu with salt and pepper. In a small bowl, combine the mustard and lemon juice. 4. Spread the mustard mixture evenly over the top and sides of the tofu, then press each slice into the bread crumb mixture. 5. Place the tofu uncoated side down on the baking sheet. Sprinkle any leftover bread crumb mixture evenly on top of the slices. Bake until the tops are browned, about 20 minutes. Serve.
Per Serving:(1 slice)
calories: 114 | fat: 7g | protein: 8g | carbs: 7g | fiber: 1g

Baked Falafel

Prep time: 15 minutes | Cook time: 30 minutes | Serves 6

1 cup dried chickpeas
½ cup packed chopped fresh parsley
½ cup packed chopped fresh cilantro (or parsley if preferred)
½ cup chopped yellow onion
3 garlic cloves, peeled
1½ tablespoons chickpea flour

or wheat flour (if gluten is not a concern)
2 teaspoons ground cumin
1 teaspoon ground coriander
½ teaspoon baking powder
2 tablespoons freshly squeezed lemon juice

1. The night before making falafel, in a large bowl, combine the dried chickpeas with enough water to cover by 3 inches. Cover the bowl and soak for at least 8 hours or overnight. Drain. 2. Preheat the oven to 375°F (190°C). Line a baking sheet with parchment paper. 3. In a high-speed blender or food processor, combine the soaked chickpeas, parsley, cilantro, onion, garlic, flour, cumin, coriander, baking powder, and lemon juice. Pulse until all ingredients are well combined but not smooth; it should have the consistency of sand but stick together when pressed. 4. Using a cookie scoop or two spoons, divide the falafel mixture into 20 balls and place them on the prepared baking sheet. Lightly flatten each ball using the bottom of a measuring cup. This will help them cook more evenly. 5. Bake for 15 minutes. Flip. Bake for 10 to 15 minutes more, until lightly browned. 6. Refrigerate in an airtight container for up to 1 week or freeze for up to 1 month.
Per Serving:
calories: 129 | fat: 2g | protein: 7g | carbs: 22g | fiber: 6g

Bulgur Chickpea Pilaf

Prep time: 15 minutes | Cook time: 35 minutes | Serves 4

1 medium yellow onion, peeled and diced small
3 cloves garlic, peeled and minced
1½ tablespoons grated ginger
1½ cups bulgur
3 cups vegetable stock, or low-sodium vegetable broth
2 cups cooked chickpeas, or 1 (15-ounce / 425-g) can, drained and rinsed
1 Roma tomato, chopped
Zest and juice of 1 lemon
Salt and freshly ground black pepper, to taste
4 green onions (white and green parts), thinly sliced

1. Place the onion in a large saucepan and sauté over medium heat for 10 minutes. Add water 1 to 2 tablespoons at a time to keep the onion from sticking to the pan. Stir in the garlic and ginger and cook for 30 seconds. Add the bulgur and vegetable stock and bring to a boil over high heat. Reduce the heat to medium and cook, covered, until the bulgur is tender, about 15 minutes. 2. Stir in the chickpeas, tomato, and lemon zest and juice and cook for another 5 minutes. Season with salt and pepper and serve garnished with the green onions.

Per Serving:
calories: 344 | fat: 2g | protein: 14g | carbs: 69g | fiber: 13g

Mujadara (Lentils with Rice and Caramelized Onions)

Prep time: 10 minutes | Cook time: 2 hours | Serves 4

1½ cups green lentils, rinsed
¾ teaspoon ground cinnamon
½ teaspoon ground allspice
¾ cup brown basmati rice
3 large yellow onions, peeled and diced
Salt and freshly ground black pepper, to taste

1. Add the lentils to a large pot with 5 cups of water and bring to a boil over high heat. Reduce the heat to medium and simmer for 30 minutes. Add the cinnamon and allspice and cook for another 15 to 20 minutes, until the lentils are tender. 2. In a separate medium saucepan, bring 1½ cups of water to a boil. Add the rice and bring the pot to a boil over high heat. Reduce the heat to medium and cook the rice, covered, for 45 minutes, or until tender. 3. Heat a large skillet over high heat. Add the onions to the skillet and cook, stirring frequently, for 10 minutes. Add water 1 to 2 tablespoons at a time to keep the onions from sticking to the pan. Reduce the heat to medium-low and continue cooking until they are browned, about 10 minutes. Add the lentils and rice to the onions and mix well. Season with salt and pepper.

Per Serving:
calories: 405 | fat: 1g | protein: 21g | carbs: 77g | fiber: 10g

Roasted Beet Biryani

Prep time: 15 minutes | Cook time: 40 minutes | Serves 4

6 cups water, plus 5 tablespoons and more as needed
2 cups basmati rice, rinsed well
1 teaspoon ground cardamom
½ teaspoon cayenne pepper
¼ teaspoon ground cinnamon
¼ teaspoon ground aniseed
¼ teaspoon ground turmeric
1 yellow onion, diced
3 garlic cloves, minced
1 (4-ounce / 113-g) can diced green chiles
1 tablespoon grated peeled fresh ginger
1 large beet, peeled and finely chopped
3 carrots, diced
1 tablespoon yellow (mellow) miso paste
Oil, for coating (optional)
1 cup green peas
1 (15-ounce /425-g) can chickpeas, drained and rinsed
¼ cup packed chopped fresh cilantro, plus more for garnish

1. Preheat the oven to 400ºF (205ºC). 2. In a large pot over high heat, bring 6 cups of water to a boil. Reduce the heat to medium-low, add the rice, and cook for 10 minutes. The rice will be parcooked. Using a fine-mesh sieve, strain the rice, lightly rinse, and set aside. 3. In a small bowl, stir together the cardamom, cayenne pepper, cinnamon, aniseed, and turmeric. Stir in 2 tablespoons of water. Set aside. 4. Heat a pot over medium heat. Add the onion, garlic, and 1 tablespoon water. Cook, stirring, for 5 minutes, adding more water, 1 tablespoon at a time, to prevent burning. The onion should be well browned. 5. Stir in the soaked spices and cook, stirring, for 1 minute. Add the green chiles and ginger. Cook for 30 seconds more. 6. Add the beet, carrots, and 2 tablespoons of water. Sauté for 3 minutes, stirring. Stir in the miso paste and turn off the heat. 7. Lightly coat a 9-by-13-inch baking dish with oil, if using. Spread half the cooked rice in the prepared dish. Top the rice with the beet and carrot mix, then the peas, and finally the chickpeas. Sprinkle the cilantro evenly across the top. Spread the remaining rice on top and cover the dish with aluminum foil. 8. Bake for 15 minutes. Lightly mix, garnish with cilantro, and serve.

Per Serving:
calories: 547 | fat: 3g | protein: 18g | carbs: 112g | fiber: 9g

Chickpea Coconut Curry

Prep time: 10 minutes | Cook time: 30 minutes | Serves 4

2 teaspoons ground coriander
1 teaspoon ground cumin
½ teaspoon ground turmeric
¼ teaspoon freshly ground black pepper
¼ teaspoon cayenne pepper
1 large red onion, thinly sliced
3 tablespoons water, divided, plus more as needed
3 garlic cloves, minced
1 tablespoon grated peeled fresh ginger
1 (14-ounce / 397-g) can diced tomatoes
1 teaspoon garam masala
1 (14-ounce / 397-g) can full-fat coconut milk
1 (15-ounce /425-g) can chickpeas, drained and rinsed
Juice of 1 lime
1 tablespoon chopped fresh cilantro, plus more for serving
Lime wedges, for serving

1. In a small bowl, stir together the coriander, cumin, turmeric, black pepper, and cayenne pepper. 2. In a large pan over medium-high heat, combine the red onion and 1 tablespoon of water. Cook until the water evaporates and add another 1 tablespoon of water. Continue this process for 3 to 5 minutes, or until the onion is soft and just starting to brown. 3. Reduce the heat to medium-low and add the garlic and ginger. Cook for 2 to 3 minutes, adding water as needed to prevent burning, until the onion is browned. Evenly sprinkle the spice mixture onto the cooked vegetables. Cook, stirring slowly to toast the spices, for 30 seconds. Add 1 tablespoon of water and cook for 30 seconds more. 4. Carefully pour the tomatoes and their juices into the pan and stir. Cook over medium-low heat for 5 minutes, stirring. The tomatoes should be simmering and the pieces of tomato

will start to soften and break down. Evenly sprinkle the garam masala on the cooked tomatoes and stir to combine. 5. Pour in the coconut milk and chickpeas. Bring the curry to a simmer and cook for 10 minutes, stirring occasionally. 6. Stir in the lime juice and 1 tablespoon of cilantro. Serve with lime wedges for squeezing and a few pinches of cilantro.

Per Serving:

calories: 324 | fat: 21g | protein: 8g | carbs: 30g | fiber: 7g

Chapter 3   Basics

Pineapple Chutney

Prep time: 25 minutes | Cook time: 15 minutes | Makes 1½ cups

½ medium yellow onion, peeled and diced small
1 tablespoon grated ginger
2 jalapeño peppers, seeded and minced
½ tablespoon cumin seeds,

toasted and ground
½ fresh pineapple, peeled, cored, and diced
½ cup finely chopped cilantro
Salt, to taste (optional)

1. Place the onion in a large skillet or saucepan and sauté over medium heat for 7 to 8 minutes. Add water 1 to 2 tablespoons at a time to keep the onion from sticking to the pan. 2. Add the ginger, jalapeño peppers, and cumin seeds and cook for another 4 minutes. Add the pineapple and remove the pan from the heat. Stir in the cilantro and salt, if using.
Per Serving: (½ cup)
calories: 98 | fat: 0g | protein: 2g | carbs: 24g | fiber: 3g

Plant-Based Fish Sauce

Prep time: 10 minutes | Cook time: 20 minutes | Makes 3 to 4 cups

4 cups water
1 (4-by-8-inch) sheet of kombu
½ cup dried shiitake mushrooms

¼ cup low-sodium soy sauce, tamari, or coconut aminos
3 garlic cloves, crushed
2 teaspoons rice vinegar

1. In a medium saucepan, combine the water, kombu, mushrooms, soy sauce, garlic, and vinegar. Bring the mixture to a boil, then reduce the heat to low. 2. Cover and simmer for 15 to 20 minutes. Remove from the heat. Keep covered and allow to steep overnight or for at least 8 hours. 3. Strain and discard any solids. Store the plant-based fish sauce in the refrigerator in a glass bottle for up to 3 weeks, shaking well before each use.
Per Serving:
calories: 4 | fat: 0g | protein: 0g | carbs: 1g | fiber: 0g

Creamy Avocado-Lime Dressing

Prep time: 5 minutes | Cook time: 0 minutes | Serves 6

1 avocado, diced
¼ cup fresh lime or lemon juice
¼ cup cilantro leaves
½ teaspoon ground cumin

¼ teaspoon salt (optional)
½ cup water, plus more as needed

1. Process all the ingredients in a high-speed blender until smooth. Adjust the seasoning and add the water, 1 tablespoon at a time, plus more as needed to achieve the desired consistency. Use within 1 day.
Per Serving:
calories: 57 | fat: 5g | protein: 1g | carbs: 4g | fiber: 2g

Hemp Mylk

Prep time: 5 minutes | Cook time: 0 minutes | Makes 3 cups

½ cup hemp hearts
3 cups purified water, for blending

½ teaspoon ground cinnamon
2 dates, pitted

1. In a blender, combine all the ingredients and blend until smooth and creamy. 2. Pour into a glass jar with a tight lid and refrigerate. Your hemp mylk will last for up to 5 days in the fridge.
Per Serving:
calories: 47 | fat: 0g | protein: 1g | carbs: 11g | fiber: 1g

Lemon-Thyme Dressing

Prep time: 5 minutes | Cook time: 0 minutes | Serves 6

⅓ cup fresh lemon juice
2 sprigs fresh thyme, leaves stripped and chopped, stems discarded
1 garlic clove, sliced in half
1 teaspoon gluten-free tahini

½ teaspoon coconut sugar (optional)
½ teaspoon salt (optional)
Pinch black pepper
¼ cup plain gluten-free hummus

1. Combine the lemon juice, thyme, garlic, tahini, sugar, salt (if desired), and pepper in a jar with a tight-fitting lid. Add the hummus in a slow, steady stream and adjust the seasoning. Refrigerate for up to 5 days. (Remove the garlic clove before serving.)
Per Serving:
calories: 7 | fat: 0g | protein: 0g | carbs: 2g | fiber: 0g

Creamy Herbed Hemp Dressing

Prep time: 10 minutes | Cook time: 0 minutes | Serves 6

½ cup hemp seeds
¼ cup chopped flat-leaf parsley
2 tablespoons raw cashews
1 scallion, sliced
1 tablespoon apple cider vinegar
1 tablespoon fresh lemon juice
2 teaspoons capers, drained
1 teaspoon nutritional yeast

½ teaspoon garlic powder
½ teaspoon coconut sugar (optional)
¼ teaspoon dried dill
Salt and black pepper (optional)
1 or 2 tablespoons water (optional)

1. Process the hemp seeds, parsley, cashews, scallion, vinegar, lemon juice, capers, nutritional yeast, garlic powder, sugar, and dill in a high-speed blender until smooth. Season with salt (if desired) and pepper and add water, 1 tablespoon at a time, as needed to achieve desired consistency. Refrigerate in an airtight container for up to 5 days.
Per Serving:
calories: 106 | fat: 9g | protein: 4g | carbs: 5g | fiber: 2g

Herbed Millet Pizza Crust

Prep time: 5 minutes | Cook time: 40 minutes | Makes 1 large thin-crust pizza crust

½ cup coarsely ground millet
1½ cups water
1 tablespoon mixed dried Italian herbs

¼ teaspoon sea salt (optional)
1 to 2 tablespoons nutritional yeast

1. Preheat the oven to 350ºF (180ºC). Line an 8-inch-round pie dish or springform pan with parchment paper so that you can lift the crust out after it's cooked. The crust will be a bit fragile until it cools and tends to stick unless you use a nonstick pan. 2. Put the millet in a small pot with the water and a pinch salt, bring it to a boil, then cover and simmer for 15 to 20 minutes. Stir it occasionally to keep it from sticking to the bottom of the pot. You can add the dried herbs to cook with the millet for a more intense flavor, or just stir them in after the millet is cooked. 3. Once the millet is cooked, add the salt (if using) and nutritional yeast. Spread the cooked and seasoned millet out in an even layer in your pan, all the way to the edges. 4. Put the crust in the oven for 20 minutes, or until lightly browned around the edges.
Per Serving: (1 crust)
calories: 378 | fat: 4g | protein: 11g | carbs: 72g | fiber: 8g

Tomato Sauce

Prep time: 10 minutes | Cook time: 40 minutes | Makes 4 cups

1 medium yellow onion, peeled and diced small
6 cloves garlic, peeled and minced
6 tablespoons minced basil

2 tablespoons minced oregano
1 (28-ounce / 794-g) can diced tomatoes, puréed
Salt, to taste (optional)

1. Place the onion in a large saucepan and sauté over medium heat for 10 minutes. Add water 1 to 2 tablespoons at a time to keep the onion from sticking to the pan. 2. Add the garlic, basil, and oregano and cook for another 3 minutes. Add the puréed tomatoes and salt (if using) and cook, covered, over medium-low heat for 25 minutes.
Per Serving: (1 cup)
calories: 48 | fat: 0g | protein: 2g | carbs: 10g | fiber: 4g

Tahini Dressing

Prep time: 5 minutes | Cook time: 0 minutes | Makes ½ cup

¼ cup tahini
1 teaspoon minced garlic
3 tablespoons lemon juice
1 tablespoon maple syrup (optional)
1 teaspoon soy sauce

1 teaspoon ground cumin
1 tablespoon olive oil (optional)
1 tablespoon hot water
Pinch of salt and pepper (optional)

1. In a small bowl, whisk together all the ingredients until well combined. 2. Store in an airtight container in the fridge for up to 7 days.
Per Serving: (½ cup)
calories: 283 | fat: 24g | protein: 6g | carbs: 16g | fiber: 3g

20-Minute Cashew Cheese Sauce

Prep time: 5 minutes | Cook time: 15 minutes | Makes about 3 cups

½ cup raw cashews
1 cup peeled and diced potatoes
¼ cup diced carrots
¼ cup diced onions
3 cups water
4 tablespoons nutritional yeast
1 tablespoon lemon juice

1 teaspoon miso paste
½ teaspoon garlic powder
½ teaspoon dry mustard
Pinch paprika
Ground black pepper
Salt (optional)

1. Soak the cashews for 30 to 60 minutes in very hot (boiled) water before use in order for your sauce to be creamy and delicious. You can omit this step if you have a high-speed blender. 2. In a medium pot, combine the potatoes, carrots, and onion and cover with the water. Bring to a boil and cook for about 15 minutes, until the vegetables are tender and easily mushed with a fork. 3. While the vegetables are boiling, drain the cashews if you soaked them. Transfer them to a blender or food processor and add the nutritional yeast, lemon juice, miso paste, garlic powder, mustard, and paprika. Season with pepper and salt (if using). 4. When the vegetables are cooked, reserve 1 cup of cooking water and add it to the blender along with the cooked vegetables. Blend for 30 to 60 seconds, until smooth. This will keep for up to 4 days in the refrigerator.
Per Serving:
calories: 55 | fat: 3g | protein: 3g | carbs: 6g | fiber: 1g

Cheesy Sprinkle

Prep time: 5 minutes | Cook time: 0 minutes | Makes ½ cup

½ cup ground sunflower seeds, or Brazil nuts, or macadamia nuts
2 teaspoons sea salt (optional)

1 to 2 tablespoons nutritional yeast
1 tablespoon olive oil (optional)

1. Place the sunflower seeds in a small bowl, then add the salt (if using) and nutritional yeast. Mix to combine. 2. Leave as is for a dry sprinkle, or add just enough olive oil (if using) to bring the mixture together into a crumbly texture.
Per Serving: (1 tablespoon)
calories: 284 | fat: 25g | protein: 9g | carbs: 9g | fiber: 4g

Maple-Dijon Dressing

Prep time: 5 minutes | Cook time: 0 minutes | Serves 4

¼ cup apple cider vinegar
2 tablespoons maple syrup
2 teaspoons gluten-free Dijon mustard

¼ teaspoon black pepper
2 tablespoons water
Salt (optional)

1. Combine the vinegar, maple syrup (if desired), mustard, pepper and water in a small jar with a tight-fitting lid. Season with salt to taste, if desired. Refrigerate for up to 5 days.
Per Serving:
calories: 31 | fat: 0g | protein: 0g | carbs: 7g | fiber: 0g

Roasted Red Pepper Sauce

Prep time: 10 minutes | Cook time: 0 minutes | Makes 2 cups

1 (12-ounce / 340-g) package extra-firm silken tofu, drained
2 large red bell peppers, roasted and seeded
3 cloves garlic, peeled and chopped

2 tablespoons chopped dill
1 teaspoon salt (optional)
½ teaspoon freshly ground black pepper
Zest of 1 lemon

1. Combine all ingredients in the bowl of a food processor and purée until smooth and creamy. Refrigerate in an airtight container until ready to use.
Per Serving: (1 cup)
calories: 205 | fat: 11g | protein: 19g | carbs: 14g | fiber: 3g

Lime-Cumin Dressing

Prep time: 5 minutes | Cook time: 0 minutes | Serves 4

1 teaspoon ground cumin
1 teaspoon coconut sugar (optional)
¼ teaspoon salt (optional)
3 tablespoons fresh lime juice

1 tablespoon apple cider vinegar
2 teaspoons extra virgin olive oil (optional)

1. Combine the cumin, sugar, and salt (if desired) in a medium jar with a tight-fitting lid. Whisk in the lime juice and vinegar. Whisk in the oil in a slow, steady stream, if desired. Refrigerate for up to 4 days. Shake to combine as needed.
Per Serving:
calories: 28 | fat: 2g | protein: 0g | carbs: 2g | fiber: 2g

Cauliflower Béchamel

Prep time: 15 minutes | Cook time: 30 minutes | Makes about 3½ cups

1 large head cauliflower, cut into florets (about 3 cups)
Unsweetened plain almond milk, as needed
1 medium yellow onion, peeled and diced small
2 cloves garlic, peeled and minced

2 teaspoons minced thyme
¼ cup finely chopped basil
¼ cup nutritional yeast (optional)
¼ teaspoon ground nutmeg
Salt and freshly ground black pepper, to taste

1. Add the cauliflower to a large pot and add water to cover. Bring to a boil over high heat and cook until the cauliflower is very tender, about 10 minutes. Drain the excess water and purée the cauliflower using an immersion blender or in a blender with a tight-fitting lid, covered with a towel, in batches if necessary. Add almond milk, if needed, to achieve a creamy consistency. Set the purée aside while you prepare the rest of the ingredients. 2. Place the onion in a large skillet or saucepan and sauté over medium heat for 10 minutes. Add water 1 to 2 tablespoons at a time to keep the onion from sticking to the pan. Add the garlic, thyme, and basil and cook for another minute. Add the nutritional yeast (if using), nutmeg, and salt and pepper and cook for 5 minutes, or until heated through. 3. Add the onion mixture to the cauliflower purée and blend until smooth, adding up to ½ cup

of water if necessary to achieve a smooth consistency.
Per Serving: (½ cup)
calories: 38 | fat: 0g | protein: 3g | carbs: 6g | fiber: 3g

Croutons

Prep time: 5 minutes | Cook time: 15 minutes | Serves 4

½ day-old baguette, sliced
2 tablespoons olive oil (optional)

½ tablespoon garlic salt (optional)

1. Preheat the oven to 350ºF (180ºC). 2. Brush the baguette slices with the olive oil and sprinkle with the garlic salt, if desired. 3. Cut the bread into cubes, place on a baking sheet, and bake for 10 to 15 minutes or until golden brown. 4. Allow the croutons to cool before serving. 5. The croutons are best if served immediately after baking.
Per Serving:
calories: 94 | fat: 7g | protein: 1g | carbs: 7g | fiber: 0g

Greener Guacamole

Prep time: 15 minutes | Cook time: 0 minutes | Makes 1 to 1½ cups

2 ripe avocados, pitted, peeled, and diced
Juice of ½ lime
2 scallions, green and white parts, chopped
1 garlic clove, minced
½ teaspoon ground cumin
½ small bunch cilantro, chopped
Ground black pepper
Salt (optional)

1. In a medium bowl, combine the avocados, lime juice, scallions, garlic, cumin, cilantro, pepper, and salt (if using). Mash together with a fork to the desired consistency. Transfer to a serving bowl and chill until serving.
Per Serving:
calories: 40 | fat: 4g | protein: 1g | carbs: 3g | fiber: 2g

Tempeh Bacon

Prep time: 5 minutes | Cook time: 10 minutes | Serves 4

2 tablespoons soy sauce
1 tablespoon water
1 tablespoon maple syrup (optional)
½ tablespoon liquid smoke

1 (8-ounce / 227-g) package tempeh
1 tablespoon canola oil (optional)

1. In a medium bowl, combine the soy sauce, water, maple syrup (if desired), and liquid smoke. Set aside. 2. Cut the tempeh block in half lengthwise and then slice it as thinly as possible. 3. In a large pan over high heat, heat the oil, if desired. Add the tempeh in a single layer and cook for 2 minutes. Flip and cook for 2 more minutes. 4. While the tempeh is still in the pan, add the liquid mixture and sauté the tempeh for 3 minutes. Flip and cook for 3 more minutes or until the liquid is absorbed. 5. The Tempeh Bacon is best if served immediately.
Per Serving:
calories: 17 | fat: 11g | protein: 11g | carbs: 11g | fiber: 0g

Mayonnaise

Prep time: 5 minutes | Cook time: 0 minutes | Makes 1½ cups

1 (12-ounce / 340-g) package extra-firm silken tofu, drained
1 teaspoon dry mustard
½ teaspoon onion powder

½ teaspoon garlic powder
½ teaspoon salt, or to taste (optional)
3 tablespoons red wine vinegar

1. Combine all ingredients in the bowl of a food processor. Purée until smooth and creamy.
Per Serving: (½ cup)
calories: 110 | fat: 6g | protein: 11g | carbs: 3g | fiber: 0g

Quinoa

Prep time: 5 minutes | Cook time: 5 minutes | Makes 3 cups

1 cup quinoa

1½ cups vegetable broth

1. Rinse the quinoa in cold water using a fine-mesh strainer. 2. Put the quinoa and broth into the pressure cooker and cook on high pressure for 5 minutes. 3. Let the pressure out, remove the lid, and fluff the quinoa with a fork. 4. Store in an airtight container in the fridge for up to 5 days.
Per Serving: (1 cup)
calories: 214 | fat: 3g | protein: 8g | carbs: 38g | fiber: 4g

Sunflower Hemp Milk

Prep time: 5 minutes | Cook time: 0 minutes | Makes 2 cups

2 cups water
3 tablespoons sunflower seeds
2 tablespoons hemp seeds or other seeds
1 to 2 dates, or 10 drops pure stevia (or vanilla stevia), or 1 to

2 tablespoons unrefined sugar (optional)
¼ teaspoon pure vanilla extract (optional)

1. Put everything in a blender, and purée until smooth. 2. Strain the fiber through a piece of cheesecloth or a fine-mesh sieve. 3. Keep in an airtight container in the fridge for up to 5 days.
Per Serving: (1 cup)
calories: 139 | fat: 11g | protein: 4g | carbs: 7g | fiber: 2g

Piecrust

Prep time: 10 minutes | Cook time: 0 minutes | Serves 4

1 cup all-purpose flour, plus more for rolling
½ teaspoon baking powder
¼ teaspoon salt (optional)
2 tablespoons canola oil, plus more if storing dough for later

(optional)
½ teaspoon lemon juice
3½ tablespoons plant-based milk
4 tablespoons water

1. In a medium bowl, thoroughly mix all the ingredients with a wooden spoon until a ball of dough forms. 2. Wrap the dough in plastic wrap and refrigerate for 1 hour. 3. If using right away, dust a work surface with flour, place the chilled dough down, and roll it out into a thin, flat 11-inch circle using a lightly floured rolling pin. Transfer to a 9-inch pie dish. Fill with your choice of fillings and bake according to the recipe's instructions. 4. If not using right away, cover the exterior of the dough with 1 teaspoon oil or less (if desired) to keep it from drying out. Place this lightly oiled ball of dough in a medium bowl and cover tightly with plastic wrap (or place the dough in an airtight container). Refrigerate for up to 7 days.
Per Serving:
calories: 183 | fat: 8g | protein: 4g | carbs: 25g | fiber: 1g

Plant-Based Parmesan

Prep time: 5 minutes | Cook time: 0 minutes | Makes 1 heaping cup

1 cup raw cashews
⅓ cup nutritional yeast

¾ teaspoon garlic powder
½ teaspoon salt (optional)

1. In a blender or food processor, combine the cashews, nutritional yeast, garlic powder, and salt (if using). 2. Blend on medium-high until the mixture has the texture of grated parmesan cheese. You may need to stop and start the blender or food processor a couple of times to make sure the nuts are not clumping together on the bottom. Store in a glass or plastic container in the refrigerator for up to 1 month.
Per Serving:
calories: 219 | fat: 15g | protein: 11g | carbs: 14g | fiber: 4g

Lemon-Tahini Dressing

Prep time: 5 minutes | Cook time: 0 minutes | Serves 8

¼ cup fresh lemon juice
1 teaspoon maple syrup (optional)
1 small garlic clove, chopped

½ cup gluten-free tahini
¼ teaspoon salt (optional)
⅛ teaspoon black pepper
¼ to ½ cup water

1. Pulse the lemon juice, sugar, garlic, tahini, salt (if desired), and pepper in a high-speed blender to combine. Slowly add the water, starting with ¼ cup, until it reaches the desired consistency. Refrigerate in an airtight container for up to 5 days.
Per Serving:
calories: 94 | fat: 8g | protein: 3g | carbs: 4g | fiber: 1g

Coriander Chutney

Prep time: 15 minutes | Cook time: 0 minutes | Makes about 1 cup

½ teaspoon cumin seeds, toasted and ground
½ teaspoon yellow mustard seeds, toasted and ground
1 large bunch cilantro
1 small yellow onion, peeled and chopped (about ½ cup)

¼ cup unsweetened coconut
3 tablespoons grated ginger
2 serrano chiles, stemmed (for less heat, remove the seeds)
Zest and juice of 2 lemons
Salt, to taste (optional)

1. Combine all ingredients in a blender and blend on high until smooth. Add water as needed to achieve a thick paste.
Per Serving:(¼ cup)
calories: 38 | fat: 1g | protein: 0g | carbs: 5g | fiber: 1g

5-Minute Tofu Cheese Sauce

Prep time: 5 minutes | Cook time: 0 minutes | Makes about 2 cups

1 (12-ounce / 340-g) package silken tofu
½ cup nutritional yeast
1½ teaspoons onion powder
½ teaspoon garlic powder
¼ teaspoon paprika

2 teaspoons Dijon mustard
1 tablespoon white wine vinegar
1 teaspoon salt (optional)
½ cup unsweetened plant-based milk

1. Place the tofu, nutritional yeast, onion powder, garlic powder, paprika, mustard, vinegar, salt (if using), and milk into a blender or food processor. Blend for 30 to 60 seconds, until well combined. 2. Heat the sauce on the stove or in the microwave. This will keep for up to 4 days in the refrigerator.
Per Serving:
calories: 54 | fat: 2g | protein: 7g | carbs: 4g | fiber: 2g

Green on Greens Dressing

Prep time: 10 minutes | Cook time: 0 minutes | Serves 10

¾ cup water, plus extra as needed
½ cup chopped flat-leaf parsley
¼ cup tahini
1 scallion, sliced
1 tablespoon apple cider

vinegar
2 umeboshi plums, pitted and roughly chopped
1 teaspoon reduced-sodium tamari

1. Process all the ingredients in a blender until smooth. The dressing will thicken upon sitting, so add additional water as desired before serving. Refrigerate in an airtight container for up to 2 days.
Per Serving:
calories: 44 | fat: 3g | protein: 2g | carbs: 3g | fiber: 1g

Date Syrup

Prep time: 30 minutes | Cook time: 0 minutes | Makes 1⅓ cups

1 cup Medjool dates, pitted (about 10 large dates)
1¼ cups purified water, for

blending
1½ teaspoons fresh lemon juice

1. In a small bowl, cover the dates with warm water (not the purified water) and let sit for 30 minutes. 2. Drain and rinse the dates. Place them in a high-speed blender together with the purified water and lemon juice. Blend for 45 to 60 seconds, or until smooth. 3. Transfer to an airtight container and store in the refrigerator for up to 2 weeks.
Per Serving:
calories: 111 | fat: 0g | protein: 1g | carbs: 30g | fiber: 2g

Fresh Tomato Salsa

Prep time: 15 minutes | Cook time: 0 minutes | Makes about 4 cups

3 large ripe tomatoes, diced small
1 small red onion, peeled and

diced small
½ cup chopped cilantro
1 to 2 jalapeño peppers, minced

(for less heat, remove the seeds)
2 cloves garlic, peeled and

minced
3 tablespoons fresh lime juice
Salt, to taste (optional)

1. Combine all ingredients in a large bowl and mix well. Store refrigerated until ready to serve.
Per Serving: (1 cup)
calories: 38 | fat: 0g | protein: 1g | carbs: 8g | fiber: 2g

Potatoes

Prep time: 0 minutes | Cook time: 5 minutes | Serves 1

1 medium potato

1. Using a fork, poke holes all over the potato for ventilation. 2. Put the potato on a microwave-safe plate and microwave it for 2 minutes. Flip it over and microwave for 2 more minutes. 3. If the potato is not soft yet, microwave again in 1-minute increments until it's soft. Store in the refrigerator in an airtight container for up to 4 days.
Per Serving:
calories: 164 | fat: 0g | protein: 4g | carbs: 37g | fiber: 5g

Green Split Peas

Prep time: 5 minutes | Cook time: 45 minutes | Makes 2 cups

1 cup split peas, rinsed

1½ cups water

1. Put the split peas and water into a large pot with a lid. 2. Over high heat, bring to a boil. 3. Cover the pot with the lid and reduce the heat to low. 4. Simmer for 45 minutes. 5. Store in an airtight container in the fridge for up to 5 days.
Per Serving: (1 cup)
calories: 347 | fat: 1g | protein: 24g | carbs: 63g | fiber: 25g

Fried Tofu

Prep time: 5 minutes | Cook time: 15 minutes | Serves 4

1 (14-ounce / 397-g) block extra-firm tofu

1½ tablespoons canola oil (optional)

1. Place the package of tofu in the freezer overnight or for at least 4 hours. 2. Bring a pot of water to a boil. Remove the completely frozen tofu from its package and add it to the pot. 3. Boil the tofu for 10 minutes. 4. Remove the tofu from the pot to cool. When cool enough to handle, gently press the water out of the tofu with a clean kitchen towel. Be careful not to break the tofu. 5. Cut the tofu into ½-inch cubes. 6. In a large pan, heat the canola oil (if desired) over high heat. Once the oil is hot, add the tofu. 7. Fry the tofu for 1 to 2 minutes on each side or until it turns golden. When you're finished frying, place the tofu on a plate lined with a kitchen towel or paper towel to soak up the excess oil. 8. Store in an airtight container in the fridge for up to 5 days.
Per Serving:
calories: 150 | fat: 12g | protein: 11g | carbs: 2g | fiber: 1g

Chipotle Peppers in Adobo Sauce

Prep time: 30 minutes | Cook time: 20 minutes | Makes 20 to 25 peppers

1 (2-ounce / 57-g) package morita chiles (about 17 to 20)
1 (2-ounce / 57-g) package chipotle chiles (about 10 to 12)
1 to 2 cups boiling water
½ onion, chopped
1 garlic clove, crushed
½ teaspoon ground cumin
½ teaspoon dried oregano
½ teaspoon dried marjoram
¼ cup apple cider vinegar
¼ cup rice vinegar
2 tablespoons date syrup (optional)
2 tablespoons tomato paste

1. Preheat the oven to 350ºF (180ºC). Line a baking sheet with aluminum foil. Place the morita and chipotle chiles on the prepared baking sheet and roast for 5 minutes. Then place them in a medium glass bowl and cover with the boiling water. Use a small plate or bowl to submerge the chiles and let them soak to rehydrate for 30 minutes. 2. Meanwhile, in a nonstick skillet over medium-high heat, dry sauté the onion for about 5 minutes, adding 1 teaspoon of water as needed to prevent sticking, until it is translucent. Add the garlic, cumin, oregano, and marjoram and sauté for 1 more minute, until fragrant. Remove from heat. 3. Transfer the onion mixture to a blender. Add the apple cider vinegar, rice vinegar, date syrup (if using), and tomato paste. After the chiles are rehydrated, remove the stem from 6 to 7 of the morita chiles and, using a paring knife, slice them open to scrape out the seeds. Add the scraped chiles to the blender along with ¾ cup of their soaking liquid. Blend well. Discard any leftover liquid. 4. Pour the sauce back into the skillet and add the remaining chiles. Cook over medium heat, stirring occasionally, for 15 minutes, until the sauce is reduced by half.
Per Serving:
calories: 30 | fat: 0g | protein: 1g | carbs: 6g | fiber: 2g

Oil-Free Hummus

Prep time: 10 minutes | Cook time: 0 minutes | Makes about 2 cups

1 (15-ounce / 425-g) can chickpeas, undrained
¼ cup raw sesame seeds
4 garlic cloves
Juice from ½ lemon
¾ teaspoon ground cumin
¼ teaspoon paprika
½ teaspoon salt (optional)

1. Put the chickpeas and about half of the liquid from the can in a blender or food processor. Add the sesame seeds, garlic, lemon juice, cumin, paprika, and salt (if using). Blend until creamy. Store in the refrigerator for up to 3 days.
Per Serving:
calories: 40 | fat: 2g | protein: 2g | carbs: 4g | fiber: 1g

Easy-Peasy Almond Milk

Prep time: 5 minutes | Cook time: 0 minutes | Makes 2 cups

2 to 3 tablespoons raw almond butter
2 cups water
Pinch sea salt (optional)
1 to 2 dates, or 10 drops pure stevia (or vanilla stevia), or 1 to 2 tablespoons unrefined sugar (optional)
¼ teaspoon pure vanilla extract (optional)

1. Put everything in a blender and purée until smooth. 2. Strain the fiber from the almonds through a piece of cheesecloth or a fine-mesh sieve. 3. Keep in an airtight container in the fridge for up to 5 days.
Per Serving: (1 cup)
calories: 110 | fat: 8g | protein: 3g | carbs: 5g | fiber: 2g

Chapter 4   Salads

Sweet Potato, Kale, and Red Cabbage Salad

Prep time: 10 minutes | Cook time: 20 minutes | Serves 2

Salad:
1 teaspoon extra-virgin olive oil (optional)
2 medium sweet potatoes, peeled and diced small
Pinch of salt (optional)
1 cup frozen corn
2 cups stemmed and chopped kale
1 cup shredded red cabbage

¼ cup pepitas
Dressing:
1 avocado, peeled and pitted
Juice of 1½ limes
Pinch of salt (optional)
Pinch red pepper flakes (optional)
3 tablespoons chopped fresh cilantro leaves
½ cup water

1. Make the Salad: Preheat the oven to 425ºF (220ºC). Grease a sheet pan with the olive oil. 2. Spread the sweet potato on the prepared sheet pan in one layer and sprinkle with salt (if using). Bake for 10 minutes. Using a spatula, turn the potatoes and continue to bake for another 5 minutes. Add the corn to the sheet pan and bake everything for 5 minutes more. 3. Make the Dressing: In a blender, combine the avocado, lime juice, salt, red pepper flakes (if using), cilantro, and water and blend until smooth. 4. Assemble the Salad: In a large bowl, combine the kale and cabbage, add half of the dressing, and toss gently. Add the sweet potatoes, corn, and the remaining dressing and toss until combined. The warm corn and sweet potatoes will help soften the kale slightly. Divide the salad between 2 bowls, top with the pepitas, and serve.
Per Serving:
calories: 488 | fat: 25g | protein: 13g | carbs: 64g | fiber: 16g

Israeli Quinoa Salad

Prep time: 10 minutes | Cook time: 15 minutes | Serves 4

½ cup quinoa
¼ teaspoon ground cumin
¼ teaspoon turmeric
1 cup finely chopped tomatoes (from 1 to 2 medium tomatoes)
1 cup finely chopped cucumber (from about 1 medium cucumber, seeded)
½ cup finely chopped roasted

red bell pepper (from about 1 medium red pepper, roasted and seeded)
1 tablespoon basil, finely chopped
Juice of 1 lemon
Salt and freshly ground black pepper, to taste

1. Rinse the quinoa under cold water and drain. Bring 1¼ cups of water to a boil in a medium saucepan over high heat. Add the quinoa, cumin, and turmeric and bring to a boil over medium-high heat. Reduce the heat to low, cover, and cook for 10 to 15 minutes, or until all the water is absorbed, stirring occasionally. Remove the pan from the heat, fluff the quinoa with a fork, and allow it to cool for 5 minutes. 2. While the quinoa cools, combine the tomato, cucumber, red pepper, basil, and lemon juice in a medium bowl. Stir in the

cooled quinoa and season with salt and pepper.
Per Serving:
calories: 96 | fat: 1g | protein: 3g | carbs: 17g | fiber: 2g

Chickpea and Avocado Salad

Prep time: 10 minutes | Cook time: 0 minutes | Serves 2

1 cup chopped romaine lettuce
1 cup arugula
1 (15-ounce /425-g) can chickpeas, drained and rinsed
1 cup diced (½-inch) English cucumber
1 cup cherry tomatoes, halved
1 large avocado, halved, pitted,

and diced
1 teaspoon dried parsley
½ teaspoon dried thyme
Freshly ground black pepper, to taste
3 tablespoons apple cider vinegar

1. In a large bowl, toss together the romaine lettuce, arugula, chickpeas, cucumber, tomatoes, avocado, parsley, and thyme. Season with pepper. 2. Sprinkle on the vinegar and toss to coat. 3. This salad is best enjoyed fresh but can be refrigerated to serve the following day.
Per Serving:
calories: 380 | fat: 19g | protein: 13g | carbs: 45g | fiber: 18g

Fiery Couscous Salad

Prep time: 5 minutes | Cook time: 5 minutes | Serves 3

1 cup cooked or canned chickpea
½ cup dry couscous
3 tangerines
1 (2-inch) piece ginger, minced
¼ cup tahini

½ cup water
Optional Toppings:
Cinnamon
Fresh mint
Raisins

1. When using dry chickpeas, soak and cook ⅓ cup of dry chickpeas if necessary. Cook the couscous for about 5 minutes. 2. Meanwhile, add the tahini, minced ginger and water to a small airtight container or bowl. Whisk the tahini and ginger in the bowl into a smooth dressing, adding more water if necessary. Alternatively, shake the container with tahini, ginger and water until everything is thoroughly mixed, adding more water if you want a thinner and less creamy dressing. 3. Add the couscous, dressing and chickpeas to a large bowl and mix thoroughly. 4. Peel and section the tangerines and set them aside to garnish the salad. 5. Divide the salad between two bowls, garnish with the tangerines and the optional toppings, serve and enjoy! 6. Store the salad in an airtight container in the fridge, and consume within 2 days. Alternatively, store in the freezer for a maximum of 30 days and thaw at room temperature. The salad can be served cold.
Per Serving:
calories: 349 | fat: 14g | protein: 14g | carbs: 41g | fiber: 8g

Roasted Root Vegetable Salad Bowl

Prep time: 15 minutes | Cook time: 35 minutes | Serves 2

Roasted Vegetables:
1 sweet potato, peeled and chopped into bite-size pieces
1 parsnip, peeled and sliced into ¼-inch rounds
2 carrots, peeled and sliced into ½-inch rounds
2 tablespoons extra virgin olive oil (optional)
½ teaspoon salt (optional)
Tahini Dressing:
¼ cup tahini
1 tablespoon maple syrup

(optional)
1 tablespoon lemon juice
1 clove garlic
¼ teaspoon salt (optional)
Pinch of ground black pepper
3 tablespoons water
Assemble:
¼ cup diced red onion
½ cup chopped red cabbage
9 ounces (255 g) baby spinach
¼ cup raw shelled hempseed
1 tablespoon black or white chia seeds

Make Roasted Vegetables: 1. Preheat the oven to 375ºF (190ºC). 2. Place the sweet potatoes, parsnips, and carrots on a baking sheet, keeping them separated. Drizzle the oil (if desired) over the top and lightly toss, still keeping the vegetables separated. Sprinkle with salt, if desired. Bake for 30 to 35 minutes or until they can be pierced with a fork. Set aside. Make Tahini Dressing: 3. Add all the dressing ingredients to a blender and blend until smooth. Assemble: 4. Prepare the salad bowls by placing half the spinach in the bottom of each bowl. Arrange all the remaining vegetables and hempseed in a circle around the edge of the bowl. Pour half of the dressing in the center of the vegetable round. Sprinkle with the chia seeds.
Per Serving:
calories: 395 | fat: 22g | protein: 24g | carbs: 26g | fiber: 8g

Succotash Salad

Prep time: 20 minutes | Cook time: 0 minutes | Serves 4

1½ cups cooked baby lima beans
3 ears corn, kernels removed (about 2 cups)
2 large tomatoes, chopped
1 medium red onion, peeled and diced
¼ cup balsamic vinegar, or to taste
¼ cup chopped parsley
Salt and freshly ground black pepper, to taste

1. Combine all ingredients in a large bowl and mix well.
Per Serving:
calories: 221 | fat: 1g | protein: 9g | carbs: 47g | fiber: 9g

Creamy Chickpea and Avocado Salad

Prep time: 20 minutes | Cook time: 0 minutes | Serves 2

1 (15-ounce / 425-g) can chickpeas, drained and rinsed
1 avocado, peeled and pitted
2 tablespoons slivered almonds
1 celery stalk, minced
1 large carrot, peeled and grated or minced
3 cherry tomatoes, diced small
6 Kalamata olives, pitted and chopped
Juice of 1 lemon
2 tablespoons chopped fresh parsley
½ teaspoon salt (optional)

1. In a medium bowl, combine the chickpeas and avocados and mash with a fork, until the avocado is smooth and the chickpeas are mostly broken but still chunky. 2. Add the almonds, celery, carrot, tomatoes, olives, lemon juice, parsley, and salt and mix until well combined. Serve immediately.
Per Serving:
calories: 396 | fat: 22g | protein: 12g | carbs: 43g | fiber: 17g

Smoky Potato Salad over Greens

Prep time: 25 minutes | Cook time: 15 minutes | Serves 6

2 pounds (907 g) waxy potatoes
¼ cup apple cider vinegar
2 scallions, sliced
1 teaspoon maple syrup (optional)
1 teaspoon tomato paste
½ teaspoon gluten-free Dijon
mustard
½ teaspoon salt (optional)
½ teaspoon smoked paprika
¼ teaspoon black pepper
2 drops liquid smoke
12 ounces (340 g) baby greens
¼ cup unsalted, roasted almonds, chopped

1. Steam or boil the potatoes in a large pot over medium-high heat until fork-tender, about 15 minutes. Drain and let cool in a single layer. 2. Meanwhile, whisk the vinegar, scallions, maple syrup, tomato paste, mustard, salt (if desired), paprika, pepper, and liquid smoke together in a large bowl. 3. Chop the potatoes into bite-size pieces. Add to the bowl and toss gently with the dressing. Serve over the greens and top with almonds if serving immediately. The salad can be refrigerated for up to 5 days (though the oil-free version will only last a day due to the avocado), then combined with the greens and almonds before eating.
Per Serving:
calories: 179 | fat: 3g | protein: 5g | carbs: 34g | fiber: 6g

Farro Salad with Italian Vinaigrette

Prep time: 10 minutes | Cook time: 0 minutes | Serves 4 to 6

Vinaigrette:
⅔ cup aquafaba (liquid from 1 can chickpeas)
⅓ cup red-wine vinegar
2 tablespoons Italian seasoning
2 tablespoons nutritional yeast
1 tablespoon red miso paste
½ teaspoon garlic powder
½ teaspoon onion powder
½ teaspoon paprika
Salad:
2 cups cooked farro, chilled
1 (15-ounce / 425-g) can chickpeas, strained (reserve the liquid for the dressing) and rinsed
1 cup diced peeled cucumber
1 cup halved grape tomatoes
½ cup diced red bell pepper
½ cup chopped broccoli florets
½ cup sliced green olives with pimentos
½ cup sliced black olives

Make the Vinaigrette: 1. In a small bowl or container with a lid, combine the aquafaba, vinegar, Italian seasoning, nutritional yeast, miso, garlic powder, onion powder, and paprika. Whisk vigorously or shake. Make the Salad: 2. In a large bowl, combine the farro, chickpeas, cucumber, tomatoes, bell pepper, broccoli, green olives, and black olives. Using a wooden spoon or rubber spatula, gently mix together. 3. Pour the dressing over the salad, and stir to coat. If you're making for the next day, refrigerate until ready to serve.
Per Serving:
calories: 497 | fat: 13g | protein: 15g | carbs: 75g | fiber: 14g

Classic French Vinaigrette

Prep time: 5 minutes | Cook time: 0 minutes | Serves 4

3 tablespoons apple cider vinegar	mustard
2 tablespoons minced shallot	½ teaspoon dried thyme
1 tablespoon balsamic vinegar	2 teaspoons olive oil (optional)
1 teaspoon gluten-free Dijon	Salt and black pepper (optional)

1. Combine the apple cider vinegar, shallot, and balsamic vinegar in a medium jar with a tight-fitting lid. Let sit for 5 minutes. Stir in the mustard and thyme. Whisk in the oil in a slow, steady stream and season with salt and pepper to taste, if desired. Refrigerate for up to 5 days.

Per Serving:
calories: 24 | fat: 2g | protein: 0g | carbs: 2g | fiber: 0g

Garden Salad with Sumac Vinaigrette

Prep time: 15 minutes | Cook time: 0 minutes | Serves 2

Dressing:	pepper, to taste (optional)
Juice of 1 lemon	Salad:
1 tablespoon cider vinegar	½ medium cucumber, chopped
2 tablespoons extra-virgin olive oil (optional)	1 small zucchini, chopped
1 tablespoon agave nectar (optional)	1 bell pepper, seeded and chopped
1 tablespoon minced or grated fresh ginger	2 small carrots, chopped
½ teaspoon sumac powder	1 cup cherry tomatoes, halved
½ teaspoon ground cumin	½ cup fresh parsley, finely chopped
Salt and freshly ground black	2 tablespoons finely chopped fresh mint

1. Prepare the dressing: In a large bowl, mix together all the dressing ingredients, including the salt (if using) and black pepper to taste. 2. Prepare the salad: Add the cucumber, zucchini, bell pepper, carrots, tomatoes and herbs to the bowl and mix everything thoroughly until the vinaigrette covers all the vegetables. 3. Serve!

Per Serving:
calories: 189 | fat: 14g | protein: 3g | carbs: 15g | fiber: 4g

Orange, Fennel and White Bean Salad

Prep time: 15 minutes | Cook time: 0 minutes | Serves 4

6 large oranges, peeled and segmented	fennel fronds
2 tablespoons fresh lemon juice	2 cups cooked navy beans, or 1 (15-ounce / 425-g) can, drained and rinsed
2 tablespoons balsamic vinegar	
1 medium fennel bulb, trimmed and thinly sliced	Salt, to taste (optional)
2 tablespoons minced fresh	Cayenne pepper, to taste
	4 cups arugula

1. Combine the orange sections, lemon juice, balsamic vinegar, fennel bulb and fronds, beans, salt (if using), and cayenne pepper in a large bowl and mix well. Let sit for 1 hour before serving. 2. To serve, divide the arugula among 4 individual plates and spoon the salad on top of the greens.

Per Serving:
calories: 267 | fat: 1g | protein: 10g | carbs: 56g | fiber: 18g

Strawberry-Pistachio Salad

Prep time: 10 minutes | Cook time: 0 minutes | Serves 6

¼ cup orange juice	chopped
2 tablespoons fresh lime juice	1½ cups cooked cannellini beans, drained and rinsed
¼ teaspoon salt, plus more to taste (optional)	1 (5 to 6 ounces / 142 to 170 g) container mixed baby greens
⅛ teaspoon black pepper, plus more to taste	½ cup chopped cilantro
½ small red onion, chopped or sliced	½ cup roasted, shelled pistachios, chopped
2 cups cooked grains, cooled	½ avocado, diced
2 cups strawberries, hulled and	High-quality balsamic vinegar

1. Combine the orange juice, lime juice, ¼ teaspoon salt (if desired), and ⅛ teaspoon pepper in a large bowl. Toss the onions in the dressing; add the grains, strawberries, and beans and toss to combine. 2. Season with salt and pepper to taste. (At this point, the salad can be refrigerated until ready to serve, up to 1 day.) 3. Add the greens and cilantro and toss to combine. Sprinkle with the pistachios, top with the avocado, and drizzle with the vinegar. Serve.

Per Serving:
calories: 393 | fat: 10g | protein: 11g | carbs: 67g | fiber: 8g

Green Mix Salad

Prep time: 10 minutes | Cook time: 0 minutes | Serves 2

1 head romaine lettuce, chopped	1 cup baby spinach
2 cups baby arugula	1 cup fresh cilantro, chopped
	1 cup fresh parsley, chopped

1. In a big salad bowl, combine all the greens. Eat fresh or store in a closed container in the fridge for 2 to 3 days.

Per Serving:
calories: 74 | fat: 1g | protein: 5g | carbs: 13g | fiber: 8g

Quinoa Arugula Salad

Prep time: 10 minutes | Cook time: 20 minutes | Serves 4

1½ cups quinoa	thinly sliced
Zest and juice of 2 oranges	1 red bell pepper, seeded and cut into ½-inch cubes
Zest and juice of 1 lime	
¼ cup brown rice vinegar	2 tablespoons pine nuts, toasted
4 cups arugula	Salt and freshly ground black pepper, to taste
1 small red onion, peeled and	

1. Rinse the quinoa under cold water and drain. Bring 3 cups of water to a boil in a pot. Add the quinoa and bring the pot back to a boil over high heat. Reduce the heat to medium, cover, and cook for 15 to 20 minutes, or until the quinoa is tender. Drain any excess water, spread the quinoa on a baking sheet, and refrigerate until cool. 2. While the quinoa cools, combine the orange zest and juice, lime zest and juice, brown rice vinegar, arugula, onion, red pepper, pine nuts, and salt and pepper in a large bowl. Add the cooled quinoa and chill for 1 hour before serving.

Per Serving:
calories: 293 | fat: 6g | protein: 10g | carbs: 50g | fiber: 5g

Tomato, Corn and Bean Salad

Prep time: 20 minutes | Cook time: 10 minutes | Serves 4

6 ears corn
3 large tomatoes, diced
2 cups cooked navy beans, or 1
(15-ounce / 425-g) can, drained
and rinsed
1 medium red onion, peeled

and diced small
1 cup finely chopped basil
2 tablespoons balsamic vinegar
Salt and freshly ground black
pepper, to taste

1. Bring a large pot of water to a boil. Add the corn and cook for 7 to 10 minutes. Drain the water from the pot and rinse the corn under cold water to cool, then cut the kernels from the cob. 2. In a large bowl, toss together the corn, tomatoes, beans, onion, basil, balsamic vinegar, and salt and pepper. Chill for 1 hour before serving.
Per Serving:
calories: 351 | fat: 2g | protein: 15g | carbs: 66g | fiber: 17g

Ancient Grains Salad

Prep time: 20 minutes | Cook time: 55 minutes | Serves 6

¼ cup farro
¼ cup raw rye berries
2 ripe pears, cored and coarsely
chopped
2 celery stalks, coarsely
chopped
1 green apple, cored and

coarsely chopped
½ cup chopped fresh parsley
¼ cup golden raisins
3 tablespoons freshly squeezed
lemon juice
¼ teaspoon ground cumin
Pinch cayenne pepper

1. In an 8-quart pot, combine the farro, rye berries, and enough water to cover by 3 inches. Bring to a boil over high heat. Reduce the heat to medium-low, cover the pot, and cook for 45 to 50 minutes, or until the grains are firm and chewy but not hard. Drain and set aside to cool. 2. In a large bowl, gently stir together the cooled grains, pears, celery, apple, parsley, raisins, lemon juice, cumin, and cayenne pepper. Serve immediately or refrigerate in an airtight container for up to 1 week.
Per Serving:
calories: 127 | fat: 1g | protein: 3g | carbs: 31g | fiber: 5g

Mango Lentil Salad

Prep time: 10 minutes | Cook time: 0 minutes | Serves 2

2 cups cooked or canned red
lentils
2 cups fresh or frozen mango
cubes
½ cup fresh spinach

8 halved cherry tomatoes
2 teaspoons cumin seeds
Optional Toppings:
Shredded coconut
Nigella seeds

1. When using dry lentils, soak and cook ⅔ cup of dry lentils if necessary. 2. Meanwhile, add the mango cubes and cumin to a blender and blend into a smooth purée. 3. Put the spinach in a strainer, rinse well to clean it thoroughly and then drain well. 4. Divide the spinach, tomatoes and lentils between two bowls, top with half of the mango purée and the optional toppings, serve and enjoy! 5. Store the salad in an airtight container in the fridge, and consume within 2 days. Alternatively, store in the freezer for a maximum of 30 days and thaw at room temperature. The salad can be served cold.
Per Serving:
calories: 355 | fat: 1g | protein: 21g | carbs: 65g | fiber: 20g

Cabbage Salad and Peanut Butter Vinaigrette

Prep time: 15 minutes | Cook time: 0 minutes | Serves 4

3 tablespoons creamy peanut
butter
2 tablespoons rice vinegar
2 tablespoons full-fat coconut
milk
1 tablespoon soy sauce
½ tablespoon maple syrup

(optional)
2 cups shredded red cabbage
1 cup shredded green or red
cabbage
1 cup chopped unsalted roasted
peanuts

1. In a medium bowl, whisk together the peanut butter, rice vinegar, coconut milk, soy sauce, and maple syrup, if desired. 2. In a large bowl, combine the red and green cabbage and peanuts. Top with the dressing and stir to coat evenly.
Per Serving:
calories: 329 | fat: 25g | protein: 14g | carbs: 17g | fiber: 5g

Thai-ish Cabbage Salad

Prep time: 20 minutes | Cook time: 0 minutes | Serves 6

Dressing:
3 tablespoons fresh lime juice
1 clove garlic, finely grated
1 (½-inch) piece of fresh
ginger, peeled and finely grated
1 tablespoon pure maple syrup
(optional)
Sriracha or other hot sauce, to
taste
Salt and pepper, to taste
(optional)
¼ cup plus 1 tablespoon
coconut oil
Salad:

½ head of green or red
cabbage, shredded
1 large carrot, peeled
1 red bell pepper
1 barely ripe mango, peeled
3 green onions, thinly sliced
¼ cup fresh mint leaves
¼ cup fresh cilantro leaves
¼ cup fresh basil leaves
Salt and pepper, to taste
½ cup roasted cashews or
peanuts or both, chopped, for
garnish

1. Make the Dressing: In a small jar with a tight-fitting lid, combine the lime juice, garlic, ginger, maple syrup, Sriracha, salt, pepper, and coconut oil, if using. Tightly secure the lid, and shake the jar vigorously until the dressing has a creamy and smooth consistency. Taste and adjust seasoning, if necessary. Set aside. 2. Make the Salad: Place the shredded cabbage in a large bowl. Using a vegetable peeler, make long strips from the carrot, and add these to the bowl with the cabbage. Remove the seeds and stem from the bell pepper, cut it into strips, and add these to the bowl. 3. Carefully cut around the large pit of the mango. After you have all of the usable mango you can get, cut the fruit into thin strips and add it to the bowl. 4. Add the sliced green onions. If you like, you can add the mint, cilantro and basil leaves whole to the salad, or you can simply give them a quick chop before adding them. Season the vegetables in the bowl with some salt and pepper, if using, and toss to mix. 5. Pour the dressing over the salad and toss to evenly coat. Garnish the salad with the chopped cashews or peanuts. Serve immediately.
Per Serving:
calories: 218 | fat: 15g | protein: 5g | carbs: 19g | fiber: 4g

Taco Tempeh Salad

Prep time: 25 minutes | Cook time: 15 minutes | Serves 3

1 cup cooked black beans
1 (8-ounce / 227-g) package tempeh
1 tablespoon lime or lemon juice
2 tablespoons extra virgin olive oil (optional)
1 teaspoon maple syrup (optional)
½ teaspoon chili powder

¼ teaspoon cumin
¼ teaspoon paprika
1 large bunch of fresh or frozen kale, chopped
1 large avocado, peeled, pitted, and diced
½ cup salsa
Salt and pepper to taste (optional)

1. Cut the tempeh into ¼-inch cubes; then add the cut tempeh, lime or lemon juice, 1 tablespoon of olive oil, maple syrup, chili powder, cumin, and paprika to a bowl. Stir well and let the tempeh marinate in the fridge for at least 1 hour, up to 12 hours. 2. Heat the remaining 1 tablespoon of olive oil in a frying pan over medium heat. Add the marinated tempeh mixture and cook until brown and crispy on both sides, around 10 minutes. Put the chopped kale in a bowl with the cooked beans and prepared tempeh. 3. Store, or serve the salad immediately, topped with salsa, avocado, and salt and pepper to taste, if desired.
Per Serving:
calories: 441 | fat: 23g | protein: 22g | carbs: 36g | fiber: 18g

Bulgur, Cucumber and Tomato Salad

Prep time: 15 minutes | Cook time: 10 minutes | Serves 4

1½ cups bulgur
1 cup cherry tomatoes, halved
1 medium cucumber, halved, seeded, and diced
3 cloves garlic, peeled and minced
4 green onions (white and green parts), sliced

Zest and juice of 2 lemons
2 tablespoons red wine vinegar
1 teaspoon crushed red pepper flakes, or to taste
¼ cup minced tarragon
Salt and freshly ground black pepper, to taste

1. Bring 3 cups of water to a boil in a medium pot and add the bulgur. Remove the pot from the heat, cover with a tight-fitting lid, and let it sit until the water is absorbed and the bulgur is tender, about 15 minutes. Spread the bulgur on a baking sheet and let cool to room temperature. 2. Transfer the cooled bulgur to a bowl, add all the remaining ingredients, and mix well to combine. Chill for 1 hour before serving.
Per Serving:
calories: 207 | fat: 0g | protein: 7g | carbs: 45g | fiber: 8g

Detox Salad

Prep time: 10 minutes | Cook time: 0 minutes | Serves 2

2 cups purple sauerkraut
1 bunch flat-leaf parsley, roughly chopped
¼ cup mixed seeds (pumpkin,

sunflower, sesame, hemp)
2 tablespoons raisins, rinsed
1 avocado, peeled, pitted and sliced

1. In a large bowl, combine the sauerkraut, parsley, seeds and raisins and toss until well combined. To serve, transfer to smaller bowls or plates and top each serving with half of the sliced avocado. 2. The salad will keep for up to 3 days in the fridge.
Per Serving:
calories: 321 | fat: 23g | protein: 9g | carbs: 25g | fiber: 12g

Zingy Melon and Mango Salad

Prep time: 5 minutes | Cook time: 0 minutes | Serves 2

1 large mango, peeled, pitted, and cut into 1-inch pieces (about 1 cup)
½ small cantaloupe or watermelon, peeled and cut

into 1-inch pieces (about 2 cups)
Juice of 1 lime
¼ cup chopped fresh cilantro
1 teaspoon chili powder

1. In a large bowl, combine the mango and cantaloupe. Add the lime juice and cilantro and gently toss until combined. To serve, spoon into bowls and sprinkle with chili powder.
Per Serving:
calories: 171 | fat: 1g | protein: 3g | carbs: 42g | fiber: 5g

Quinoa, Corn and Black Bean Salad

Prep time: 25 minutes | Cook time: 0 minutes | Serves 4

2½ cups cooked quinoa
3 ears corn, kernels removed (about 2 cups)
1 red bell pepper, roasted, seeded, and diced
½ small red onion, peeled and diced
2 cups cooked black beans, or 1 (15-ounce / 425-g) can, drained and rinsed

1 cup finely chopped cilantro
6 green onions (white and green parts), thinly sliced
1 jalapeño pepper, minced (for less heat, remove the seeds)
Zest of 1 lime and juice of 2 limes
1 tablespoon cumin seeds, toasted and ground
Salt, to taste (optional)

1. Combine all ingredients in a large bowl and mix well. Chill for 1 hour before serving
Per Serving:
calories: 366 | fat: 3g | protein: 16g | carbs: 70g | fiber: 14g

Winter Sunshine Salad

Prep time: 15 minutes | Cook time: 0 minutes | Serves 6

2 small fennel bulbs, cored and thinly sliced
2 ruby red grapefruits with juice reserved
2 cups shredded red cabbage
1 red or orange bell pepper, thinly sliced

1 tablespoon fresh lime juice
Salt and black pepper (optional)
½ cup chopped cilantro
1 avocado, diced or sliced
¼ cup walnut pieces

1. Combine the fennel, grapefruit segments and juice, cabbage, bell pepper, and lime juice in a large bowl. Season with salt (if desired) and pepper to taste, then toss to combine. 2. When ready to serve, add the cilantro and toss to combine. Divide into bowls, then divide avocado and walnuts evenly between salads.
Per Serving:
calories: 157 | fat: 8g | protein: 4g | carbs: 21g | fiber: 7g

Crunchy Curry Salad

Prep time: 20 minutes | Cook time: 0 minutes | Serves 4

1 head napa cabbage	milk
1 cup shredded carrots	¼ cup rice vinegar
1 red bell pepper, julienned	¼ cup diced yellow onion
½ cup thinly sliced scallions	2 tablespoons white miso paste
½ cup fresh cilantro, roughly chopped	2 tablespoons pure maple syrup (optional)
½ cup sunflower seeds	1 tablespoon red curry paste
1 jalapeño chile pepper, thickly sliced	1 garlic clove, minced
½ cup creamy almond butter	½-inch piece fresh ginger, peeled
¼ cup canned full-fat coconut	

1. Trim the end of the cabbage, halve and core it, and cut into very thin ribbons, or shred. Place in a bowl with the carrots, bell pepper, scallions, cilantro, sunflower seeds, and chile pepper. Set aside. 2. In a blender, make a curry sauce by combining the almond butter, coconut milk, vinegar, onion, miso, maple syrup (if using), curry paste, garlic, and ginger and purée until smooth. Stop to scrape down the sides as needed. If the mixture is too thick, add a little more coconut milk and blend again. 3. Pour the sauce over the cabbage mixture. Toss well to combine. Serve immediately or store in an airtight container for up to 5 days.

Per Serving:
calories: 478 | fat: 31g | protein: 16g | carbs: 42g | fiber: 15g

Larb Salad

Prep time: 15 minutes | Cook time: 5 minutes | Serves 4

1 teaspoon canola oil (optional)	1 green onion, sliced
1 (14-ounce / 397-g) block extra-firm tofu, pressed and crumbled	½ tablespoon minced jalapeño
	¼ cup thinly sliced red, white, or yellow onion
3 tablespoons lime juice, divided	2 tablespoons minced mint
2½ tablespoons minced cilantro	8 iceberg or romaine lettuce leaves
2 tablespoons soy sauce	

1. Heat the oil (if desired) in a saucepan over medium heat. Add the tofu and 1 tablespoon of the lime juice, and sauté for 4 to 5 minutes or until the tofu is light brown. 2. Place the tofu in a medium bowl and combine with the remaining 2 tablespoons lime juice, cilantro, soy sauce, green onion, jalapeño, onion, and mint. Mix well. 3. Serve in the lettuce leaves.

Per Serving:
calories: 245 | fat: 10g | protein: 18g | carbs: 26g | fiber: 9g

Meyer Lemon Romanesco Glow Salad

Prep time: 20 minutes | Cook time: 0 minutes | Serves 6

Dressing:	Salt and pepper, to taste (optional)
½ teaspoon Meyer lemon zest	Salad:
1 tablespoon fresh Meyer lemon juice	1 medium head Romanesco broccoli or cauliflower, broken up into florets
½ teaspoon Dijon mustard	
2 tablespoons coconut oil (optional)	1 medium sweet apple, cored

and chopped
1 stalk celery, small diced
1 cup seedless grapes, halved
3 green onions, thinly sliced
2 teaspoons minced fresh sage

⅓ cup walnut halves, toasted and chopped
Salt and pepper, to taste (optional)

1. Make the Dressing: In a small bowl, whisk together the lemon zest, lemon juice, Dijon mustard, coconut oil, salt, if using, and pepper until combined. Set aside. 2. Make the Salad: In batches, use a food processor to blitz the Romanesco florets until you have a couscous-like size and texture. Place the processed Romanesco in a large bowl. 3. To the large bowl, add the apples, celery, grapes, green onions, sage, and walnuts. Season everything with salt and pepper, if using and toss to combine. 4. Pour the dressing over the salad and toss to combine. Serve the salad immediately or store in a container in the refrigerator for up to 3 days.

Per Serving:
calories: 129 | fat: 8g | protein: 3g | carbs: 15g | fiber: 4g

Red Beet Salad

Prep time: 15 minutes | Cook time: 0 minutes | Serves 2

4 medium red beets	¼ cup finely chopped pecans
¼ cup water	1 tablespoon balsamic vinegar
2 celery stalks, finely chopped	

1. Place the beets in a microwave-safe dish with a lid. Pierce the skin of the beets in several places to prevent them from exploding. Add the water, cover the dish, and microwave on full power for 7 minutes. 2. Turn the beets; then microwave for 7 minutes more, until soft. 3. Allow the beets to cool on ice or under cold water for at least 5 minutes before peeling them. 4. Peel the beets; then shred them using the large hole size of a box grater, into a large bowl. 5. Add the celery, pecans, and balsamic vinegar and toss. 6. Enjoy chilled.

Per Serving:
calories: 175 | fat: 10g | protein: 4g | carbs: 20g | fiber: 6g

Beet, Cabbage, and Black Bean Salad

Prep time: 2 minutes | Cook time: 20 minutes | Serves 4 to 6

3 or 4 medium beets, peeled and cut into ½-inch dice	parts, thinly sliced
	½ cup seasoned rice vinegar
½ cup water	¼ teaspoon freshly ground black pepper
1 (15-ounce / 425-g) can black beans, drained and rinsed	4 to 6 cups cooked brown rice
1 cup shredded cabbage	1 ripe avocado, pitted, peeled, and diced
1 cup shredded spinach	
1 cup halved grape tomatoes	Fresh cilantro, for garnish
2 scallions, green and white	

1. In a sauté pan or skillet, combine the beets and water. Bring to a simmer over high heat. 2. Reduce the heat to medium-low. Cover, and cook for 10 to 15 minutes, or until the beets are slightly soft. Remove from the heat. 3. Stir in the beans, cabbage, spinach, tomatoes, scallions, vinegar, and pepper. 4. Serve the vegetables over the rice. 5. Top with the avocado, and garnish with cilantro.

Per Serving:
calories: 179 | fat: 7g | protein: 7g | carbs: 26g | fiber: 10g

Lentil, Lemon and Mushroom Salad

Prep time: 10 minutes | Cook time: 25 minutes | Serves 2

½ cup dry lentils of choice
2 cups vegetable broth
3 cups mushrooms, thickly sliced
1 cup sweet or purple onion, chopped
4 teaspoons extra virgin olive oil (optional)

2 tablespoons garlic powder or 3 garlic cloves, minced
¼ teaspoon chili flakes
1 tablespoon lemon juice
2 tablespoons cilantro, chopped
½ cup arugula
Salt and pepper to taste (optional)

1. Sprout the lentils for 2 to 3 days. 2. Place the vegetable stock in a deep saucepan and bring it to a boil. Add the lentils to the boiling broth, cover the pan, and cook for about 5 minutes over low heat until the lentils are a bit tender. Remove the pan from heat and drain the excess water. 3. Put a frying pan over high heat and add 2 tablespoons of olive oil. Add the onions, garlic, and chili flakes, and cook until the onions are almost translucent, around 5 to 10 minutes while stirring. Add the mushrooms to the frying pan and mix in thoroughly. Continue cooking until the onions are completely translucent and the mushrooms have softened; remove the pan from the heat. Mix the lentils, onions, mushrooms, and garlic in a large bowl. Add the lemon juice and the remaining olive oil. Toss or stir to combine everything thoroughly. 4. Serve the mushroom and onion mixture over some arugala in bowl, adding salt and pepper to taste, if desired, or, store and enjoy later!
Per Serving:
calories: 262 | fat: 10g | protein: 16g | carbs: 28g | fiber: 15g

Pineapple Quinoa Salad

Prep time: 10 minutes | Cook time: 15 minutes | Serves 3

2 cups cooked or canned black beans
½ cup dry quinoa
1 cup fresh or frozen pineapple chunks
8 halved cherry tomatoes

1 red onion, minced
Optional Toppings:
Chili flakes
Soy sauce
Shredded coconut

1. When using dry beans, soak and cook ⅔ cup of dry black beans if necessary and cook the quinoa for about 15 minutes. 2. Add all of the ingredients to a large bowl and mix thoroughly. 3. Divide the salad between 3 bowls, serve with the optional toppings and enjoy! 4. Store the salad in an airtight container in the fridge, and consume within 2 days. Alternatively, store in the freezer for a maximum of 30 days and thaw at room temperature. The salad can be served cold.
Per Serving:
calories: 310 | fat: 2g | protein: 16g | carbs: 56g | fiber: 14g

Creamy Fruit Salad

Prep time: 15 minutes | Cook time: 0 minutes | Serves 4

4 red apples, cored and diced
1 (15-ounce / 425-g) can pineapple chunks, drained, or 2 cups fresh pineapple chunks
¼ cup raisins

¼ cup chopped pecans or walnuts
1 cup plain plant-based yogurt
2 teaspoons maple syrup (optional)

1. In a large bowl, combine the apples and pineapples and toss well to make sure the apples are covered in pineapple juice to prevent browning. Add the raisins, nuts, yogurt, and maple syrup (if using) and mix well. Cover and refrigerate for at least 2 hours to develop the flavors.
Per Serving:
calories: 267 | fat: 5g | protein: 6g | carbs: 54g | fiber: 6g

Bean and Corn Salad

Prep time: 15 minutes | Cook time: 0 minutes | Serves 6

1 (15-ounce / 425-g) can pinto beans, drained and rinsed
1 (15-ounce / 425-g) can black beans, drained and rinsed
1 (15-ounce / 425-g) can chickpeas, drained and rinsed
1 (15-ounce / 425-g) can

unsalted corn, drained and rinsed
¾ cup diced tomato
¼ cup chopped cilantro
3 to 4 tablespoons lemon or lime juice
Salt, to taste (optional)

1. In a large bowl, mix together all the ingredients. The salad can be served chilled or at room temperature.
Per Serving:
calories: 200 | fat: 30g | protein: 10g | carbs: 38g | fiber: 9g

Chapter 5 Desserts

Poached Pears

Prep time: 10 minutes | Cook time: 20 minutes | Serves 2 to 4

2 cups apple juice
¼ cup unsweetened raisins
½ teaspoon ground cinnamon
½ teaspoon vanilla extract
4 to 6 slightly ripe Bosc pears, peeled

1. In a large pan with a flat bottom, combine the apple juice, raisins, cinnamon, and vanilla. Place over high heat. 2. Quarter the pears. Using a melon baller, scoop out the seeds (or trim them out with a paring knife). 3. Add the pears to the liquid. Bring to a boil. Reduce the heat to medium. Partially cover, and simmer for 20 minutes, or until the pears are tender (a paring knife should easily slide into the pears). Remove from the heat. 4. Serve the poached pears with a drizzle of the cooking liquid.
Per Serving:
calories: 343 | fat: 2g | protein: 0g | carbs: 89g | fiber: 4g

Mango-Peach Sorbet

Prep time: 2 minutes | Cook time: 0 minutes | Serves 4

2 cups frozen mango
2 cups frozen peaches
1 cup fresh orange juice
Pure maple syrup (optional)

1. In a high-powered blender, combine the mango, peaches, and orange juice. Purée, stopping to scrape down the sides as needed. Add a little extra liquid if the blender is struggling. Taste; add maple syrup if the mixture needs sweetening. 2. Serve immediately for soft serve sorbet, or, for scoopable sorbet, transfer to an airtight container and freeze until firm enough to scoop. Store leftovers in the freezer.
Per Serving:
calories: 107 | fat: 0g | protein: 1g | carbs: 26g | fiber: 2g

Cherry Chocolate Bark

Prep time: 5 minutes | Cook time: 0 minutes | Serves 8

1 cup vegan semisweet chocolate chips
1 cup sliced almonds
1 cup dried tart cherries,
chopped
½ teaspoon flaky sea salt, for sprinkling (optional)

1. Line a rimmed baking sheet with parchment paper and place in the fridge or freezer to get very cold. 2. In a heatproof glass bowl set over a pan of simmering water, melt the chocolate, stirring occasionally. Be careful not to let water droplets get into the bowl or the chocolate will seize. 3. Remove the bowl from the heat (or the microwave) when some pieces of unmelted chocolate still remain. Stir well until the remaining chocolate melts, but do not stir too vigorously or air bubbles will form. 4. Pour the melted chocolate onto the chilled prepared pan and use a thin spatula to spread it evenly almost to the edges of the pan. Immediately sprinkle the almonds and cherries

evenly over the chocolate, followed by a sprinkling of salt (if using). Refrigerate until firm. 5. Break the bark into pieces and store in an airtight container in the refrigerator for up to 1 week.
Per Serving:
calories: 189 | fat: 12g | protein: 3g | carbs: 17g | fiber: 3g

Chocolate Tahini Muffins

Prep time: 10 minutes | Cook time: 20 minutes | Makes 12 muffins

½ teaspoon plus 2 tablespoons coconut oil, divided (optional)
2 tablespoons ground flaxseeds
6 tablespoons cold water
2 tablespoons tahini
2 tablespoons plain plant-based yogurt
1½ cups unsweetened plant-
based milk
2 teaspoons baking powder
½ cup maple syrup (optional)
¼ cup unsweetened cocoa powder
½ teaspoon salt (optional)
2½ cups whole-wheat flour

1. Preheat the oven to 375°F (190°C). Lightly oil a 12-cup muffin tin with ½ tablespoon of coconut oil. 2. In a large bowl, mix together the flaxseed and cold water to make 2 "flax eggs." Let sit for 10 minutes. 3. In a microwave-safe bowl, microwave the remaining 2 tablespoons coconut oil until melted, about 35 seconds. Be careful when removing the bowl so as not to splash hot coconut oil. 4. Add the coconut oil, tahini, yogurt, plant-based milk, baking powder, and maple syrup to the bowl with the flax eggs and mix well with a fork. Add the cocoa powder, salt (if using), and flour and mix until combined. 5. Divide the batter evenly among the 12 muffin cups, filling each about three-fourths full. Put the muffin pan in the oven and lower the heat to 350°F (180°C). Bake for 20 minutes, until a toothpick inserted in the middle comes out clean.
Per Serving:
calories: 187 | fat: 6g | protein: 5g | carbs: 31g | fiber: 4g

Peanut Butter Cookies

Prep time: 10 minutes | Cook time: 15 minutes | Makes 10 cookies

2 tablespoons ground flaxseeds
6 tablespoons cold water
¼ cup maple syrup (optional)
1 tablespoon baking powder
1 cup natural peanut butter
½ cup whole-wheat flour

1. Preheat the oven to 350°F (180°C). Line a sheet pan with parchment paper. 2. In a large bowl, mix together the ground flaxseeds and water to make "flax eggs" and let sit until it gels, about 10 minutes. 3. Add the maple syrup (if using), baking powder, peanut butter, and flour to the bowl and mix well with a fork. 4. Put rounded tablespoons of the batter onto the prepared sheet pan. Flatten each cookie and, using the back of a fork, press a crisscross pattern into each one. Bake for 13 to 15 minutes, or until they are firm and slightly golden.
Per Serving:
calories: 409 | fat: 28g | protein: 14g | carbs: 33g | fiber: 5g

Two-Ingredient Peanut Butter Fudge

Prep time: 5 minutes | Cook time: 5 minutes | Serves 8

1 cup chocolate chips
½ cup natural peanut butter
Sea salt (optional)

1. Place the chocolate chips and peanut butter in a small saucepan over medium-low heat. Cook, stirring often, until the chocolate is melted and the mixture is thoroughly combined, about 5 minutes. Use a spatula to scrape the mixture into a pie plate or small glass container lined with parchment paper. Sprinkle with sea salt, if desired. 2. Refrigerate until set, at least 1 hour or overnight. Slice into squares and serve, or refrigerate for up to 1 week.

Per Serving:
calories: 194 | fat: 12g | protein: 6g | carbs: 21g | fiber: 2g

Pear Chia Pudding

Prep time: 10 minutes | Cook time: 10 minutes | Makes 3 cups

3 firm but ripe pears, peeled, cored, and cut into 1-inch dice
½ cup freshly squeezed orange juice or ¼ cup filtered water
Pinch of fine sea salt (optional)
½ cup raw cashews or macadamia nuts
2 tablespoons coconut butter
1 teaspoon vanilla extract
6 tablespoons chia seeds

1. Combine the pears, orange juice or water, and salt, if using, in a medium pot and bring to a boil over high heat. Cover, reduce the heat to low, and simmer for 8 to 10 minutes, until the pears have cooked through. Remove from the heat and allow to cool slightly. Transfer the mixture to an upright blender, add the cashews, coconut butter, and vanilla, and blend until completely smooth. Pour into a widemouthed quart jar or a medium bowl, add the chia seeds, and whisk thoroughly, making sure there are no clumps of seeds hiding anywhere. Allow to sit for a few minutes and then whisk again. Leave the whisk in place and refrigerate for at least 1 hour, or until completely chilled, whisking every now and then to distribute the chia seeds evenly and to help cool the pudding quickly. The pudding will thicken further overnight; if it gets too thick, stir in a splash of water or nut milk. Store the pudding in an airtight glass jar or other container in the fridge for up to 5 days.

Per Serving: (½ cup)
calories: 188 | fat: 13g | protein: 2g | carbs: 18g | fiber: 5g

Stone Fruit Compote

Prep time: 5 minutes | Cook time: 10 minutes | Makes 2½ cups

1½ pounds (680 g) ripe peaches, plums, apricots, or cherries
½ cup freshly squeezed orange juice or filtered water
Tiny pinch of fine sea salt (optional)
1 teaspoon arrowroot powder
2 teaspoons filtered water
½ teaspoon vanilla extract

1. If using peaches, plums, or apricots, halve and pit them. Cut each half into ½-inch wedges and slice the wedges in half crosswise. If using cherries, pit them. Put the fruit in a medium pot, add the orange juice and salt, and bring to a simmer over high heat. Cover the pot, reduce the heat to low, and simmer for 8 to 10 minutes, until the fruit is soft. Dissolve the arrowroot in the water in a small cup, then drizzle it into the pot, stirring constantly. Once the compote has returned to a simmer and thickened, remove from the heat and stir in the vanilla. 2. Serve warm or at room temperature. Store the cooled compote in a sealed jar in the fridge for up to 5 days.

Per Serving: (½ cup)
calories: 77 | fat: 0g | protein: 1g | carbs: 19g | fiber: 2g

Chocolate's Best Friends Brownies

Prep time: 15 minutes | Cook time: 3½ hours | Makes about 2 dozen brownies

1¼ cups oats
¾ cup white beans, drained, and rinsed
¾ cup plus 3 tablespoons maple syrup (optional)
¼ cup plus 2 tablespoons unsweetened applesauce
1½ teaspoons vanilla extract
1½ teaspoons baking powder
½ teaspoon salt (optional)
¾ cup unsweetened cocoa powder
½ teaspoon ground cinnamon
1 teaspoon instant coffee

1. Crumple two pieces of aluminum foil to form a ring around the interior base of the slow cooker. Add a liner or piece of parchment and set the slow cooker to Low to preheat. 2. Put the oats in a blender or food processor and process into oat flour. Pour it into a small bowl and set aside. 3. Add the beans, maple syrup (if using), applesauce, and vanilla to the blender and blend until well combined, about 1 minute. Add the oat flour, baking powder, salt (if using), cocoa powder, cinnamon, and instant coffee. Blend until smooth and thick, scraping down the sides as needed. 4. Spread the batter into the prepared slow cooker. Cover and cook on Low for 3½ hours. Turn off the slow cooker, remove the cover, and let the brownies cool completely before slicing, at least 1 hour. Store at room temperature for 2 to 3 days.

Per Serving:
calories: 63 | fat: 1g | protein: 2g | carbs: 14g | fiber: 2g

Coconut Chia Pudding

Prep time: 5 minutes | Cook time: 0 minutes | Makes 3 cups

1 pound (454 g) raw young coconut meat, defrosted if frozen, any liquid reserved
1¼ cups unpasteurized coconut
water
1 tablespoon vanilla extract
6 tablespoons chia seeds

1. Put the coconut meat (and any liquid that accumulated as it defrosted, if frozen) in an upright blender. Add the coconut water and vanilla and blend on high speed until completely smooth. Pour into a widemouthed quart jar or a medium bowl, add the chia seeds, and whisk thoroughly, making sure there are no clumps of seeds hiding anywhere. Allow to sit for a few minutes and then whisk again. Leave the whisk in place and refrigerate for at least 1 hour, or until completely chilled, whisking every now and then to distribute the chia seeds evenly. The pudding will thicken further overnight; if it gets too thick, stir in a splash of water, coconut water, or nut milk. Store the pudding in an airtight glass jar or other container in the fridge for up to 3 days.

Per Serving: (½ cup)
calories: 296 | fat: 26g | protein: 3g | carbs: 15g | fiber: 8g

Stone Fruit Chia Pudding

Prep time: 10 minutes | Cook time: 10 minutes | Makes 3 cups

1¼ pounds (567 g) stone fruit, halved, pitted, and cut into 1-inch dice
¾ cup freshly squeezed orange juice or ½ cup filtered water
Pinch of fine sea salt (optional)
½ cup raw cashews or macadamia nuts
2 tablespoons coconut butter
1 teaspoon vanilla extract
¼ cup chia seeds

1. Combine the fruit, orange juice, and salt, if using, in a medium pot and bring to a boil over high heat. Cover, reduce the heat to low, and simmer for 8 to 10 minutes, until the fruit has cooked through. Remove from the heat and allow to cool slightly. 2. Transfer the mixture to an upright blender, add the cashews, coconut butter, and vanilla, and blend until completely smooth. Pour into a widemouthed quart jar or a medium bowl, add the chia seeds, and whisk thoroughly, making sure there are no clumps of seeds hiding anywhere. Allow to sit for a few minutes and then whisk again. Leave the whisk in place and refrigerate for at least 1 hour, or until completely chilled, whisking every now and then to distribute the chia seeds evenly and to help cool the pudding quickly. The pudding will thicken further overnight; if it gets too thick, stir in a splash of water or nut milk. Store the pudding in an airtight glass jar or other container in the fridge for up to 5 days.
Per Serving: (½ cup)
calories: 199 | fat: 15g | protein: 3g | carbs: 17g | fiber: 5g

Stone Fruit Pecan Crumble

Prep time: 15 minutes | Cook time: 255 minutes | Serves 6

Filling:
1¾ pounds (794 g) ripe stone fruit, pitted and sliced into ½-inch wedges
2 tablespoons pure maple syrup (optional)
2 teaspoons fresh lemon juice
1 teaspoon arrowroot powder
½ teaspoon ground cinnamon
¼ teaspoon fine sea salt (optional)
Crumble Topping:
1¼ cups raw pecan halves
2 tablespoons pure maple syrup (optional)
¼ teaspoon ground cinnamon
¼ teaspoon fine sea salt (optional)

1. Preheat the oven to 375ºF (190ºC). 2. Make the Filling: In an 8-inch ovenproof dish, add the stone fruit, maple syrup, lemon juice, arrowroot powder, cinnamon, and sea salt, if using, and lightly toss to combine. Set aside. 3. Make the Crumble Topping: In a food processor, combine the pecans, maple syrup, cinnamon, and sea salt, if using. Pulse the mixture until you have a crumbly consistency. 4. Sprinkle the crumble mixture on top of the stone fruit. Bake the crumble until the fruit is tender and the topping has browned, 22 to 25 minutes. Serve warm or at room temperature.
Per Serving:
calories: 252 | fat: 15g | protein: 3g | carbs: 25g | fiber: 4g

Basic Vanilla Chia Pudding

Prep time: 5 minutes | Cook time: 0 minutes | Serves 4

1 cup almond milk
½ cup full-fat coconut milk

⅓ cup chia seeds
1 tablespoon coconut sugar (optional)
1 teaspoon vanilla bean powder
Pinch of salt (optional)

1. Whisk all the ingredients together in a medium bowl. Stir every few minutes until thickened, about 15 minutes. Serve, or refrigerate for up to 48 hours.
Per Serving:
calories: 153 | fat: 14g | protein: 5g | carbs: 14g | fiber: 6g

Protein Chocolate Chip Cookies

Prep time: 10 minutes | Cook time: 20 minutes | Makes 12 cookies

1 teaspoon canola oil, for greasing (optional)
1 (15-ounce / 425-g) can chickpeas, drained and rinsed
½ cup creamy or chunky peanut butter
1½ teaspoons vanilla extract
¼ teaspoon baking powder
⅛ teaspoon salt (optional)
¾ cup vegan semisweet chocolate chips

1. Preheat the oven to 350ºF (180ºC), and lightly grease a baking sheet. 2. In a food processor or high-powered blender, blend the chickpeas, peanut butter, vanilla, baking powder, and salt (if desired) until smooth. 3. Using a spoon, mix in the chocolate chips. 4. Scoop out 1 tablespoon cookie dough and roll the scoop into a tight ball. Place the ball on the prepared baking sheet and flatten using your fingertips. Repeat until all the cookie dough is used. 5. Bake for 20 minutes or until the cookies turn golden brown.
Per Serving: (2 cookies)
calories: 302 | fat: 20g | protein: 9g | carbs: 27g | fiber: 5g

Berry Chia Pudding

Prep time: 5 minutes | Cook time: 5 minutes | Makes 3 cups

4 cups fresh or frozen berries
1½ cups freshly squeezed orange juice
Pinch of fine sea salt (optional)
½ cup raw cashews or
macadamia nuts
2 tablespoons coconut butter
2 teaspoons vanilla extract
6 tablespoons chia seeds

1. Combine the berries, orange juice, and salt, if using, in a medium pot and bring to a boil over high heat. Cover, reduce the heat to low, and simmer for 5 minutes, or until the berries have softened and released their juices. Remove from the heat and allow to cool slightly. 2. Transfer the mixture to an upright blender, add the cashews, coconut butter, and vanilla, and blend until completely smooth. Pour into a widemouthed quart jar or a medium bowl, add the chia seeds, and whisk thoroughly, making sure there are no clumps of seeds hiding anywhere. Allow to sit for a few minutes and then whisk again. Leave the whisk in place and refrigerate for at least 1 hour, or until completely chilled, whisking every now and then to distribute the chia seeds evenly and to help cool the pudding quickly. The pudding will thicken further overnight; if it gets too thick, stir in a splash of water or nut milk. Store the pudding in an airtight glass jar or other container in the fridge for up to 5 days.
Per Serving: (½ cup)
calories: 211 | fat: 14g | protein: 2g | carbs: 21g | fiber: 5g

Molasses-Ginger Oat Cookie Balls

Prep time: 10 minutes | Cook time: 15 minutes | Makes 1 dozen cookies

1 cup pitted dates
3 tablespoons unsalted, unsweetened almond butter
2 tablespoons blackstrap molasses
1 teaspoon vanilla extract
1 cup oat flour
¼ cup rolled oats
½ teaspoon baking powder
1 teaspoon ground ginger
½ teaspoon ground cinnamon
⅛ teaspoon ground nutmeg
⅛ teaspoon ground cardamom

1. Preheat the oven to 350°F (180°C). Line a baking sheet with parchment paper. 2. In a food processor, combine the dates and almond butter. Blend to a creamy paste. Transfer to a large bowl. 3. Stir in the molasses and vanilla. 4. In a medium bowl, thoroughly combine the flour, oats, baking powder, ginger, cinnamon, nutmeg, and cardamom. 5. Fold the flour mixture into the molasses mixture. 6. Drop 12 (1-tablespoon) dough balls about 1 inch apart onto the prepared baking sheet. 7. Bake for 12 to 15 minutes, or until the edges are golden brown and the cookie balls are slightly firm to the touch. Remove from the oven.
Per Serving:
calories: 275 | fat: 10g | protein: 6g | carbs: 44g | fiber: 6g

"Here Comes Autumn" Apple Crisp

Prep time: 15 minutes | Cook time: 2 to 3 hours | Serves 4 to 6

Apple Base:
6 apples (about 2 pounds / 907 g), any variety, cored and thinly sliced
1 tablespoon lemon juice
2 tablespoons maple syrup (optional)
1 teaspoon ground cinnamon
½ teaspoon grated nutmeg

Topping:
¾ cup chopped pecans
½ cup almond meal or almond flour
½ cup rolled oats
3 tablespoons maple syrup (optional)
½ teaspoon ground cinnamon
¼ teaspoon grated nutmeg

1. Make the apple base: Put the apples in the slow cooker and sprinkle with the lemon juice, tossing well to coat the apples completely. Stir in the maple syrup (if using), cinnamon, and nutmeg until the syrup and spices cover every apple slice. Spread the apples out in an even layer. 2. Make the topping and cook: In a medium bowl, combine the pecans, almond meal or flour, oats, maple syrup (if using), cinnamon, and nutmeg. Mix well until crumbles form. Spoon the mixture evenly over the apples. 3. To keep the condensation that forms on the inside of the lid away from the topping, stretch a clean dish towel or several layers of paper towels across the top of the slow cooker, but not touching the food, and place the lid on top of the towel(s). If you skip this step, you will have a soggy result rather than a crunchy crumble. 4. Cook on High for 2 to 3 hours or on Low for 4 to 5 hours, until the apples are soft and cooked through.
Per Serving:
calories: 469 | fat: 23g | protein: 7g | carbs: 68g | fiber: 12g

Caramelized Banana with Yogurt and Toasted Coconut

Prep time: 5 minutes | Cook time: 5 minutes | Serves 1

1 tablespoon maple syrup (optional)
1 small banana, cut into ¼-inch-thick slices
¼ cup plain unsweetened
cashew milk yogurt
1 tablespoon toasted shredded coconut
Pinch ground cinnamon

1. Pour the maple syrup (if using) into a small skillet and heat over medium-low heat. Add the bananas and caramelize for 3 to 5 minutes. 2. Put the yogurt on a small plate or in a small bowl. Place the caramelized bananas on top of the yogurt, and sprinkle with the shredded coconut and cinnamon.
Per Serving:
calories: 196 | fat: 3g | protein: 3g | carbs: 43g | fiber: 3g

Vanilla Corn Cake with Roasted Strawberries

Prep time: 20 minutes | Cook time: 50 minutes | Makes 1 cake

¾ cup full-fat coconut milk
1 teaspoon fresh lemon juice
1 cup cornmeal
1 cup whole spelt flour
1 teaspoon lemon zest
1 tablespoon aluminum-free baking powder
¼ teaspoon baking soda
1 teaspoon fine sea salt (optional)
½ teaspoon ground turmeric (optional)
½ cup plus 2 tablespoons pure maple syrup (optional)
½ cup coconut oil, plus extra to grease pan
1 teaspoon vanilla bean paste or pure vanilla extract
4 cups whole strawberries

1. Preheat the oven to 350°F (180°C). Lightly grease a 9-inch round cake pan with coconut oil. Cut a circle of parchment paper to fit in the bottom of the pan and press it in. Lightly grease the parchment, and set aside. 2. In a medium bowl, whisk together the coconut milk and lemon juice. Let this mixture sit for 5 minutes so that the milk can curdle slightly. 3. In a large bowl, whisk together the cornmeal, spelt flour, lemon zest, baking powder, baking soda, sea salt, and turmeric, if using. 4. Make a well in the center of the cornmeal mixture. Add the maple syrup, oil, if using, vanilla, and coconut milk mixture. With a spatula, gently mix until you have a smooth and unified batter. Avoid overmixing. 5. Scrape the batter into the prepared cake pan and slide the pan into the oven. Bake the cake for 25 to 28 minutes or until the top is golden and a toothpick inserted into the center comes out clean. Let the cake cool completely. Raise the oven temperature to 400°F (205°C). 6. Cut the strawberries into halves or quarters (depending on size), and place them on a parchment-lined baking sheet. Slide the baking sheet into the oven and roast the strawberries until they become juicy and jammy, about 20 minutes. 7. Serve slices of the corn cake with a few roasted strawberries.
Per Serving: (⅛ cake)
calories: 394 | fat: 20g | protein: 6g | carbs: 52g | fiber: 5g

Chocolate Dirt Yogurt Cup

Prep time: 15 minutes | Cook time: 0 minutes | Serves 2

¼ cup vegan chocolate chips
3 tablespoons sliced almonds
3 teaspoons cocoa powder, divided
2 teaspoons plus 2 tablespoons

pure maple syrup, divided
1 cup nondairy vegan yogurt
2 tablespoons tahini
½ teaspoon vanilla extract
½ cup blueberries

1. In a food processor, combine the chocolate chips, almonds, 2 teaspoons of cocoa powder, and 2 teaspoons of maple syrup. Process until crumbly, like dirt. 2. In a medium bowl, mix together the yogurt, remaining 2 tablespoons of maple syrup, the tahini, vanilla, and remaining 1 teaspoon of cocoa powder. 3. In a small serving dish, layer 1 tablespoon of the chocolate "dirt" mixture, ¼ cup of blueberries, and a layer of chocolate yogurt. Repeat with a second layer, and top with the remaining "dirt mixture." Refrigerate until ready to serve.

Per Serving:
calories: 299 | fat: 17g | protein: 15g | carbs: 50g | fiber: 6g

Tea Scones

Prep time: 5 minutes | Cook time: 24 minutes | Makes 1 dozen scones

½ cup unsweetened plant-based milk
1 teaspoon apple cider vinegar
1 teaspoon pure vanilla extract
3 cups oat flour

2 tablespoons baking powder
½ cup date sugar (optional)
½ teaspoon salt (optional)
½ cup unsweetened applesauce
⅓ cup almond butter

1. Preheat oven to 350ºF (180ºC). Line a baking sheet with parchment paper or a Silpat baking mat. 2. In a glass measuring cup, whisk together the plant-based milk and apple cider vinegar. Set aside to curdle for a few minutes and then add the vanilla. 3. In a medium bowl, sift together the oat flour, baking powder, date sugar, and salt (if using). 4. In a small bowl, mix together the applesauce and almond butter with a fork. Use the fork to cut the applesauce mixture into the flour mixture, until crumbly. Add the milk mixture and stir until just moistened. Do not overmix. 5. Use a ¼-cup measuring cup (or ice-cream scoop) to scoop the scones out onto the baking sheet. Mist it with a little water first so that the batter comes out easier. Bake for 20 to 24 minutes, or until a knife inserted through the center comes out clean. 6. Allow the scones to cool on the baking sheet for a few minutes before transferring them to a cooling rack to cool completely.

Per Serving:
calories: 173 | fat: 5g | protein: 5g | carbs: 20g | fiber: 2g

Poppy's Carrot Cake

Prep time: 20 minutes | Cook time: 3 hours | Serves 6 to 8

Carrot Cake:
Nonstick cooking spray (optional)
1 tablespoon ground flaxseed
2½ tablespoons water
2¼ cups rolled oats, divided

1¾ teaspoons ground cinnamon
¾ teaspoon ground nutmeg
¾ teaspoon ground ginger
2 teaspoons baking powder
1 teaspoon baking soda
1 cup unsweetened plant-based

milk
¾ cup raisins, divided
¼ cup unsweetened applesauce
⅓ cup date syrup or maple syrup (optional)
1 medium banana, peeled and broken into pieces
1 teaspoon vanilla extract
2 cups grated carrots

½ cup walnut pieces (optional)
Frosting:
¾ cup raw cashews
6 pitted Medjool dates, chopped
½ teaspoon ground ginger
⅓ to ½ cup water
2 tablespoons coconut cream

1. Prepare the slow cooker by folding two long sheets of aluminum foil and placing them perpendicular to each other (crisscross) in the bottom of the slow cooker to create "handles" that will come out over the top of the slow cooker. Coat the inside of the slow cooker and foil with cooking spray (if using) or line it with a slow cooker liner. 2. Make the carrot cake: Make a flax egg in a small bowl by mixing together the flaxseed and the water. Set aside. 3. In a blender or food processor, combine 1¾ cups of oats, the cinnamon, nutmeg, ginger, baking powder, and baking soda. Blend until the oats are turned into a flour. Pour into a large bowl and set aside. Add the remaining ½ cup of whole oats to the dry ingredients. 4. Without rinsing the blender or food processor, add the milk, ¼ cup of raisins, applesauce, syrup (if using), banana, vanilla, and the flax egg. Process until smooth and the raisins are broken down. Pour over the dry ingredients. Add the carrots, the remaining ½ cup of raisins, and the walnuts (if using), and stir well to combine. 5. Pour the mixture into the prepared slow cooker. Stretch a clean dish towel or a few layers of paper towels over the top of the slow cooker and cover. Cook on Low for 3 hours. The carrot cake is ready when a toothpick inserted in the center comes out clean. Remove the insert from the slow cooker and cool on a wire rack for at least 30 minutes before removing the cake from the insert. Allow to cool completely before frosting. 6. Make the frosting: Put the cashews, dates, and ginger in a blender or food processor. Cover with just enough water to submerge the cashews and dates. Let the mixture soak for up to 1 hour to soften. Add the coconut cream and blend well until creamy. The frosting will thicken slightly as it sits.

Per Serving:
calories: 436 | fat: 11g | protein: 9g | carbs: 81g | fiber: 9g

Sweet Potato Pie Nice Cream

Prep time: 5 minutes | Cook time: 0 minutes | Serves 2

2 medium cooked sweet potatoes
½ cup plant-based milk
1 tablespoon maple syrup

(optional)
1 teaspoon vanilla extract
½ teaspoon ground cinnamon

1. Line a baking sheet with parchment paper. 2. Remove the skin from the cooked sweet potatoes, and cut the flesh into 1-inch cubes. Place on the baking sheet in an even layer, then place in the freezer overnight, or for a minimum of 4 hours. 3. In a food processor, combine the frozen sweet potato, milk, maple syrup (if desired), vanilla, and cinnamon. 4. Process on medium speed for 1 to 2 minutes, or until the mixture has been blended into a smooth soft-serve consistency, and serve. (If you notice any sweet potato pieces stuck toward the top and sides of the food processor, you may need to stop and scrape them down with a spatula, then pulse until smooth.)

Per Serving:
calories: 155 | fat: 1g | protein: 2g | carbs: 34g | fiber:5 g

Two-Minute Turtles

Prep time: 5 minutes | Cook time: 0 minutes | Makes 12 turtles

12 pitted dates
12 toasted pecans

¼ cup chocolate chips

1. Slice lengthwise into each date, making sure to only go halfway through. Carefully widen the opening, then stuff in 1 pecan and a couple of chocolate chips. 2. Repeat with the remaining dates, pecans, and chocolate chips and serve. The turtles can be stored in an airtight container for up to 2 days.

Per Serving: (2 turtles)
calories: 95 | fat: 41g | protein: 16g | carbs: 2g | fiber: 2g

Seasonal Fruit Crumble

Prep time: 5 minutes | Cook time: 40 to 50 minutes | Serves 6 to 8

Crumble:
1 cup certified gluten-free oat flour (ground oats)
½ cup certified gluten-free rolled oats
¼ cup ground flaxseeds
½ teaspoon Himalayan pink salt (optional)
1 teaspoon ground cinnamon, plus more for coating (optional)
½ teaspoon ground cardamom
1½ teaspoons grated fresh ginger

Zest and juice of ½ lemon
¼ cup organic raw coconut oil (optional)
¼ cup pure maple syrup, plus more for coating (optional)
Filling:
4 to 5 cups fresh seasonal fruit, such as 5 large organic peaches, 3 organic pears and 2 cups of mixed berries, or 5 large organic apples
Coconut oil, for pan (optional)

1. Preheat the oven to 350ºF (180ºC). 2. Prepare the crumble: In a large bowl, combine the oat flour, oats, ground flaxseeds, salt (if using), cinnamon, cardamom, ginger, lemon zest and juice, coconut oil and maple syrup (if using) until fully combined with a crumble-like texture that sticks together. Set aside. 3. Prepare the filling: Wash, peel and slice the fruit, if necessary. Coat a 10-inch cast-iron baking pan or casserole dish with coconut oil. 4. If you wish, coat the fruit with cinnamon and a touch of maple syrup, depending on how tart or how sweet the fruit is and also your preference. 5. Spread the fruit evenly into the pan and cover with the crumble topping. Using a spatula or clean hands, gently press the topping down to compact it. 6. Bake for 40 to 50 minutes, or until lightly browned.

Per Serving:
calories: 214 | fat: 10g | protein: 4g | carbs: 30g | fiber: 4g

Salted Chocolate Truffles

Prep time: 5 minutes | Cook time: 5 minutes | Makes 18 truffles

12 ounces (340 g) vegan dark chocolate
⅔ cup full-fat coconut milk
1 teaspoon fine sea salt

(optional)
½ cup unsweetened cocoa powder

1. Set up a double boiler with a medium saucepan and medium, nonreactive bowl. Break up the chocolate into pieces, and transfer them to the bowl along with the coconut milk and sea salt, if using. 2. Place the bowl over the simmering water. Let it sit for about a minute. Then, start stirring occasionally with a spatula. Once you have a melted, smooth mixture, remove the bowl from the heat. Let the truffle mixture cool to room temperature, and then place it in the refrigerator for at least 6 hours, preferably overnight. 3. Line a small baking sheet with parchment paper. 4. Once the truffle mixture is set and fully chilled, scoop out full tablespoons onto the parchment-lined sheet. Once you've scooped out all the truffles, transfer the baking sheet to the refrigerator for 30 minutes. 5. Place the cocoa powder in a shallow bowl. 6. Remove the scooped truffle mixture from the refrigerator. Working quickly, roll the portioned mixture into balls. Then, roll those balls in the cocoa powder. Try to gently shake off any excess cocoa powder, and then place the truffles back on the baking sheet. 7. The truffles will keep in a sealed container in the refrigerator for about 1 week.

Per Serving: (2 truffles)
calories: 278 | fat: 21g | protein: 4g | carbs: 21g | fiber: 6g

Berry Compote

Prep time: 5 minutes | Cook time: 5 minutes | Makes 2 cups

3 to 4 cups fresh or frozen berries,
½ cup freshly squeezed orange juice
1 teaspoon vanilla extract

Tiny pinch of fine sea salt (optional)
2 teaspoons arrowroot powder
1 tablespoon filtered water

1. Combine the berries, orange juice, vanilla, and salt, if using, in a medium pot and bring to a boil over high heat. Cover the pan, reduce the heat to low, and simmer for 5 minutes, or until the berries have softened and released their juice. Dissolve the arrowroot in the water in a small cup, then slowly drizzle into the simmering berries, stirring constantly. Once the compote has returned to a simmer and thickened, remove from the heat. 2. Serve warm or at room temperature. Store the cooled compote in a sealed jar in the fridge for up to 5 days.

Per Serving: (½ cup)
calories: 81 | fat: 1g | protein: 1g | carbs: 19g | fiber: 3g

Chocolate-Covered Strawberries

Prep time: 10 minutes | Cook time: 1 minute | Serves 20 strawberries

1 (12-ounce / 340-g) bag vegan semisweet chocolate chips

1 (1-pound / 454-g) carton strawberries, washed and dried

1. Line a baking sheet with parchment paper. 2. In a medium, microwave-safe bowl, microwave the chocolate chips in 30-second increments, stirring between each time, until the chocolate is smooth and creamy. 3. Grab each strawberry by its stem and dip it in chocolate, then place it on the prepared baking sheet. Repeat until all the strawberries have been dipped. 4. Place the baking tray in the fridge and refrigerate for 20 to 25 minutes or until the chocolate solidifies. These are best kept in the fridge until you're ready to serve.

Per Serving: (5 strawberries)
calories: 439 | fat: 25g | protein: 4g | carbs: 62g | fiber: 7g

Apple Crisp

Prep time: 10 minutes | Cook time: 50 minutes | Serves 6 to 8

Filling:
3 pounds (1.4 kg) Granny Smith apples (about 8 apples), peeled, cored, and cut into ¼-inch slices
2 tablespoons cornstarch
1 teaspoon ground cinnamon
½ teaspoon ground ginger
⅛ teaspoon ground cloves
½ cup 100% pure maple syrup (optional)

Topping:
¼ cup 100% pure maple syrup (optional)
3 tablespoons cashew butter
2 tablespoons unsweetened applesauce
1 teaspoon pure vanilla extract
1½ cup rolled oats
½ teaspoon ground cinnamon
¼ teaspoon salt (optional)

1. Preheat the oven to 400ºF (205ºC). Line an 8 × 8-inch pan with parchment paper, making sure that the parchment goes all the way up the sides of the pan, or have ready an 8 × 8-inch nonstick or silicone baking pan. Make the Filling: 2. Place the apples in a large mixing bowl. 3. Sprinkle the cornstarch, cinnamon, ginger, and cloves over the apple slices and toss well to coat. Pour the maple syrup (if using) over the mixture and stir to combine. Place the apple mixture into the prepared baking pan. Make the Topping: 4. In a small bowl, use a fork to stir together the maple syrup (if using), cashew butter, applesauce, and vanilla, until relatively smooth. Add the oats, cinnamon, and salt (if using), and toss to coat. Assemble the Crisp: 5. Spread the topping over the apple mixture. Place the pan in the preheated oven and bake for 20 minutes. Reduce the oven temperature to 350ºF (180ºC) and bake for an additional 30 minutes, or until the topping is golden and filling is bubbly. 6. Remove the pan from the oven and transfer it to a cooling rack. Serve the crisp warm.

Per Serving:
calories: 232 | fat: 4g | protein: 4g | carbs: 45g | fiber: 8g

Pumpkin Spice Bread

Prep time: 5 minutes | Cook time: 1 hour | Makes one 8 × 4-inch loaf

2 cups whole wheat pastry flour
2 teaspoons baking powder
1 teaspoon baking soda
2 teaspoons ground cinnamon
½ teaspoon ground ginger
¼ teaspoon ground allspice
⅛ teaspoon ground cloves
1 (15-ounce / 425-g) can

pumpkin purée (about 2 cups)
½ cup 100% pure maple syrup (optional)
⅓ cup apple butter
1 teaspoon pure vanilla extract
½ cup golden raisins (optional)
½ cup chopped walnuts (optional)

1. Preheat the oven to 350ºF (180ºC). Have ready an 8 × 4-inch nonstick or silicone baking pan. 2. In a large mixing bowl sift together the flour, baking powder, baking soda, cinnamon, ginger, allspice, and cloves. 3. In a separate mixing bowl, vigorously mix together the pumpkin, maple syrup (if using), apple butter, and vanilla. 4. Pour the wet mixture into the dry mixture and combine until everything is evenly moistened (the batter will be stiff). Fold in the raisins and walnuts, if using. 5. Spoon the batter into the prepared loaf pan. Distribute the batter evenly along the length of the pan but don't spread the batter to the edges; the batter will spread as it bakes. Bake for 50 to 60 minutes, or until a knife inserted through the center

comes out clean. 6. Remove the pan from the oven and let the bread cool for at least 30 minutes, then run a knife around the edges and carefully invert the loaf onto a cooling rack. Be sure it is fully cooled before slicing.

Per Serving:
calories: 180 | fat: 3g | protein: 4g | carbs: 30g | fiber: 4g

Almond Anise Biscotti

Prep time: 5 minutes | Cook time: 40 minutes | Makes 18 slices

⅓ cup unsweetened plant-based milk
2 tablespoons ground flaxseeds
¾ cup date sugar (optional)
¼ cup unsweetened applesauce
¼ cup almond butter
½ teaspoon pure vanilla extract
½ teaspoon almond extract

1⅔ cups whole wheat pastry flour
2 tablespoons cornstarch
2 teaspoons baking powder
2 teaspoons anise seeds
½ teaspoon salt (optional)
1 cup slivered almonds

1. Preheat the oven to 350ºF (180ºC). Line a baking sheet with parchment paper or a Silpat baking mat. 2. In a large mixing bowl, use a fork to vigorously mix together the plant-based milk and flaxseeds until frothy. Mix in the date sugar (if using), applesauce, almond butter, vanilla, and almond extract. 3. Sift in the flour, cornstarch, and baking powder. Add the anise seeds and salt (if using) and mix until well combined. Knead in the almonds using your hands because the dough will be stiff. 4. On the prepared baking sheet, form the dough into a rectangle about 12 inches long by 3 to 4 inches wide. Bake for 26 to 28 minutes, or until lightly puffed and browned. Remove the sheet from the oven and let cool for 30 minutes. 5. Turn the oven temperature up to 375ºF (190ºC). With a heavy, very sharp knife, slice the biscotti loaf into ½-inch-thick slices. The best way to do this is in one motion, pushing down; don't "saw" the slices or they may crumble. Lay the slices down on the baking sheet and bake for 10 to 12 minutes, flipping the slices halfway through. Allow to cool for a few minutes on the baking sheet before transferring the slices to cooling racks.

Per Serving:
calories: 127 | fat: 5g | protein: 3g | carbs: 16g | fiber: 2g

Vanilla Bean Whip

Prep time: 5 minutes | Cook time: 0 minutes | Makes 2 cups

1 (12-ounce / 340-g) package extra-firm silken tofu, drained
½ cup cashews, soaked overnight and drained
½ cup 100% pure maple syrup

(optional)
2 tablespoons fresh lemon juice
Pinch salt (optional)
1 vanilla bean

1. Combine the tofu, cashews, maple syrup (if using), lemon juice, and salt (if using) in a blender. Purée until smooth. Scrape down the sides of the blender to incorporate all the ingredients. 2. Slice the vanilla bean in half lengthwise with a sharp knife and scrape the seeds into the blender. Blend the mixture until very smooth. 3. Transfer the mixture to a bowl and cover with plastic wrap. Chill for several hours in the refrigerator, or until firm.

Per Serving:
calories: 143 | fat: 6g | protein: 5g | carbs: 17g | fiber: 0g

Black Sesame–Ginger Quick Bread

Prep time: 20 minutes | Cook time: 50 minutes | Make 12 muffins

⅔ cup black sesame seeds
1 cup candied ginger
1½ cups plus 2 tablespoons whole wheat pastry flour
1 cup almond meal
2½ teaspoons baking powder
½ teaspoon salt (optional)
¾ cup almond milk, room temperature
¾ cup coconut sugar (optional)
½ cup melted coconut oil (optional)
2 tablespoons chia seeds
1 tablespoon fresh lemon juice
1 tablespoon ginger juice

1. Adjust an oven rack to the middle position, and preheat the oven to 350°F (180°C). Line two muffin pans with liners. 2. Pulse the sesame seeds in a food processor until ground. Transfer to a large bowl and set aside. 3. Add the ginger and 2 tablespoons of the flour to the food processor; pulse until the ginger is roughly chopped. (The flour will help keep it suspended in the batter as it bakes.) 4. Add the remaining flour, almond meal, baking powder, and salt (if desired) to the bowl with the ground sesame seeds. Stir to combine, then stir in the ginger. Make a well in the center. 5. Process the almond milk, sugar, coconut oil (if desired), chia seeds, lemon juice, and ginger juice in the now-empty food processor until completely combined. Transfer to the bowl with the dry ingredients and gently fold in the wet ingredients until just combined. (The batter will be quite thick.) 6. Scoop the batter into the muffin pans. Smooth the tops with a wet spatula. Bake for 30 minutes, until a toothpick inserted in the center comes out clean. 7. Allow to cool for 10 minutes in the pans, then allow to cool completely on a rack before slicing or peeling off the liners.

Per Serving: (2 muffins)
calories: 449 | fat: 30g | protein: 9g | carbs: 42g | fiber: 6g

Cranberry Orange Biscotti

Prep time: 5 minutes | Cook time: 40 minutes | Makes 18 slices

⅓ cup fresh orange juice
2 tablespoons ground flaxseeds
¾ cup date sugar (optional)
¼ cup unsweetened applesauce
¼ cup almond butter
1 teaspoon pure vanilla extract
1⅔ cups whole wheat pastry flour
2 tablespoons cornstarch
2 teaspoons baking powder
½ teaspoon ground allspice
½ teaspoon salt (optional)
¾ cup fruit-sweetened dried cranberries

1. Line a baking sheet with parchment paper or a Silpat baking mat. Preheat the oven to 350°F (180°C). 2. In a large mixing bowl, use a fork to vigorously mix together orange juice and flaxseeds until frothy. Mix in the date sugar (if using), applesauce, almond butter, and vanilla. 3. Sift in the flour, cornstarch, baking powder and allspice, then add the salt (if using) and mix until well combined. Knead in the cranberries using your hands because the dough will be stiff. 4. On the prepared baking sheet, form the dough into a rectangle about 12 inches long by 3 to 4 inches wide. Bake for 26 to 28 minutes, or until lightly puffed and browned. Remove the sheet from the oven and let cool for 30 minutes. 5. Turn the oven temperature up to 375°F (190°C). With a heavy, very sharp knife, slice the biscotti into ½-inch-thick slices. The best way to do this is in one motion, pushing down; don't "saw" the slices or they may crumble. Lay the slices down on the cookie sheet and bake for 10 to 12 minutes, flipping the slices halfway through. Allow to cool for a few minutes on the baking sheet before transferring the slices to cooling racks.

Per Serving:
calories: 108 | fat: 2g | protein: 2g | carbs: 19g | fiber: 2g

Blueberry Muffin Loaf

Prep time: 25 minutes | Cook time: 1 hour | Makes 1 loaf

Topping:
¼ cup maple sugar or coconut palm sugar (optional)
4 tablespoons whole spelt flour
Small pinch of fine sea salt (optional)
¼ teaspoon ground cinnamon
2 tablespoons coconut oil (optional)
Loaf:
⅓ cup unsweetened almond milk
1 tablespoon fresh orange juice
1½ cups whole spelt flour
½ cup almond flour
2 teaspoons aluminum-free baking powder
¼ teaspoon baking soda
½ teaspoon fine sea salt (optional)
1 teaspoon ground cinnamon
¼ cup unsweetened applesauce
⅓ cup coconut oil, plus extra for greasing the pan
⅓ cup plus 2 tablespoons maple sugar (optional)
1 teaspoon pure vanilla extract
1 cup fresh blueberries or frozen blueberries

1. Preheat the oven to 375°F (190°C). Lightly grease an 8- × 4-inch loaf pan with coconut oil. Line the pan with parchment paper, leaving an overhang on the two long sides, and set aside. 2. Make the Crumble Topping: In a small bowl, combine maple sugar, spelt flour, sea salt, cinnamon, and oil, if using. Lightly mix the topping with a fork until it starts clumping. Place the topping in the refrigerator while you make the loaf. 3. Make the Loaf: In a measuring cup, lightly whisk the almond milk with the orange juice, and set aside to curdle. 4. In a large bowl, whisk together the spelt flour, almond flour, baking powder, baking soda, sea salt, and cinnamon. Add the almond milk mixture to the flour mixture. Add the applesauce, oil, maple sugar, if using, and vanilla. Gently mix with a spatula until you have a unified batter, being careful not to overmix. 5. Gently fold the blueberries into the batter. Quickly scrape the batter into the prepared loaf pan, and top it with the crumble mixture. Gently press the crumble mixture into the surface of the loaf with your fingers. The crumble pieces should be surrounded by batter without being submerged. Slide the loaf pan into the oven, and bake for 55 to 60 minutes or until evenly browned on the top and a toothpick inserted into the center of the loaf comes out clean. 6. Cool the loaf completely in the pan before slicing and serving.

Per Serving: (⅛ loaf)
calories: 280 | fat: 11g | protein: 6g | carbs: 42g | fiber: 5g

Chapter 6 Vegetables and Sides

Baked Spaghetti Squash with Spicy Lentil Sauce

Prep time: 15 minutes | Cook time: 55 minutes | Serves 4

2 small spaghetti squash (about 1 pound / 454 g each), halved	2 teaspoons crushed red pepper flakes, or to taste
Salt and freshly ground black pepper, to taste	¼ cup tomato paste
1 medium yellow onion, peeled and diced small	1 cup cooked green lentils
3 cloves garlic, peeled and minced	1 cup vegetable stock, or low-sodium vegetable broth, plus more as needed
	Chopped parsley

1. Preheat the oven to 350ºF (180ºC). 2. Season the cut sides of the squash with salt and pepper. Place the squash halves, cut side down, on a baking sheet, and bake them for 45 to 55 minutes, or until the squash is very tender (it is done when it can be easily pierced with a knife). 3. While the squash bakes, place the onion in a large saucepan and sauté over medium heat for 5 minutes. Add water 1 to 2 tablespoons at a time to keep the onion from sticking to the pan. Add the garlic, crushed red pepper flakes, tomato paste, and ½ cup of water and cook for 5 minutes. Add the lentils to the pan and cook until heated through. Season with additional salt. Purée the lentil mixture using an immersion blender or in a blender with a tight-fitting lid, covered with a towel, until smooth and creamy. Add some of the vegetable stock, as needed, to make a creamy sauce. 4. To serve, scoop the flesh from the spaghetti squash (it should come away looking like noodles) and divide it among 4 plates. Top with some of the lentil sauce and garnish with the parsley.

Per Serving:

calories: 94 | fat: 0g | protein: 6g | carbs: 18g | fiber: 5g

Stir-Fried Vegetables with Miso and Sake

Prep time: 25 minutes | Cook time: 10 minutes | Serves 4

¼ cup mellow white miso	strips
½ cup vegetable stock, or low-sodium vegetable broth	1 large head broccoli, cut into florets
¼ cup sake	½ pound (227 g) snow peas, trimmed
1 medium yellow onion, peeled and thinly sliced	2 cloves garlic, peeled and minced
1 large carrot, peeled, cut in half lengthwise, and then cut into half-moons on the diagonal	½ cup chopped cilantro (optional)
1 medium red bell pepper, seeded and cut into ½-inch	Salt and freshly ground black pepper, to taste

1. Whisk together the miso, vegetable stock, and sake in a small bowl and set aside. 2. Heat a large skillet over high heat. Add the onion, carrot, red pepper, and broccoli and stir-fry for 4 to 5 minutes. Add water 1 to 2 tablespoons at a time to keep the vegetables from sticking to the pan. Add the snow peas and stir-fry for another 4 minutes. Add the garlic and cook for 30 seconds. Add the miso mixture and cook until heated through. 3. Remove the pan from the heat and add the cilantro (if using). Season with salt and pepper.

Per Serving:

calories: 135 | fat: 1g | protein: 7g | carbs: 24g | fiber: 7g

Sweet Potato Biscuits

Prep time: 5 minutes | Cook time: 10 minutes | Makes 12 biscuits

1 medium sweet potato	(optional)
3 tablespoons melted coconut oil, divided (optional)	1 cup whole-grain flour
1 tablespoon maple syrup	2 teaspoons baking powder
	Pinch sea salt (optional)

1. Bake the sweet potato at 350ºF (180ºC) for about 45 minutes, until tender. Allow it to cool, then remove the flesh and mash. 2. Turn the oven up to 375ºF (190ºC) and line a baking sheet with parchment paper or lightly grease it. 3. Measure out 1 cup potato flesh. In a medium bowl, combine the mashed sweet potato with 1½ tablespoons of the coconut oil and the maple syrup, if using. 4. Mix together the flour and baking powder in a separate medium bowl, then add the flour mixture to the potato mixture and blend well with a fork. 5. On a floured board, pat the mixture out into a ½-inch-thick circle and cut out 1-inch rounds, or simply drop spoonfuls of dough and pat them into rounds. Put the rounds onto the prepared baking sheet. Brush the top of each with some of the remaining 1½ tablespoons melted coconut oil. 6. Bake 10 minutes, or until lightly golden on top. Serve hot.

Per Serving: (1 biscuit)

calories: 77 | fat: 3g | protein: 1g | carbs: 10g | fiber: 1g

Radish Turmeric Pickle

Prep time: 5 minutes | Cook time: 0 minutes | Serves 6

1 pound (454 g) medium radishes	1 teaspoon fine sea salt, or more to taste (optional)
6 tablespoons raw apple cider vinegar	1 (2-inch) piece fresh turmeric

1. Trim the tail ends of the radishes and thinly slice the radishes on a mandoline, holding them by their greens, or slice paper-thin with a sharp knife. Transfer to a medium bowl, add the vinegar and salt, if using, and mix until well combined. 2. Peel and finely grate the turmeric, then stir it into the radishes and season with more salt if necessary. Serve immediately, or transfer to a jar, cover, and store in the fridge for up to 2 weeks. Invert the jar after an hour or two to make sure all the radishes are combined with liquid and evenly colored by the turmeric.

Per Serving:

calories: 20 | fat: 0g | protein: 1g | carbs: 4g | fiber: 2g

Yellow Bell Pepper Boats

Prep time: 30 minutes | Cook time: 50 minutes | Serves 6

Bell Pepper Boats:
2 medium potatoes, halved
1 ear corn, kernels removed (about ½ cup)
½ small onion, peeled and finely chopped
1 small green bell pepper, seeded and finely chopped (about ¼ cup)
¼ teaspoon grated ginger
½ clove garlic, peeled and minced
½ teaspoon minced serrano chile, or to taste (for less heat, remove the seeds)
½ teaspoon salt, or to taste (optional)
1 teaspoon fresh lime juice
2 yellow bell peppers
¼ cup sunflower seeds, toasted
Hot Sauce:
1 large tomato, chopped (about 2 cups)
½ teaspoon cayenne pepper
½ teaspoon salt, or to taste (optional)
½ clove garlic, peeled and mashed to a paste
½ tablespoon finely chopped cilantro

Make the Bell Pepper Boats: 1. Preheat the oven to 350ºF (180ºC). 2. Boil the potatoes in a saucepan of water for 15 minutes over medium heat, until tender. Remove from the heat, drain, and let cool. Mash the potatoes in a mixing bowl. 3. Place the corn and 1 cup of water in a small pan. Cook on medium heat until the corn is tender, 5 to 7 minutes. Drain and add to the potatoes along with the onion, green pepper, ginger, garlic, serrano chile, salt (if using), and lime juice. Mix well. 4. Cut the yellow peppers into 3 long slices each, making boat shapes, and remove the seeds. Divide the potato mixture among the slices and, sprinkle with sunflower seeds. Bake, covered, for 30 to 35 minutes, until the yellow peppers are soft when poked with a fork. Make the Hot Sauce: 5. Purée the tomato in a blender. Add the purée to a saucepan with the cayenne pepper, salt (if using), and garlic, bring to a boil, and cook for 5 minutes. Reduce the heat to low and simmer for 5 more minutes. 6. To serve, spread the hot sauce on top of the baked bell peppers. Garnish with cilantro.

Per Serving:
calories: 138 | fat: 3g | protein: 4g | carbs: 25g | fiber: 4g

Fennel and Cherry Tomato Gratin

Prep time: 15 minutes | Cook time: 55 minutes | Serves 6

2 fennel bulbs, long fronds and top stalks trimmed off
1 cup whole cherry tomatoes
⅓ cup vegetable stock
2 tablespoons dry white wine
1 tablespoon virgin olive oil (optional)
2 teaspoons minced fresh thyme leaves
Salt and pepper, to taste
(optional)
Topping:
½ cup raw pine nuts
½ cup raw walnut halves
1 tablespoon virgin olive oil
1 tablespoon nutritional yeast
½ teaspoon garlic powder
2 teaspoons minced fresh thyme leaves

1. Preheat the oven to 375ºF (190ºC). 2. Cut the fennel bulbs into 2-inch wedges, removing pieces of the core as you go. Arrange the fennel wedges facing up in a 13- × 9-inch glass or metal baking dish. 3. Place the tomatoes in the crevices between the fennel wedges in the pan. Carefully pour the vegetable stock and white wine into the pan so that they distribute themselves evenly. Carefully drizzle the olive oil over the fennel wedges. Season the fennel with the minced thyme, salt, and pepper, if using. Cover the dish tightly with foil, and bake in the oven for 35 minutes. 4. Make the Topping: In the bowl of a food processor, combine the pine nuts, walnut halves, olive oil, nutritional yeast, garlic powder, and minced thyme. Pulse until you have a crumbly topping that holds together in small chunks. 5. After baking for 35 minutes, remove the fennel from the oven. Remove the foil, and sprinkle the topping all over the surface. Slide the gratin back into the oven and bake, uncovered, for another 20 minutes or until the topping is golden brown and the fennel is fork-tender. Serve the gratin hot.

Per Serving:
calories: 196 | fat: 16g | protein: 5g | carbs: 10g | fiber: 4g

Braised Red Cabbage with Beans

Prep time: 25 minutes | Cook time: 38 minutes | Serves 4

1 large yellow onion, peeled and diced
2 large carrots, peeled and diced
2 celery stalks, diced
2 teaspoons thyme
1½ cups red wine
2 tablespoons Dijon mustard
1 large head red cabbage, cored
and shredded
4 cups cooked navy beans, or 2 (15-ounce / 425-g) cans, drained and rinsed
2 tart apples (such as Granny Smith), peeled, cored, and diced
Salt and freshly ground black pepper, to taste

1. Place the onion, carrots, and celery in a large saucepan and sauté over medium heat for 7 to 8 minutes. Add water 1 to 2 tablespoons at a time to keep the vegetables from sticking to the pan. Add the thyme, red wine, and mustard and cook until the wine is reduced by half, about 10 minutes. 2. Add the cabbage, beans, and apples. Cook, covered, until the cabbage is tender, about 20 minutes. Season with salt and pepper.

Per Serving:
calories: 315 | fat: 1g | protein: 14g | carbs: 60g | fiber: 20g

Broccolini on Fire

Prep time: 5 minutes | Cook time: 20 minutes | Serves 2

1 bunch broccoli
2 tablespoons extra-virgin coconut oil (optional)
4 large garlic cloves, cut into ¼-inch slices
¼ teaspoon fine sea salt (optional)
½ teaspoon red chili pepper flakes

1. Trim the bottom ends of the broccolini stems. Cut the florets off the stems and cut each floret into 2 or 3 pieces. Slice the stems in half lengthwise. 2. Warm the oil in a large heavy skillet, preferably cast iron, over medium heat. Add the garlic and sauté for 4 to 5 minutes, until golden. Using a slotted spoon, remove the garlic from the pan, leaving the oil behind, and set aside. Add the broccolini and stems to the pan and sauté for 12 to 15 minutes, stirring every couple of minutes, until it is tender and starting to brown in parts. Remove from the heat and stir in the salt, if using, and red chili pepper flakes and reserved garlic. 3. Serve warm. Any leftovers can be stored in an airtight container in the fridge for up to 3 days.

Per Serving:
calories: 234 | fat: 14g | protein: 9g | carbs: 23g | fiber: 8g

Maple-Glazed Butternut Squash and Brussels Sprouts

Prep time: 15 minutes | Cook time: 2 to 2½ hours | Serves 4 to 6

1 medium butternut squash (about 2 to 3 pounds / 907 g to 1.4 kg), peeled, seeded, and cut into 1-inch cubes	(optional)
	½ teaspoon ground cinnamon
	Ground black pepper
¾ pound (340 g) Brussels sprouts, halved	Salt (optional)
¼ cup apple cider vinegar	1 cup chopped pecans
2 tablespoons maple syrup	4 to 5 Medjool dates, pitted and chopped

1. Put the butternut squash and Brussels sprouts in the slow cooker. Cover and cook on High for 2 to 2½ hours or on Low for 4 to 6 hours, checking for doneness each hour, until the squash is tender but not mushy and the Brussels sprouts still have some texture. 2. In a measuring cup or medium bowl, make the glaze by stirring together the vinegar, maple syrup (if using), and cinnamon. Pour the mixture over the vegetables and stir gently to coat. Season with pepper and salt (if using). Toss with the pecans and dates and serve immediately.

Per Serving:

calories: 372 | fat: 20g | protein: 7g | carbs: 50g | fiber: 12g

Sautéed Collard Greens

Prep time: 10 minutes | Cook time: 25 minutes | Serves 4

1½ pounds (680 g) collard greens	½ teaspoon onion powder
1 cup vegetable broth	⅛ teaspoon freshly ground black pepper
½ teaspoon garlic powder	

1. Remove the hard middle stems from the greens, then roughly chop the leaves into 2-inch pieces. 2. In a large saucepan, mix together the vegetable broth, garlic powder, onion powder, and pepper. Bring to a boil over medium-high heat, then add the chopped greens. Reduce the heat to low, and cover. 3. Cook for 20 minutes, stirring well every 4 to 5 minutes, and serve. (If you notice that the liquid has completely evaporated and the greens are beginning to stick to the bottom of the pan, stir in a few extra tablespoons of vegetable broth or water.)

Per Serving:

calories: 28 | fat: 1g | protein: 3g | carbs: 4g | fiber: 2g

Lemony Roasted Cauliflower with Coriander

Prep time: 15 minutes | Cook time: 50 minutes | Serves 6

1 medium cauliflower, cut into 1-inch florets	virgin coconut oil (optional)
	2 teaspoons ground coriander
¼ cup raw cashew butter	1 teaspoon fine sea salt (optional)
2 tablespoons filtered water	
Grated zest of 1 lemon	1 large garlic clove, grated or pressed
2 tablespoons freshly squeezed lemon juice	
	¼ teaspoon ground turmeric
2 tablespoons melted extra-	

1. Preheat the oven to 400ºF (205ºC). Line a rimmed baking sheet with parchment paper and set aside. 2. Set up a steamer and fill the pot with about 1 inch of filtered water. Bring to a boil over high heat and set the steamer basket in place. Arrange the cauliflower evenly in the basket and steam for 5 minutes, or until a knife slides easily into a floret. Transfer to a bowl and set aside. 3. Combine the cashew butter, water, lemon zest, and lemon juice in a small bowl and stir until smooth. Add the coconut oil, coriander, salt, if using, garlic, and turmeric and stir to combine. Pour over the cauliflower and use your hands to gently and thoroughly mix, making sure every floret is thoroughly coated. 4. Spread the cauliflower out on the parchment-lined baking sheet and roast for 20 to 25 minutes, until browned on the bottom. Remove from the oven and turn each piece over, then roast for another 10 to 15 minutes, until golden brown. Serve warm. This is best served right away, but any leftovers can be stored in an airtight container in the fridge for 2 to 3 days.

Per Serving:

calories: 130 | fat: 10g | protein: 4g | carbs: 9g | fiber: 2g

Sautéed Root Vegetables with Parsley, Poppy Seeds, and Lemon

Prep time: 10 minutes | Cook time: 10 minutes | Serves 4

2 tablespoons extra-virgin coconut oil (optional)	more to taste (optional)
	1 tablespoon poppy seeds
2 large garlic cloves, finely chopped	Grated zest of 1 small lemon
	1 tablespoon freshly squeezed lemon juice
1 pound (454 g) root vegetables, grated	
	1½ cups fresh flat-leaf parsley leaves, coarsely chopped
1 teaspoon fine sea salt, plus	

1. Warm the oil in a large skillet over medium heat. Add the garlic and sauté for 1 minute, or until golden. Stir in the grated vegetables and salt, if using, and cook for 8 minutes, or until the vegetables are softened. Remove from the heat and stir in the poppy seeds, lemon zest, lemon juice, and parsley. Season to taste with more salt and serve warm or at room temperature. Any leftovers can be stored in an airtight container in the fridge for up to 3 days.

Per Serving:

calories: 130 | fat: 8g | protein: 2g | carbs: 14g | fiber: 4g

Jicama-Citrus Pickle

Prep time: 15 minutes | Cook time: 0 minutes | Serves 6

1 small-medium jicama, peeled	juice
2 tablespoons raw apple cider vinegar, or more to taste	2 teaspoons freshly squeezed lime juice
1 teaspoon grated orange zest	2 teaspoons freshly squeezed lemon juice
1 teaspoon grated lime zest	
1 teaspoon grated lemon zest	1¼ teaspoons fine sea salt, or
¼ cup freshly squeezed orange	more to taste (optional)

1. Cut the jicama crosswise into 1-inch slices. Shave lengthwise on a mandoline or slice paper-thin with a sharp knife. Transfer to a medium bowl, add the vinegar, citrus zest and juice, and salt, and mix well to combine. Add more vinegar or salt to taste if necessary. Serve immediately, or store in a jar in the fridge for up to 1 week.

Per Serving:

calories: 49 | fat: 0g | protein: 1g | carbs: 11g | fiber: 6g

Savory Sweet Potato Casserole

Prep time: 15 minutes | Cook time: 30 minutes | Serves 6

8 cooked sweet potatoes	1 teaspoon dried thyme
½ cup vegetable broth	1 teaspoon dried rosemary
1 tablespoon dried sage	

1. Preheat the oven to 375ºF (190ºC). 2. Remove and discard the skin from the cooked sweet potatoes, and put them in a baking dish. Mash the sweet potatoes with a fork or potato masher, then stir in the broth, sage, thyme, and rosemary. 3. Bake for 30 minutes and serve.

Per Serving:

calories: 154 | fat: 0g | protein: 3g | carbs: 35g | fiber: 6g

Loaded Frijoles

Prep time: 10 minutes | Cook time: 20 minutes | Serves 6

1 tablespoon avocado oil (optional)	1 teaspoon ground cumin
1 yellow onion, finely chopped	2 (15-ounce / 425-g) cans pinto beans, undrained
3 garlic cloves, minced	¼ cup tomato sauce
2 teaspoons chili powder	Sea salt, to taste (optional)

1. In a 4-quart pan, warm the avocado oil (if using) over medium-high heat. Add the onion and sauté for 5 minutes. 2. Add the garlic and cook for 30 seconds, then add the chili powder and cumin and cook for 30 seconds. 3. Stir in the beans and tomato sauce. Taste and add salt (if using), if needed. 4. Mash the beans, or purée them with an immersion blender, until the desired consistency is reached. Cook over medium-low heat for 15 minutes, or until the beans thicken. If the beans become too thick, add a little water. 5. Store in an airtight container in the fridge for up to 1 week or in the freezer for several months.

Per Serving:

calories: 142 | fat: 3g | protein: 7g | carbs: 22g | fiber: 6g

Vegetable Spring Rolls with Spicy Peanut Dipping Sauce

Prep time: 15 minutes | Cook time: 10 minutes | Serves 2

Spicy Peanut Dipping Sauce:	Spring Rolls:
2 tablespoons defatted peanut powder	6 rice paper wraps
1 tablespoon maple syrup (optional)	6 large lettuce leaves
1 tablespoon rice vinegar	1½ cups cooked brown rice
½ teaspoon onion powder	1 cup shredded carrots
½ teaspoon garlic powder	1 bunch fresh cilantro
½ teaspoon red pepper flakes	1 bunch fresh mint
	1 bunch fresh basil

Make Spicy Peanut Dipping Sauce: 1. In a small saucepan over medium heat, combine the peanut powder, maple syrup (if desired), rice vinegar, onion powder, garlic powder, and red pepper flakes. Cook for 10 minutes, stirring occasionally. Remove the sauce from the heat, and set aside to cool. Make Spring Rolls: 1. Fill a shallow bowl or pan with warm water, and dip a rice paper wrap in the water

for 10 to 15 seconds. Remove and place on a cutting board or other clean, smooth surface. 2. Lay a lettuce leaf down flat on a rice paper wrap, then add ¼ cup of brown rice, 2 to 3 tablespoons of shredded carrots, and a few leaves each of cilantro, mint, and basil. 3. Wrap the sides of the rice paper halfway into the center, then roll the wrap from the bottom to the top to form a tight roll. 4. Repeat for the remaining spring rolls. Serve with the sauce in a dipping bowl on the side.

Per Serving:

calories: 263 | fat: 3g | protein: 11g | carbs: 46g | fiber: 5g

Summer Squash and Blossom Sauté with Mint and Peas

Prep time: 10 minutes | Cook time: 10 minutes | Serves 4

½ cup fresh or frozen peas	15 large zucchini blossoms, stems removed and chopped into ½-inch pieces
1 pound (454 g) mixed zucchini and pattypan squash	
1 tablespoon extra-virgin coconut oil (optional)	A handful of fresh mint leaves, torn

1. If you're using fresh peas, bring a small saucepan of water to a boil, add the peas, and simmer for 3 minutes, or until tender. Drain and set aside. 2. Cut the zucchini into ½-inch slices. Cut pattypan squash into ½-inch wedges. Warm the oil in a wide skillet over medium-high heat. Add the squash and sauté, stirring frequently, until tender and beginning to brown in parts, 2 to 3 minutes. Add the peas and zucchini blossoms and cook for another minute or so, until the blossoms have softened and the peas are heated through. Remove from the heat and serve. This is best served fresh, but any leftovers can be stored for a day or two in the fridge.

Per Serving:

calories: 262 | fat: 8g | protein: 17g | carbs: 42g | fiber: 14g

Grilled Vegetable Kabobs

Prep time: 25 minutes | Cook time: 15 minutes | Serves 6

½ cup balsamic vinegar	1 red bell pepper, seeded and cut into 1-inch pieces
3 cloves garlic, peeled and minced	1 pint cherry tomatoes
1½ tablespoons minced rosemary	1 medium zucchini, cut into 1-inch rounds
1½ tablespoons minced thyme	1 medium yellow squash, cut into 1-inch rounds
Salt and freshly ground black pepper, to taste	1 medium red onion, peeled and cut into large chunks
1 green bell pepper, seeded and cut into 1-inch pieces	

1. Prepare the grill. 2. Soak 12 bamboo skewers in water for 30 minutes. 3. Combine the balsamic vinegar, garlic, rosemary, thyme, and salt and pepper in a small bowl. 4. Skewer the vegetables, alternating between different-colored vegetables for a nice presentation. Place the skewers on the grill and cook, brushing the vegetables with the vinegar mixture and turning every 4 to 5 minutes, until the vegetables are tender and starting to char, 12 to 15 minutes.

Per Serving:

calories: 50 | fat: 0g | protein: 1g | carbs: 10g | fiber: 2g

Spring Steamed Vegetables with Savory Goji Berry Cream

Prep time: 15 minutes | Cook time: 10 minutes | Serves 6

Savory Goji Berry Cream:	(optional)
¼ cup dried goji berries	Salt and pepper, to taste
1 tablespoon apple cider vinegar	(optional)
	Vegetables:
1 tablespoon mellow or light miso	1½ pounds (680 g) trimmed spring vegetables
1 tablespoon fresh lemon juice	Salt and pepper, to taste
1(1-inch) piece of fresh ginger, peeled and chopped	(optional)
	Garnishes:
1 teaspoon pure maple syrup (optional)	Scant ¼ cup walnut halves, toasted and chopped
3 tablespoons virgin olive oil	1 green onion, thinly sliced

1. Make the Savory Goji Berry Cream: Place the goji berries in a small bowl and cover them with boiling water. Let the berries sit for 5 minutes or until they've plumped and softened. Spoon the goji berries into a blender, reserving the soaking water. 2. Add the apple cider vinegar, miso, lemon juice, ginger, maple syrup, olive oil, salt, and pepper, if using, to the blender. Add 3 tablespoons of the goji soaking water, and then whiz the mixture on high until creamy and smooth. Set aside. 3. Make the Vegetables: After you've trimmed the vegetables, set a large pot with about 1 inch of water on the stove. Bring the water to a simmer. Arrange the vegetables in a steamer basket and set them into the pot. Cover and steam until all the vegetables are just tender, about 8 minutes. 4. Arrange the steamed vegetables on your serving platter and top with the Savory Goji Berry Cream. Garnish with the chopped walnuts and sliced green onions.

Per Serving:
calories: 136 | fat: 9g | protein: 5g | carbs: 17g | fiber: 5g

Garlicky Winter Vegetable and White Bean Mash

Prep time: 20 minutes | Cook time: 25 minutes | Serves 4

Vegetable and Bean Mash:	1 tablespoon virgin olive oil
2 cups peeled and diced celery root	(optional)
	5 cups sliced mushrooms
2 cups chopped cauliflower	2 teaspoons chopped fresh
1 cup chopped parsnips	thyme leaves
5 cloves garlic, peeled	4 cloves garlic, minced
1 cup cooked and drained white beans, such as navy or cannellini	Salt and pepper, to taste (optional)
	2 teaspoons balsamic vinegar
¾ cup unsweetened almond milk	1¼ cups vegetable stock
1 teaspoon virgin olive oil (optional)	1 tablespoon mellow or light miso
Salt and pepper, to taste (optional)	2 teaspoons arrowroot powder
	Freshly ground black pepper,
Mushroom Miso Gravy:	for serving (optional)

1. Make the Vegetable And Bean Mash: Place the diced celery root, cauliflower, parsnips, and garlic cloves in a medium saucepan. Cover the vegetables with cold water and then place the pot over medium heat. Bring to a boil and then simmer until the vegetables are tender, about 15 minutes. 2. Drain the vegetables and place them in the bowl of a food processor along with the white beans. Pulse the vegetables and beans a couple of times to lightly chop them. Add the almond milk, olive oil, salt, and pepper, if using. Run the motor on high speed until you have a creamy and smooth mixture. Keep it warm. 3. Make the Mushrom Miso Gravy: Heat the olive oil in a large sauté pan over medium heat. Add the mushrooms, and let them sit for 2 full minutes. Stir them up and let them sear for another full minute. Add the thyme and garlic, and stir. After the mushrooms start to glisten slightly, season them with salt and pepper, if using. Add the balsamic vinegar and stir. 4. In a small bowl, whisk together the vegetable stock, miso, and arrowroot powder until no lumps of miso remain. Pour this mixture into the pan with the mushrooms, and stir. 5. Bring the gravy to a light simmer, and cook until the gravy has thickened slightly. 6. Serve the Mushroom Miso Gravy piping hot on top of the vegetable mash. Sprinkle with freshly ground black pepper if you like.

Per Serving:
calories: 225 | fat: 6g | protein: 10g | carbs: 36g | fiber: 8g

Fermented Carrots with Turmeric and Ginger

Prep time: 15 minutes | Cook time: 0 minutes | Makes 8 cups

10 medium-large carrots, grated	peeled and finely grated
	1 (2-inch) piece fresh ginger,
½ medium cabbage, cored and thinly sliced with 1 leaf reserved	peeled and finely grated
	1 small shallot, finely chopped
	5 teaspoons fine sea salt
1 (3-inch) piece fresh turmeric,	(optional)

1. Combine the carrots, cabbage, turmeric, ginger, shallot, and salt, if using, in a large bowl and use clean hands to mix the vegetables together, squeezing and softening them until they are juicy and wilted. Transfer a handful of the mixture to a large widemouthed jar or a fermentation crock and press it down well with your fist. Repeat with the remaining carrot mixture, a handful at a time, and then add any liquid left in the bowl. The liquid should completely cover the mixture; if it does not, keep pressing the mixture down until it does. If they don't create enough liquid, add cooled brine to cover. You should have at least 3 inches of headspace above the vegetables. Clean the edges of the jar or crock of any stray pieces of vegetable. Place the reserved cabbage leaf on top of the vegetables. Add a weight, such as a small glass jar filled with water, a flat glass plate or lid, or a fermentation weight, to keep the vegetables submerged, then seal the jar or crock. Label and date it and put it in a cool, dark place for 10 days. 2. After 10 days, carefully remove the lid, as it might pop off because of the gases that have built up, then remove the weight and cabbage leaf and use a clean fork to remove a little of the carrots to taste. If the level of tanginess and complexity of flavor are to your liking, transfer the jar or crock to the fridge, or transfer the mixture to smaller jars and refrigerate. If not, replace the leaf and the weight, tighten the lid, set aside for a few more days, and taste again. Usually 2 to 3 weeks of fermentation results in a good flavor. The fermented carrots will keep in the fridge for months. The flavor will continue to develop, but at a much slower rate.

Per Serving: (1 cup)
calories: 37 | fat: 0g | protein: 1g | carbs: 9g | fiber: 3g

Aloo Gobi (Potato and Cauliflower Curry)

Prep time: 25 minutes | Cook time: 27 minutes | Serves 4

1 medium yellow onion, peeled and diced	other waxy potatoes, cut into ½-inch dice
1 tablespoon grated ginger	1 teaspoon ground cumin
2 cloves garlic, peeled and minced	1 teaspoon ground coriander
½ jalapeño pepper, seeded and minced	1 teaspoon crushed red pepper flakes
2 medium tomatoes, diced	½ teaspoon turmeric
1 medium head cauliflower, cut into florets	¼ teaspoon ground cloves
	2 bay leaves
1 pound (454 g) Yukon Gold or	1 cup green peas
	¼ cup chopped cilantro or mint

1. Place the onion in a large saucepan and sauté over medium heat for 7 to 8 minutes. Add water 1 to 2 tablespoons at a time to keep the onion from sticking to the pan. Add the ginger, garlic, and jalapeño pepper and cook for 3 minutes. Add the tomatoes, cauliflower, potatoes, cumin, coriander, crushed red pepper flakes, turmeric, cloves, and bay leaves and cook, covered, for 10 to 12 minutes, until the vegetables are tender. Add the peas and cook for 5 minutes longer. 2. Remove the bay leaves, and serve garnished with the cilantro or mint.

Per Serving:
calories: 163 | fat: 0g | protein: 6g | carbs: 34g | fiber: 7g

Stuffed Eggplant

Prep time: 25 minutes | Cook time: 1 hour 40 minutes | Serves 4

2 cups vegetable stock, or low-sodium vegetable broth	1 medium red bell pepper, seeded and diced small
1 cup brown basmati rice	2 cloves garlic, peeled and minced
1 cinnamon stick	
2 medium eggplants, stemmed and halved lengthwise	¼ cup finely chopped basil
	¼ cup finely chopped cilantro
1 medium yellow onion, peeled and diced small	Salt and freshly ground black pepper, to taste
1 celery stalk, diced small	

1. Bring the vegetable stock to a boil in a medium saucepan. Add the rice and cinnamon stick and bring the pot back to a boil. Cover and cook over medium heat for 45 minutes, or until tender and the stock is absorbed. 2. Carefully scoop the flesh out of the eggplant halves, leaving a ¼-inch-thick shell. Coarsely chop the pulp and set it aside with the shells. 3. Preheat the oven to 350ºF (180ºC). 4. Place the onion, celery, and red pepper in a large saucepan and sauté over medium heat for 7 to 8 minutes, or until the vegetables start to brown. Add water 1 to 2 tablespoons at a time to keep the vegetables from sticking to the pan. Add the garlic and eggplant pulp and cook for 5 more minutes, or until the eggplant is tender. Remove from the heat. Add the cooked rice, basil, and cilantro to the eggplant mixture. Season with salt and pepper. 5. Divide the rice mixture evenly among the eggplant shells and place the stuffed eggplants in a baking dish. Cover with aluminum foil and bake for 40 minutes.

Per Serving:
calories: 250 | fat: 1g | protein: 6g | carbs: 54g | fiber: 9g

Beet Sushi and Avocado Poke Bowls

Prep time: 20 minutes | Cook time: 20 minutes | Serves 2

2 red beets, trimmed and peeled	1 cup cooked brown rice
3 cups water	1 cucumber, peeled and cut into matchsticks
2 teaspoons low-sodium soy sauce or gluten-free tamari	2 carrots, cut into matchsticks
½ teaspoon wasabi paste (optional)	1 avocado, peeled, pitted, and sliced
1 tablespoon maple syrup (optional)	1 scallion, green and white parts, chopped small, for garnish
1 teaspoon sesame oil (optional)	2 tablespoons sesame seeds, for garnish (optional)
1 teaspoon rice vinegar	
1 cup frozen shelled edamame	

1. In a medium saucepan, combine the beets and water and bring to a boil over high heat. Lower the heat to medium and cook until they are tender but not mushy, about 15 minutes. Drain, rinse, and set aside to cool. 2. In a small bowl, make the dressing by mixing together the soy sauce, wasabi (if using), maple syrup, sesame oil, and rice vinegar and set aside. 3. When the beets are cooled, slide off the skins. Using a sharp knife, cut the beets into very thin slices to resemble tuna sashimi. Put the beet slices in a small bowl and top with 1 teaspoon of the dressing. Set aside to marinate. 4. Put the edamame in a microwave-safe bowl, add water to cover, and cook in the microwave for 1 minute. Drain and set aside. 5. To assemble the bowls, divide the rice between 2 bowls. Top each bowl with the sliced beets, rice, cucumbers, carrots, edamame, and avocado and drizzle with the remaining dressing. Garnish with the scallions and sesame seeds (if using).

Per Serving:
calories: 488 | fat: 22g | protein: 16g | carbs: 63g | fiber: 18g

Roasted Balsamic Beets

Prep time: 5 minutes | Cook time: 50 minutes | Serves 6

6 medium beets, scrubbed	1½ tablespoons virgin olive oil (optional)
¼ cup plus 2 tablespoons balsamic vinegar, divided	Salt and pepper, to taste (optional)
2 teaspoons pure maple syrup (optional)	

1. Preheat the oven to 400ºF (205ºC). 2. Trim both ends of the beets and peel them. Cut the beets into ½-inch dices. Arrange the diced beets in a single layer in a large glass baking dish. 3. Drizzle the diced beets with ¼ cup of the balsamic vinegar, the maple syrup, and the olive oil, if using. Season the beets with salt and pepper, if using, and gently toss them until they're evenly coated. Cover the dish with foil and place in the oven. 4. Roast the covered beets for 25 minutes. Then, remove them from the oven and add the remaining 2 tablespoons of the balsamic vinegar. Carefully toss the beets to coat. Roast the beets uncovered for another 25 minutes or until fork-tender. 5. Serve beets immediately or allow them to cool thoroughly on the counter. Beets can be stored in a sealed container in the refrigerator for up to 5 days.

Per Serving:
calories: 84 | fat: 4g | protein: 1g | carbs: 12g | fiber: 2g

Sweet and Savory Root Veggies and Butternut Squash

Prep time: 20 minutes | Cook time: 3½ to 5 hours | Serves 4 to 6

1 large sweet potato (about ½ pound / 227 g), peeled and cut into 1½-inch chunks	2 apples, any variety, peeled and cut into 1-inch chunks
2 red or yellow potatoes (about ⅔ pound / 272 g), unpeeled and cut into 1½-inch chunks	½ cup golden raisins
	½ cup pitted dates, quartered
1 medium yam (about ⅓ pound / 136 g), scrubbed, peeled, and cut into 1½-inch chunks	¼ cup maple syrup or date syrup (optional)
	Juice from 2 oranges (about 1 cup)
1 small butternut squash (about 1 pound / 454 g), peeled and cut into 1½-inch chunks	Zest from 1 orange
	1 cup store-bought low-sodium vegetable broth
1 medium onion, diced	2 teaspoons ground cinnamon
4 carrots, cut into 1-inch rounds	1 teaspoon ground ginger

1. Put the sweet potato, potatoes, yam, squash, onion, carrots, apples, raisins, dates, syrup (if using), orange juice, orange zest, broth, cinnamon, and ginger in the slow cooker. 2. Cover and cook on High for 3½ to 5 hours or on Low for 8 to 10 hours, until the vegetables are tender.

Per Serving:

calories: 460 | fat: 1g | protein: 7g | carbs: 116g | fiber: 15g

Rosemary-and-Garlic Beet Salad

Prep time: 15 minutes | Cook time: 3 to 4 hours | Serves 4 to 6

Salad:	¼ cup chopped walnuts (optional)
2 large red or golden beets (about ½ pound / 227 g)	Dressing:
3 garlic cloves, crushed	3 tablespoons balsamic vinegar
1 fresh rosemary sprig	1 tablespoon Dijon mustard
1 (5-ounce / 142-g) package fresh arugula	1 tablespoon maple syrup (optional)
2 tablespoons raw sunflower seed kernels	Ground black pepper
¼ cup currants	Salt (optional)

1. Make the salad: Rinse the beets, dry them with a paper towel, and cut off and discard the stem end. Pierce each beet 10 to 12 times with a fork. 2. Lay a large piece of aluminum foil on your prep surface. Place the beets and garlic on the foil. Cut the rosemary sprig into several pieces and add to the beets. Pull up all sides of the foil, enclosing everything into a packet that is gathered and twisted on top. 3. Place the packet into the slow cooker, cover, and cook for 3 to 4 hours on High or 4 to 6 hours on Low, depending on the size of your beets. Test for doneness by carefully opening the packet and piercing the beets with a fork or paring knife. It should easily slide in. 4. When done, use tongs or a fork to gently remove the beets from the foil. Once cool enough to handle, rub the beets with a paper towel to remove the skins. Slice the peeled beets into bite-size chunks and place into a large bowl. 5. Discard the rosemary. Mince the garlic and add it to the bowl, then add the arugula, sunflower seeds, currants, and walnuts (if using). 6. Make the dressing: In a small jar with a lid, combine the vinegar, Dijon mustard, and maple syrup (if using). Shake until well blended. Pour the dressing over the salad and toss. Season with pepper and salt (if using).

Per Serving:

calories: 94 | fat: 3g | protein: 3g | carbs: 15g | fiber: 3g

Lemony Steamed Kale with Olives

Prep time: 10 minutes | Cook time: 20 minutes | Serves 4

1 bunch kale, leaves chopped and stems minced	2 tablespoons vegetable broth
½ cup celery leaves, roughly chopped	¼ cup pitted Kalamata olives, chopped
½ bunch flat-leaf parsley, stems and leaves roughly chopped	Grated zest and juice of 1 lemon
4 garlic cloves, chopped	Salt and pepper (optional)

1. Place the kale, celery leaves, parsley, and garlic in a steamer basket set over a medium saucepan. Steam over medium-high heat, covered, for 15 minutes. Remove from the heat and squeeze out any excess moisture. 2. Place a large skillet over medium heat. Add the broth, then add the kale mixture to the skillet. Cook, stirring often, for 5 minutes. 3. Remove from the heat and add the olives and lemon zest and juice. Season with salt (if desired) and pepper and serve.

Per Serving:

calories: 41 | fat: 1g | protein: 2g | carbs: 7g | fiber: 2g

Vegan Goulash

Prep time: 20 minutes | Cook time: 50 minutes | Serves 5

5 tablespoons olive oil (optional)	½ cup dry red wine
12 medium onions, finely chopped	3 to 6 cups vegetable broth
	10 medium potatoes, skinned, cubed
1 head garlic, minced	1 (7-ounce / 198-g) pack tempeh
4 red bell peppers, cored and chopped	Salt and pepper to taste (optional)
10 small tomatoes, cubed	¼ cup fresh parsley, chopped
4 tablespoons paprika powder	

1. Heat the olive oil, in a large pot over medium heat. Sauté the onions until brown. Add the minced garlic and stir for 1 minute. Continue to add the chopped bell peppers and cook the ingredients for another 3 minutes while stirring. Blend in the tomatoes, paprika powder, salt (if desired), pepper and the dry red wine. Stir thoroughly while letting the mixture cook for another 2 minutes. Add the vegetable broth and the potato cubes to the pot and stir to combine all ingredients. Put a lid on the pot and allow the goulash to cook for another 5 minutes. 2. Turn the heat down to low and continue to gently cook the goulash for 15 minutes. The goulash will thicken and the potatoes will get cooked properly. Add the tempeh and taste to see if the goulash needs more salt and pepper. Let the goulash cook for another 15 minutes. Check if the potatoes have softened with a fork. Cook the mixture a few minutes more if the potatoes are hard to penetrate. Once the potatoes are soft, add the parsley, stir and take the goulash off the heat. 3. Allow the goulash to cool down for about 10 minutes and serve or allow the goulash to cool down longer before storing.

Per Serving:

calories: 591 | fat: 18g | protein: 16g | carbs: 74g | fiber: 14g

Tandoori-Rubbed Portobellos with Cool Cilantro Sauce

Prep time: 25 minutes | Cook time: 10 minutes | Serves 4

Cool Cilantro Sauce:
½ cup raw sunflower seeds, soaked for at least 4 hours
¼ cup plus 2 tablespoons filtered water
1 clove garlic, finely grated
1 tablespoon fresh lime juice
1 tablespoon virgin olive oil (optional)
¼ cup finely chopped fresh cilantro leaves
1 green onion, white and light-green parts only, thinly sliced
Salt and pepper, to taste (optional)
Portobellos:

4 large portobello mushroom caps
2 tablespoons virgin olive oil (optional)
1 tablespoon fresh lime juice
1 tablespoon tandoori spice blend
1 (1-inch) piece of fresh ginger, peeled and finely grated
1 clove garlic, finely grated
Salt and pepper, to taste (optional)
Serve:
Warm cooked brown rice
Chopped fresh cilantro leaves

1. Make the Cool Cilantro Sauce: Drain the sunflower seeds and transfer them to a blender. Add the filtered water, garlic, lime juice, and olive oil, if using. Whiz the mixture on high until you have a mostly smooth purée. Stop to scrape down the sides or add another tablespoon of water if necessary. Scrape the sauce base out of the blender into a small bowl. Stir in the cilantro, green onions, salt, and pepper, if using. Cover and place in the refrigerator until you're ready to use it. 2. Preheat a grill to high. 3. Prepare the Portobellos: Take the portobello mushroom caps and, using a spoon, scrape out the gills—the dark brown strips that line the underside of the mushroom. Transfer the scraped mushrooms to a plate. 4. In a medium bowl, whisk together the olive oil, lime juice, tandoori spice, ginger, garlic, salt, and pepper. Rub this wet spice mixture on both sides of the portobello mushrooms. 5. Lightly rub some oil on the grill with a wad of paper towel. Place the spice-rubbed portobello caps on the grill and close the lid. Let the portobellos cook for 4 minutes, then flip them over. Cook for another 4 minutes. The mushrooms should be tender, be lightly glistening, and have char marks on both sides. Remove from the grill. 6. Slice the grilled portobellos, and serve with Cool Cilantro Sauce, warm rice, and extra chopped cilantro.
Per Serving:
calories: 261 | fat: 20g | protein: 6g | carbs: 18g | fiber: 3g

Cumin-Citrus Roasted Carrots

Prep time: 10 minutes | Cook time: 30 minutes | Serves 6

8 large carrots, sliced into ½-inch rounds
¼ cup orange juice
¼ cup vegetable broth
1 teaspoon ground cumin
¼ teaspoon ground turmeric

Salt and black pepper (optional)
1 tablespoon fresh lime juice
Chopped flat-leaf parsley (optional)

1. Preheat the oven to 400ºF (205ºC). 2. Place the carrots in a large baking dish, then add the orange juice, broth, cumin, and turmeric. Season with salt and pepper, if desired. 3. Bake, uncovered, until the carrots are lightly browned and the juices have reduced slightly, about 30 minutes, stirring halfway through. Drizzle with the lime juice and parsley, if desired, and serve.
Per Serving:
calories: 47 | fat: 0g | protein: 1g | carbs: 11g | fiber: 3g

Roasted Carrots with Ginger Maple Cream

Prep time: 10 minutes | Cook time: 25 minutes | Serves 6

Carrots:
1 pound (454 g) medium carrots, cut into ½-inch batons
1 teaspoon minced fresh thyme leaves
2 teaspoons virgin olive oil (optional)
Salt and pepper, to taste (optional)
Ginger Maple Cream:

2 tablespoons raw cashew butter
1½ tablespoons filtered water
1 tablespoon pure maple syrup (optional)
1½ teaspoons fresh lemon juice
1 piece of fresh ginger, peeled and finely grated
Salt, to taste (optional)

1. Preheat the oven to 400ºF (205ºC). Line a baking sheet with parchment paper. 2. Make the Carrots: Place the carrots on the baking sheet. Toss them with the thyme, olive oil, salt, and pepper, if using. Arrange the carrots in a single layer, and slide the baking sheet into the oven. Roast the carrots until just tender, about 25 minutes. Flip and toss the carrots at the halfway mark. 3. Make the Ginger Maple Cream: In a medium bowl, stir the cashew butter with the water until no big chunks of cashew butter remain. Press the cashew butter on the side of the bowl and slowly work it into the water. Whisk in the maple syrup, lemon juice, and grated ginger. Season the cream with salt, if using. 4. Arrange the carrots on a serving platter. Drizzle the Ginger Maple Cream over the carrots, and serve warm.
Per Serving:
calories: 85 | fat: 4g | protein: 2g | carbs: 11g | fiber: 2g

Spiced Green Peas and Yams

Prep time: 15 minutes | Cook time: 20 minutes | Serves 4

3 medium white yams, cut into ½-inch dice (about 2 cups)
½ cup green peas
¾ teaspoon cumin seeds, toasted
1 pinch asafetida (optional)
¼ teaspoon cayenne pepper
¼ teaspoon garam masala

½ teaspoon ground coriander
½ teaspoon ground cumin
½ teaspoon salt, or to taste (optional)
½ tablespoon fresh lime juice
½ tablespoon finely chopped cilantro

1. Steam the yams in a double boiler or steamer basket for 5 to 7 minutes, or until tender. Set aside. 2. In a small saucepan, bring 1 cup of water to a boil, add the peas, and cook for 5 to 10 minutes, until the peas are soft. Drain and set aside. 3. In a large skillet over medium heat, place the cumin seeds, asafetida, white yams, peas, cayenne pepper, garam masala, coriander, cumin, and salt (if using). Add 2 tablespoons of water, mix well, and cook for another 2 to 3 minutes, or until the water has evaporated. Stir in the lime juice and mix well. Serve garnished with the cilantro.
Per Serving:
calories: 107 | fat: 0g | protein: 2g | carbs: 24g | fiber: 4g

Chickpea of the Sea Salad

Prep time: 15 minutes | Cook time: 4 hours | Serves 3 to 4

1 (1-pound / 454-g) bag dried chickpeas, rinsed and sorted to remove small stones and debris
7 cups water
¼ teaspoon baking soda
5 tablespoons plant-based mayonnaise
1 tablespoon yellow mustard
¼ cup diced dill pickles
¼ cup finely diced onions
1 celery stalk, diced
2 tablespoons rice vinegar
½ teaspoon kelp powder
Ground black pepper
Salt (optional)

1. Put the chickpeas, water, and baking soda in the slow cooker. Cover and cook on High for 4 hours or on Low for 8 to 9 hours. Strain and discard the liquid. 2. Transfer 2 cups of the cooked chickpeas to a food processor and pulse 5 to 10 times to break them up but not turn them to mush. Transfer the pulsed chickpeas to a medium bowl. Save the remaining chickpeas for another recipe. 3. Add the mayonnaise, mustard, pickles, onions, celery, vinegar, kelp powder, pepper, and salt (if using). Stir well to form a salad and chill until serving.
Per Serving:
calories: 313 | fat: 21g | protein: 8g | carbs: 25g | fiber: 7g

Vegetable Korma Curry

Prep time: 10 minutes | Cook time: 20 minutes | Serves 4

1 tablespoon extra-virgin olive oil (optional)
2 garlic cloves, minced
2 tablespoons minced fresh ginger
½ small yellow onion, diced small
1 medium sweet potato, peeled and cut into small cubes
½ head cauliflower, cut into small florets (about 2 cups)
3 medium tomatoes, diced small
Pinch of salt (optional)
2 cups water, divided
1 cup softened cashews
1 tablespoon curry powder
2 tablespoons tomato paste
½ cup frozen green beans
½ cup frozen peas
1 (15-ounce / 425-g) can light unsweetened coconut milk
2 cups cooked brown rice or quinoa, for serving
Chopped fresh cilantro, for garnish
Black pepper

1. In a large sauté pan, heat the oil over medium heat. Add the garlic, ginger, and onion and cook until browned and fragrant, about 5 minutes. Add the sweet potato, cauliflower, tomatoes, and salt (if using) and cook until the tomatoes begin to break down, about 5 minutes. Add 1 cup of water, stir until combined, and bring the mixture to a boil. Cook until the sweet potatoes are soft, about 10 minutes. 2. In a blender or food processor, combine the cashews with the remaining 1 cup water and blend until you have a smooth paste. 3. Add the blended cashews, curry powder, tomato paste, green beans, peas, and coconut milk to the pan and stir well to combine. Lower the heat to medium-low and simmer for 5 minutes. Taste and adjust the seasoning as desired. 4. Put ½ cup of rice into each serving bowl and top with the curry. Sprinkle with fresh cilantro and black pepper.
Per Serving:
calories: 535 | fat: 29g | protein: 14g | carbs: 55g | fiber: 8g

Tangy Cabbage, Apples, and Potatoes

Prep time: 15 minutes | Cook time: 3 to 4 hours | Serves 4 to 6

6 red or yellow potatoes (about 2 pounds / 907 g), unpeeled and cut into 1½-inch chunks
½ medium onion, diced
2 apples, peeled, cored, and diced
½ teaspoon ground cinnamon
½ medium head green cabbage, sliced
1 cup store-bought low-sodium vegetable broth
½ cup apple juice, apple cider, or hard apple cider
2 tablespoons apple cider vinegar
2 teaspoons ground mustard, or 1 tablespoon spicy brown mustard
1 teaspoon fennel seeds
1 bay leaf
Ground black pepper
Salt (optional)

1. In the slow cooker, layer the potatoes, onion, and apples, in that order. Sprinkle the cinnamon over the apples. Top with the cabbage. 2. In a small bowl, whisk together the broth, apple juice, vinegar, mustard, fennel, bay leaf, pepper, and salt (if using). Pour over the cabbage. 3. Cover and cook on High for 3 to 4 hours or on Low for 6 to 8 hours. Remove and discard the bay leaf and serve.
Per Serving:
calories: 266 | fat: 1g | protein: 7g | carbs: 62g | fiber: 10g

Delicata Squash Boats

Prep time: 20 minutes | Cook time: 1 hour 20 minutes | Serves 4

2 delicata squash, halved and seeded
Salt and freshly ground black pepper, to taste
1 shallot, peeled and minced
½ red bell pepper, seeded and diced small
6 cups chopped spinach
2 cloves garlic, peeled and minced
1 tablespoon minced sage
2 cups cooked cannellini beans, or 1 (15-ounce / 425-g) can, drained and rinsed
¾ cup whole-grain bread crumbs
3 tablespoons nutritional yeast (optional)
3 tablespoons pine nuts, toasted
Zest of 1 lemon

1. Preheat the oven to 350ºF (180ºC). Line a baking sheet with parchment paper. 2. Season the cut sides of the squash with salt and pepper. Place the halves on the prepared baking sheet, cut sides down. Bake until the squash is tender, about 45 minutes. 3. Place the shallot and red pepper in a large saucepan and sauté over medium heat for 2 to 3 minutes. Add water 1 to 2 tablespoons at a time to keep the vegetables from sticking to the pan. Add the spinach, garlic, and sage and cook until the spinach is wilted, 4 to 5 minutes. Add the beans and season with salt and pepper. Cook for another 2 to 3 minutes. Remove from the heat. Add the bread crumbs, nutritional yeast (if using), pine nuts, and lemon zest. Mix well. 4. Divide the bean mixture among the baked squash halves. Place the stuffed squash halves in a baking dish and cover with aluminum foil. Bake for 15 to 20 minutes, or until heated through.
Per Serving:
calories: 194 | fat: 5g | protein: 10g | carbs: 29g | fiber: 7g

Fluffy Mashed Potatoes with Gravy

Prep time: 10 minutes | Cook time: 15 minutes | Serves 6

Mashed Potatoes:
8 red or Yukon Gold potatoes, cut into 1-inch cubes
½ cup plant-based milk (here or here)
1 teaspoon garlic powder
1 teaspoon onion powder
Gravy:
2 cups vegetable broth, divided

¼ cup gluten-free or whole-wheat flour
½ teaspoon garlic powder
½ teaspoon onion powder
¼ teaspoon freshly ground black pepper
¼ teaspoon dried thyme
¼ teaspoon dried sage

Make Mashed Potatoes: 1. Bring a large stockpot of water to a boil over high heat, then gently and carefully immerse the potatoes. Cover, reduce the heat to medium, and boil for 15 minutes, or until the potatoes are easily pierced with a fork. 2. Drain the liquid, and return the potatoes to the pot. Using a potato masher or large mixing spoon, mash the potatoes until smooth. 3. Stir in the milk, garlic powder, and onion powder. Make Gravy: 1. Meanwhile, in a medium saucepan, whisk together ½ cup of broth and the flour. Once no dry flour is left, whisk in the remaining 1½ cups of broth. 2. Stir in the garlic powder, onion powder, pepper, thyme, and sage. Bring the gravy to a boil over medium-high heat, then reduce the heat to low. 3. Simmer for 10 minutes, stirring every other minute, and serve with the mashed potatoes.
Per Serving:
calories: 260 | fat: 1g | protein: 8g | carbs: 56g | fiber: 4g

Chili-Lime Corn

Prep time: 10 minutes | Cook time: 3 hours | Serves 4 to 6

4½ cups frozen corn
1 small red onion, diced
1 small green bell pepper, diced
Juice and zest of 2 limes

2 teaspoons chili powder
1 teaspoon ground cumin
1 teaspoon garlic powder
Salt (optional)

1. Put the corn, onion, bell pepper, lime juice and zest, chili powder, cumin, garlic powder, and salt (if using) in the slow cooker. Stir to combine. 2. Cover and cook on Low for 3 hours. Refrigerate leftovers in an airtight container for 3 to 4 days or freeze for up to 1 month, and reheat in the microwave.
Per Serving:
calories: 188 | fat: 2g | protein: 7g | carbs: 44g | fiber: 7g

Cauliflower and Pine Nut "Ricotta" Toasts

Prep time: 15 minutes | Cook time: 15 minutes | Makes 1½ cups

3 cups chopped cauliflower
1 teaspoon fresh thyme leaves
¼ cup raw pine nuts, soaked for at least 4 hours
2 tablespoons virgin olive oil (optional)
1 teaspoon lemon zest
1 tablespoon fresh lemon juice

½ teaspoon nutritional yeast
½ teaspoon sea salt (optional)
Serve:
Toasted baguette slices
Fruit
Good quality balsamic vinegar

1. Set up a steamer basket over a large pot of simmering water. Place the chopped cauliflower in the basket, and cover the pot with a tight-fitting lid. Let the cauliflower steam for 15 minutes, or until tender. 2. Remove the cauliflower from the pot, and carefully transfer the florets to the bowl of a food processor. To the cauliflower, add the thyme, pine nuts, olive oil, lemon zest, lemon juice, nutritional yeast, and sea salt, if using. 3. Pulse a few times to break up the cauliflower and nuts. Then run on high until you have a smooth, almost purée-like texture. You may have to stop the food processor and scrape the bowl down a couple of times. 4. Scrape the ricotta into a small bowl, and cover it with plastic wrap. Chill for at least 30 minutes before serving with toasted baguette slices and fruit.
Per Serving: (½ cup)
calories: 186 | fat: 17g | protein: 4g | carbs: 8g | fiber: 3g

Chapter 7 Staples, Sauces, Dips, and Dressings

Beer "Cheese" Dip

Prep time: 10 minutes | Cook time: 10 minutes | Serves 12

¾ cup brown ale
¾ cup water
½ cup raw cashews, soaked in hot water for at least 15 minutes, then drained
½ cup raw walnuts, soaked in hot water for at least 15 minutes, then drained
2 tablespoons fresh lemon juice

2 tablespoons tomato paste or 1 roasted red pepper
1 tablespoon apple cider vinegar
½ cup nutritional yeast
1 tablespoon arrowroot powder
½ teaspoon sweet or smoked paprika
1 tablespoon red miso

1. Purée the beer, water, cashews, walnuts, lemon juice, tomato paste, and vinegar in a high-speed blender until completely smooth. 2. Transfer to a medium saucepan set over medium heat. Whisk in the nutritional yeast, arrowroot powder, and paprika. Cook, whisking often, until the mixture thickens, about 7 minutes. Remove from the heat, whisk in the miso paste, and serve immediately. 3. Store in an airtight container in the refrigerator for up to 5 days.
Per Serving:
calories: 85 | fat: 5g | protein: 5g | carbs: 7g | fiber: 1g

Perfect Marinara Sauce

Prep time: 10 minutes | Cook time: 20 minutes | Makes 7 cups

2 (28-ounce / 794-g) cans crushed tomatoes in purée
4 garlic cloves, minced
2 tablespoons Italian seasoning
2 teaspoons pure maple syrup

2 teaspoons onion powder
2 teaspoons paprika
¼ teaspoon freshly ground black pepper

1. In a medium saucepan, stir together the tomatoes, garlic, Italian seasoning, maple syrup, onion powder, paprika, and pepper. Bring to a simmer. 2. Reduce the heat to low. Cover, and simmer for 15 to 20 minutes, or until the sauce is fragrant and the flavors have melded together. Remove from the heat.
Per Serving:
calories: 39 | fat: 0g | protein: 2g | carbs: 8g | fiber: 2g

B-Savory Sauce and Marinade

Prep time: 5 minutes | Cook time: 0 minutes | Makes 1¼ cups

½ cup nutritional yeast
¼ cup reduced-sodium, gluten-

free tamari
2 tablespoons apple cider

vinegar
2 tablespoons balsamic vinegar
2 tablespoons gluten-free Worcestershire sauce
1 tablespoon plus 1 teaspoon

maple syrup (optional)
2 teaspoons gluten-free Dijon mustard
½ teaspoon ground turmeric
¼ teaspoon black pepper

1. Combine all the ingredients in a resealable container. The sauce can be refrigerated for up to 3 weeks, and it yields enough to marinate 4 blocks of tempeh or tofu, or 16 portobello caps.
Per Serving: (¼ cup)
calories: 84 | fat: 0g | protein: 9g | carbs: 11g | fiber: 2g

Lemon Mint Tahini Cream

Prep time: 5 minutes | Cook time: 0minutes | Serves 6

½ cup tahini
3 pitted dates
½ cup water

¼ cup lemon juice
2 cloves garlic
6 leaves mint

1. Add all the ingredients to a blender or food processor and blend to form a thick and smooth sauce. 2. Store the tahini cream in the fridge, using an airtight container, and consume within 3 days. Alternatively, store the tahini cream in the freezer for a maximum of 60 days and thaw at room temperature.
Per Serving:
calories: 141 | fat: 11g | protein: 5g | carbs: 5g | fiber: 1g

Tofu Veggie Gravy Bowl

Prep time: 15 minutes | Cook time: 10 minutes | Serves 4

Gravy:
6 tablespoons water
¼ cup diced red, white, or yellow onion
2 tablespoons whole wheat or all-purpose flour
1 cup vegetable broth
Veggie Base:

1 cup evenly sliced broccoli, steamed
1 cup evenly chopped zucchini, steamed
1 cup chopped carrots, steamed
½ (14-ounce / 397-g) block extra-firm tofu, pressed and cut into ½-inch cubes

1. In a medium pan over medium heat, heat the water and onion and cook for 3 minutes or until the onion becomes tender and translucent. 2. Reduce the heat to low, add the flour, and stir until your roux has a smooth consistency, 2 to 3 minutes. It should resemble a paste. 3. Add broth and stir over low heat until the gravy thickens, 3 to 4 minutes. 4. On a plate, arrange the broccoli, zucchini, carrots, and tofu, and pour the gravy over this base. Serve immediately.
Per Serving:
calories: 86 | fat: 4g | protein: 7g | carbs: 9g | fiber: 2g

Roasted Bell Pepper Wedges

Prep time: 5 minutes | Cook time: 25 minutes | Makes 1½ cups

2 large red bell peppers, seeded and cut into wedges
1 tablespoon freshly squeezed lemon juice
Pinch freshly ground black pepper
½ teaspoon garlic powder (optional)
½ teaspoon cumin seeds (optional)

1. Preheat the oven to 425ºF (220ºC). 2. Place the bell pepper wedges in a large mixing bowl; then add the lemon juice, black pepper, garlic powder (if using), and cumin seeds (if using). Toss to combine. 3. Place the bell pepper wedges cut-side down on a baking sheet lined with nonstick foil or parchment paper. 4. Bake for 20 to 25 minutes until soft and lightly charred. Remove from the oven and cool for up to 20 minutes. Store in the refrigerator in an airtight container for up to 5 days.
Per Serving:
calories: 53 | fat: 1g | protein: 2g | carbs: 10g | fiber: 4g

Dulse Rose Za'atar

Prep time: 5 minutes | Cook time: 0 minutes | Makes 6 tablespoons

¼ cup raw unhulled sesame seeds, toasted
2 tablespoons dried organic rose petals
½ teaspoon flaky sea salt (optional)
1 tablespoon toasted dulse flakes
1 teaspoon ground sumac
1 teaspoon dried thyme

1. Combine the sesame seeds, rose petals, dulse, sumac, thyme, and salt, if using, in a small jar or bowl and stir to combine. Store in a tightly sealed jar for up to 3 months.
Per Serving: (1 tablespoon)
calories: 44 | fat: 4g | protein: 1g | carbs: 2g | fiber: 1g

Tahini-Maple Granola

Prep time: 10 minutes | Cook time: 40 minutes | Makes 2½ cups

1 cup rolled oats
¼ cup unsweetened raisins
¼ cup pecan pieces
¼ cup walnut pieces
¼ cup sliced almonds
¼ cup vegan chocolate chips
3 tablespoons tahini
3 tablespoons pure maple syrup

1. Preheat the oven to 350ºF (180ºC). Line a baking sheet with parchment paper. 2. In a large bowl, combine the oats, raisins, pecans, walnuts, almonds, and chocolate chips. 3. Add the tahini and maple syrup. Mix thoroughly. 4. Spread the mixture out in a thin layer on the prepared baking sheet (for a chunkier granola, leave small chunks together). 5. Transfer the baking sheet to the oven, and bake for 35 to 40 minutes, stirring halfway through, or until the granola is crispy and golden brown. Remove from the oven. Store in an airtight container for up to 1 week.
Per Serving:
calories: 145 | fat: 8g | protein: 4g | carbs: 3g | fiber: 2g

Crispy, Crunchy Granola

Prep time: 5 minutes | Cook time: 20 minutes | Makes 4 cups

3 cups rolled oats
¼ cup extra-virgin olive oil (optional)
¼ cup maple syrup (optional)
½ teaspoon salt (optional)
1 tablespoon pumpkin pie spice
½ cup chopped pecans
½ cup raisins

1. Preheat the oven to 350ºF (180ºC). Line a sheet pan with parchment paper. 2. In a large bowl mix together the oats, olive oil, and maple syrup (if using) and stir well until the oats are slightly wet. Add the salt (if using) and pumpkin pie spice and stir well. 3. Spread out the mixture gently on the sheet pan. It's okay if it's clumpy (granola clusters are delicious!). Bake for 10 minutes. Stir gently, being careful not to break up the clusters. Sprinkle the pecans on top and bake for another 10 minutes, or until it is golden and smells amazing. Since oven temperatures vary, if the granola is not ready, continue to bake and check every 2 minutes so the granola does not burn. 4. Let the granola cool completely. Add the raisins and stir gently until combined. Store the granola in an airtight container at room temperature for up to 2 weeks.
Per Serving:
calories: 138 | fat: 7g | protein: 3g | carbs: 18g | fiber: 2g

Mexican Salsa

Prep time: 5 minutes | Cook time: 0 minutes | Serves 5

3 large quartered tomatoes
¼ chopped red onion
¼ cup fresh cilantro
1 jalapeño
1 clove garlic, minced

1. Remove the stem, seeds and placenta of the jalapeño and cut the flesh into slices. 2. Add all of the ingredients to a food processor or blender and blend until smooth. 3. Serve the salsa chilled and enjoy as a topping or a side! 4. Store the salsa in the fridge, using an airtight container, and consume within 3 days. Alternatively, store it in the freezer for a maximum of 60 days and thaw at room temperature.
Per Serving:
calories: 27 | fat: 0g | protein: 1g | carbs: 5g | fiber: 1g

Chickenless Bouillon Base

Prep time: 5 minutes | Cook time: 0 minutes | Makes 2 cups

2 cups nutritional yeast
¼ cup sea salt (optional)
2 tablespoons onion powder
1 tablespoon Italian seasoning
2 teaspoons garlic powder
1 teaspoon ground turmeric
1 teaspoon celery salt
1 teaspoon dried thyme

1. In a small blender, food processor, spice grinder, or mortar and pestle, combine the nutritional yeast, salt (if using), onion powder, Italian seasoning, garlic powder, turmeric, celery salt, and thyme. Blend to a powder. 2. Store the bouillon powder in a sealable jar or container at room temperature. Use 1 tablespoon per 1 cup of water for a flavorful stock.
Per Serving: (1 tablespoon)
calories: 23 | fat: 0g | protein: 3g | carbs: 3g | fiber: 1g

Raw Date Paste

Prep time: 10 minutes | Cook time: 0 minutes | Makes 2½ cups

1 cup Medjool dates, pitted and chopped

1½ cups water

1. In a blender, combine the dates and water and blend until smooth. Store in an airtight container in the refrigerator for up to 7 days.
Per Serving:
calories: 21 | fat: 0g | protein: 0g | carbs: 5g | fiber: 1g

Barbecue Sauce

Prep time: 10 minutes | Cook time: 0 minutes | Makes 2 cups

1 (8-ounce / 227-g) can tomato sauce
3 pitted dates
¼ cup apple cider vinegar
3 tablespoons blackstrap molasses

2 tablespoons whole-grain mustard
1½ teaspoons onion powder
1½ teaspoons smoked paprika
½ teaspoon garlic powder
⅛ teaspoon cayenne

1. In a high-efficiency blender or food processor, combine the tomato sauce, dates, vinegar, molasses, mustard, onion powder, paprika, garlic powder, and cayenne. Process until smooth. Store leftovers in an airtight container in the refrigerator for up to 1 week.
Per Serving:
calories: 45 | fat: 0g | protein: 1g | carbs: 11g | fiber: 1g

Potato Wedges

Prep time: 10 minutes | Cook time: 40 minutes | Serves 2 to 4

3 or 4 medium red potatoes, cut into ½-inch wedges (about 1

pound / 454 g)

1. Preheat the oven to 450°F (235°C). Line a baking sheet with parchment paper. 2. Spread the potatoes out in a single layer on the prepared baking sheet. 3. Bake for 15 to 20 minutes, or until the potatoes are browned and crispy. 4. Flip the potatoes over, and bake for 15 to 20 minutes, or until crispy. Remove from the oven. Serve immediately.
Per Serving:
calories: 149 | fat: 0g | protein: 4g | carbs: 34g | fiber: 4g

Creamy Nut Sauce

Prep time: 15 minutes | Cook time: 20 minutes | Makes 2 cups

1 tablespoon extra-virgin coconut oil (optional)
1 medium onion, diced
3 large garlic cloves, finely chopped
½ teaspoon fine sea salt, plus more to taste (optional)

1 tablespoon mirin
¼ cup filtered water
1 cup raw or toasted cashews, walnuts, or almonds
¾ cup boiling filtered water
1 teaspoon tamari

1. Warm the oil in a medium skillet over medium-high heat. Add the onion and cook for 6 to 8 minutes, until golden. Stir in the garlic and salt, if using, and cook for 3 to 4 minutes, until the garlic is golden and fragrant. Add the mirin and the ¼ cup water, then raise the heat and bring to a simmer, stirring for a couple of minutes to deglaze the pan. 2. Remove from the heat and transfer the mixture to an upright blender, scraping the skillet with a rubber spatula. Add the nuts, boiling water, and tamari and blend until smooth, scraping the sides as necessary. Season to taste with more salt and serve immediately, or let cool and store in an airtight jar in the fridge for up to 4 days.
Per Serving: (½ cup)
calories: 188 | fat: 16g | protein: 4g | carbs: 9g | fiber: 2g

Fresh Mango Salsa

Prep time: 15 minutes | Cook time: 0 minutes | Makes 2 cups

1 large mango, diced
1 medium tomato, diced
1 garlic clove, pressed
Juice of ½ lime
1 scallion, chopped

1 tablespoon chopped jalapeño pepper (optional)
¼ cup fresh cilantro, parsley, mint, and/or basil, chopped
Pinch sea salt (optional)

1. Mix everything together in a bowl, or pulse in a food processor if you want a smoother texture.
Per Serving: (1 cup)
calories: 129 | fat: 0g | protein: 2g | carbs: 31g | fiber: 4g

Whipped Coconut Cream

Prep time: 5 minutes | Cook time: 0 minutes | Makes 1 cup

1 can (13½ ounces / 383 g) full-fat coconut milk, chilled overnight

1 tablespoon pure maple syrup (optional)
½ teaspoon pure vanilla extract

1. Remove the chilled can of coconut milk from the refrigerator. When you open it, there should be a thick layer of pure coconut cream on top. Scoop this coconut cream into a medium bowl, being careful to avoid the water at the bottom of the can. Reserve the water for smoothies or discard. 2. To the coconut cream, add the maple syrup and vanilla and whisk vigorously by hand until you have a smooth and light cream. You could also whip this in a blender, food processor, or with a hand mixer.
Per Serving: (¼ cup)
calories: 235 | fat: 22g | protein: 2g | carbs: 9g | fiber: 2g

Homemade Beans

Prep time: 5 minutes | Cook time: 2 hours | Makes 3 cups

8 ounces (227 g) dried black beans, picked over and rinsed

3½ cups water
Pinch kelp granules

1. In a Dutch oven or saucepan, combine the beans, water, and kelp. Bring to a boil over high heat. 2. Reduce the heat to low. Cover, and simmer for about 1½ hours. Remove from the heat.
Per Serving:
calories: 110 | fat: 1g | protein: 11g | carbs: 29g | fiber: 16g

Cilantro Chutney

Prep time: 5 minutes | Cook time: 0 minutes | Makes ¾ cup

1 big bunch cilantro
½ cup green raisins
⅓ cup cubed fresh pineapple
1 (½-inch) piece fresh ginger, grated
¼ teaspoon ground cumin

2 teaspoons cider vinegar
Pinch of freshly ground black pepper
½ teaspoon Celtic sea salt (optional)

1. Clean the cilantro under running water and remove any thick stalks (for this recipe, we only want leaves and extremely thin stalks). 2. In a small food processor or blender, combine all the ingredients. Blend well to create a smooth fine chutney. 3. Transfer to a bowl or glass jar and serve. 4. Keep leftovers in an airtight container in the fridge for 3 to 4 days.
Per Serving:
calories: 66 | fat: 0g | protein: 1g | carbs: 16g | fiber: 1g

Chipotle Relish

Prep time: 15 minutes | Cook time: 0 minutes | Makes 1½ cups

½ cup diced Persian cucumber
½ cup diced red bell pepper
1 small seedless orange, peeled and diced
½ tablespoon freshly squeezed

lime juice
¼ teaspoon chipotle chili powder
¼ cup diced jicama (optional)

1. In a medium bowl, combine the cucumber, bell pepper, orange, lime juice, chili powder, and jicama (if using). 2. Serve immediately with chips, or cover and refrigerate until serving time.
Per Serving:
calories: 17 | fat: 0g | protein: 0g | carbs: 4g | fiber: 1g

Oat Milk

Prep time: 5 minutes | Cook time: 0 minutes | Makes 4 cups

1 cup rolled oats
3 dates, pitted (optional)

4 cups water

1. In a blender, combine the oats, dates (if using), and water and blend on high for 45 seconds, until the oats are pulverized and the liquid looks creamy. Be careful not to overblend, as the texture will become slimy and unpleasant. 2. Pour the mixture through a nut milk bag, cheesecloth, or fine-mesh sieve to strain out all the small pieces. Pour it into an airtight storage container and chill for up to 4 days.
Per Serving:
calories: 90 | fat: 3g | protein: 1g | carbs: 13g | fiber: 0g

Oil-Free Sundried Tomato and Oregano Dressing

Prep time: 10 minutes | Cook time: 5 minutes | Makes 3 cups

2 cups filtered water

½ cup sundried tomato halves

1 clove garlic, chopped
1 small shallot, chopped
2 tablespoons Dijon mustard
2 tablespoons pure maple syrup

(optional)
¼ teaspoon dried oregano
salt and pepper, to taste
(optional)

1. Bring the 2 cups of water to a boil. In a small bowl, combine the sundried tomatoes and boiling water. Let the sundried tomatoes soften for about 10 minutes. 2. Pour the sundried tomatoes and the soaking liquid into a blender. Add the garlic, shallots, Dijon mustard, maple syrup, oregano, salt, and pepper, if using. Whiz the mixture on high until it has a smooth and creamy consistency. This takes a full 3 minutes with a couple of pauses for scraping down. Store the dressing in the refrigerator for up to 1 week.
Per Serving: (½ cup)
calories: 37 | fat: 0g | protein: 1g | carbs: 8g | fiber: 1g

Roasted Beet Dip

Prep time: 5 minutes | Cook time: 30 to 40 minutes | Makes 2 cups

2 medium or 3 small red beets
½ cup sunflower seeds, soaked in water for 8 hours
1 tablespoon hemp oil (optional)
Juice of 1 lemon

2 tablespoons balsamic vinegar
1 teaspoon fennel seeds
½ teaspoon sea salt (optional)
½ teaspoon freshly ground black pepper

1. Preheat the oven to 400ºF (205ºC). Wrap the beets in unbleached parchment paper and place them on a baking sheet. Roast for 30 to 40 minutes, or until the beets are fork-tender. 2. When cool enough to handle, peel away the beet skins, using your hands. Chop the beets and place them in a blender or food processor. Add the remaining ingredients and blend until smooth. 3. Store in an airtight container in the fridge for up to 5 days. Leftovers make the perfect weekday lunch solution or take-along snacks.
Per Serving:
calories: 81 | fat: 6g | protein: 2g | carbs: 4g | fiber: 1g

Spanish Red Pepper Spread (Romesco)

Prep time: 5 minutes | Cook time: 10 minutes | Serves 12

½ cup raw almonds or walnuts
1 slice whole wheat bread, chopped
2 garlic cloves
1 (15-ounce / 425-g) jar roasted

red peppers, drained with liquid reserved, and rinsed
3 tablespoons chopped flat-leaf parsley
¼ cup olive oil (optional)

1. Toast the almonds in a small skillet over medium heat for about 3 minutes, shaking occasionally, until golden brown and fragrant. Remove from the heat and transfer to a food processor. 2. Add the bread and garlic to the now-empty skillet. Cook until the bread is toasted and the garlic is soft, about 3 minutes. 3. Transfer to the food processor with the almonds and pulse a few times. Add the red peppers and parsley and pulse until well blended, then drizzle in the olive oil and liquid from the red pepper jar until the dip is uniform in texture but quite thick. Serve. 4. Store in an airtight container in the refrigerator for up to 5 days.
Per Serving:
calories: 81 | fat: 7g | protein: 1g | carbs: 4g | fiber: 1g

Coconut "Bacon" Bits

Prep time: 15 minutes | Cook time: 12 minutes | Makes 2 cups

2 tablespoons tamari or low-sodium soy sauce
1 tablespoon liquid hickory smoke
1 tablespoon pure maple syrup (optional)
½ teaspoon smoked paprika
¼ teaspoon onion powder
¼ teaspoon ground white pepper
2 cups unsweetened coconut flakes (not desiccated)

1. Preheat the oven to 350ºF (180ºC). Line a baking sheet with parchment paper or aluminum foil. Avoid using a silicone mat, because the ingredients will stain the surface. 2. In a large bowl, stir together the tamari, liquid smoke, maple syrup (if using), paprika, onion powder, and ground white pepper. Add the coconut flakes. Stir and toss gently to combine until the coconut flakes are thoroughly coated. Let sit for 10 minutes. Stir again, then spread the coconut evenly on the prepared baking sheet. 3. Bake for 12 minutes. The coconut flakes should look dry and golden brown rather than dark. 4. Let cool completely on the baking sheet. 5. Store in an airtight container at room temperature for 2 weeks or freeze for up to 2 months.

Per Serving: (1 tablespoon)
calories: 36 | fat: 3g | protein: 1g | carbs: 2g | fiber: 1g

Quick Mole Sauce

Prep time: 40 minutes | Cook time: 25 minutes | Makes 4 cups

4 dried pasilla chiles
2 dried ancho chiles
Boiling water, for soaking the peppers
1 yellow onion, cut into slices
6 garlic cloves, coarsely chopped
1 tablespoon water, plus more as needed
2 tablespoons tomato paste
1 jalapeño pepper, seeded and chopped
2 ounces (57 g) vegan dark chocolate
2 tablespoons whole wheat flour
2 tablespoons cocoa powder
2 tablespoons almond butter
2 teaspoons smoked paprika
1 teaspoon ground cumin
1 teaspoon ground cinnamon
½ teaspoon dried oregano
2½ cups no-sodium vegetable broth

1. Cut off the stem ends from the pasilla and ancho chiles and shake out the seeds. Cut the chiles in half, transfer to a medium bowl, and cover with the boiling water. Let soak for 20 minutes. Drain. 2. In a large nonstick sauté pan or skillet over medium-high heat, combine the onion and garlic. Cook for 5 to 7 minutes, adding water, 1 tablespoon at a time, to prevent burning. The onions should be dark brown but not burned. Stir in the tomato paste and cook for 2 minutes to caramelize. Transfer to a high-speed blender. 3. Add the soaked chiles, jalapeño pepper, chocolate, flour, cocoa powder, almond butter, paprika, cumin, cinnamon, oregano, and vegetable broth. Purée for about 3 minutes until smooth. 4. Return the sauté pan or skillet to medium-high heat. Pour in the sauce and cover the pan. Cook until the sauce begins to bubble. Reduce the heat to low and simmer, uncovered, for 5 minutes, stirring occasionally. 5. Serve immediately, refrigerate in an airtight container for up to 1 week, or freeze for up to 6 months.

Per Serving: (½ cup)
calories: 114 | fat: 7g | protein: 4g | carbs: 13g | fiber: 4g

Peanut Butter

Prep time: 15 minutes | Cook time: 10 minutes | Makes 2 cups

2 cups raw and unsalted peanuts
½ teaspoon sea salt (optional)

1. Preheat the oven to 375ºF (190ºC). 2. Roast the peanuts for about 10 minutes. Transfer them to a food processor and process for about 1 minute. Scrape down the sides of the food processor, add the sea salt (if desired), and blend again for 1 minute; continue until the desired consistency is reached. 3. For the best flavor, chill the mix before serving.

Per Serving:
calories: 153 | fat: 11g | protein: 5g | carbs: 8g | fiber: 1g

Italian Spices

Prep time: 5 minutes | Cook time: 0 minutes | Makes ½ cup

¼ cup dried oregano
3 tablespoons fennel seeds
1 tablespoon garlic powder

1. Shake all the ingredients together in a jar with a tight-fitting lid. Store for up to 6 months.

Per Serving: (½ cup)
calories: 132 | fat: 3g | protein: 6g | carbs: 26g | fiber: 14g

Chipotle–Pumpkin Seed Salsa

Prep time: 5 minutes | Cook time: 10 minutes | Serves 12

½ cup raw pumpkin seeds
1 yellow onion, diced
3 garlic cloves, minced
1 or 2 gluten-free chipotles chiles in adobo sauce, chopped
1 (28-ounce / 794-g) can diced tomatoes with juice
¼ teaspoon salt, plus more to taste (optional)

1. Place a medium skillet over low heat and add the pumpkin seeds. Toast, stirring often, until fragrant and light brown, about 3 minutes. Transfer to a medium bowl and set aside. 2. Increase the heat to medium-high, then add the onion and garlic. (Add a splash of water if the pan looks dry or garlic begins to brown.) Cook, stirring occasionally to avoid burning, about 3 minutes. Stir in the chipotles and cook for 1 minute. Stir in the tomatoes with their juice and cook, without stirring, for 5 minutes. Remove from the heat and stir again. 3. While the tomato mixture is cooking, transfer the pumpkin seeds to a food processor. Pulse several times, until the seeds are partially ground with some larger pieces. Return the seeds to the bowl. 4. Add the tomato mixture to the now-empty food processor. Pulse several times, add ¼ teaspoon salt (if desired), and pulse until the salsa is uniform in texture. 5. Transfer to the bowl with the pumpkin seeds, stir to combine, and season with salt. Serve or refrigerate in an airtight container for up to 3 days.

Per Serving:
calories: 44 | fat: 3g | protein: 2g | carbs: 4g | fiber: 2g

Chili Spice Blend

Prep time: 5 minutes | Cook time: 0 minutes | Makes 7½ tablespoons

¼ cup chili powder
4 teaspoons onion powder
4 teaspoons ground cumin
1 teaspoon ground coriander
1 teaspoon garlic powder
½ teaspoon cayenne

1. In an airtight container with a lid (or repurposed spice jar), combine the chili powder, onion powder, cumin, coriander, garlic powder, and cayenne. Shake or mix well.
Per Serving:
calories: 24 | fat: 1g | protein: 1g | carbs: 4g | fiber: 2g

Vegan Basil Pesto

Prep time: 5 minutes | Cook time: 0 minutes | Serves 6

2 bunches basil, leaves only
1 cup spinach
¼ cup roasted almonds
¼ cup toasted pine nuts
4 raw Brazil nuts, chopped
2 garlic cloves
¼ cup water
¼ to ½ teaspoon salt (optional)

1. Pulse the basil, spinach, almonds, pine nuts, Brazil nuts, and garlic in a food processor until combined and finely chopped. With the food processor running, stream in the water, stopping when it reaches the desired consistency. Add ¼ teaspoon salt, then added more to taste if desired. 2. The pesto can be refrigerated in an airtight container for up to 5 days. It can also be frozen in single portions for up to 6 months: Scoop into ice cube trays, freeze, then transfer to an airtight container.
Per Serving:
calories: 81 | fat: 8g | protein: 2g | carbs: 2g | fiber: 1g

Spicy Italian Vinaigrette

Prep time: 5 minutes | Cook time: 0 minutes | Makes 1 cup

1 cup apple cider vinegar
½ cup extra-virgin olive oil (optional)
2 teaspoons maple syrup (optional)
2 teaspoons Italian seasoning
¼ teaspoon salt (optional)
¼ teaspoon black pepper
½ teaspoon garlic powder
Pinch red pepper flakes

1. Combine the apple cider vinegar, olive oil, maple syrup, Italian seasoning, salt (if using), black pepper, garlic powder, and red pepper flakes in a jar, cover, and shake until well blended. The dressing can be stored in the refrigerator for up to 2 weeks.
Per Serving:
calories: 131 | fat: 14g | protein: 0g | carbs: 2g | fiber: 0g

Coconut Butter

Prep time: 5 minutes | Cook time: 0 minutes | Makes 1 cup

4 cups unsweetened shredded dried coconut or 7 cups
unsweetened flaked dried coconut

1. Put the coconut in a food processor and process for 10 to 15

minutes, scraping down the sides every couple of minutes, until the butter is completely smooth and quite liquid. Store in a tightly sealed glass jar at room temperature for up to 1 month.
Per Serving: (½ cup)
calories: 280 | fat: 28g | protein: 3g | carbs: 10g | fiber: 7g

Quick Tahini Sauce

Prep time: 10 minutes | Cook time: 0 minutes | Makes 1¼ cups

½ cup tahini
½ cup filtered water
2 tablespoons extra-virgin olive oil (optional)
2 tablespoons freshly squeezed
lemon juice
1 small garlic clove, finely grated or pressed
½ teaspoon fine sea salt, plus more to taste (optional)

1. Combine the tahini, water, olive oil, lemon juice, garlic, and salt, if using, in a food processor and blend until smooth. Season to taste. Serve immediately, or store the sauce in a glass jar in the fridge for up to 5 days. Bring to room temperature before using and add water to thin if needed.
Per Serving: (¼ cup)
calories: 193 | fat: 18g | protein: 4g | carbs: 6g | fiber: 2g

Jerk Spices

Prep time: 5 minutes | Cook time: 0 minutes | Makes ⅓ cup

1 tablespoon garlic powder
2 teaspoons dried thyme
2 teaspoons onion powder
1 teaspoon black pepper
1 teaspoon dried parsley
1 teaspoon sweet paprika
1 teaspoon whole allspice
½ teaspoon cayenne pepper
½ teaspoon crushed red pepper
¼ teaspoon cumin seeds
¼ teaspoon freshly grated nutmeg
¼ teaspoon ground cinnamon

1. Pulse all the ingredients in a clean coffee grinder until thoroughly combined. Store in an airtight container for up to 6 months.
Per Serving: (☐ cup)
calories: 83 | fat: 1g | protein: 3g | carbs: 18g | fiber: 5g

Sweet Peanut Butter Dipping Sauce

Prep time: 10 minutes | Cook time: 0 minutes | Makes 1 cup

½ cup creamy peanut butter (no added sugar or salt)
2 tablespoons rice vinegar
¼ cup unsweetened coconut milk
1 tablespoon maple syrup
(optional)
2 garlic cloves
½-inch piece fresh ginger, peeled and grated
¼ teaspoon red pepper flakes

1. In a food processor, combine the peanut butter, rice vinegar, coconut milk, maple syrup (if using), garlic, ginger, and red pepper flakes. Blend until smooth. 2. Store in an airtight container in the refrigerator for up to 5 days.
Per Serving:
calories: 107 | fat: 8g | protein: 4g | carbs: 6g | fiber: 1g

Anytime "Cheese" Sauce

Prep time: 5 minutes | Cook time: 15 minutes | Makes 6 cups

1 medium Yukon Gold potato, cut into 1-inch cubes	1 tablespoon freshly squeezed lemon juice
1 medium sweet potato, cut into 1-inch cubes	2 teaspoons garlic powder
¼ cup rolled oats	2 teaspoons onion powder
¼ cup nutritional yeast	1 teaspoon smoked paprika

1. Bring a large stockpot of water to a boil over high heat. Gently and carefully immerse the Yukon Gold potato and sweet potato in the boiling water. Cook for 12 minutes. Strain, reserving 3 cups of cooking liquid. 2. In a blender, combine the reserved cooking liquid with the boiled potato and sweet potato, oats, nutritional yeast, lemon juice, garlic powder, onion powder, and paprika. Blend on high for 3 to 5 minutes, and serve.

Per Serving: (½ cup)
calories: 53 | fat: 1g | protein: 4g | carbs: 10g | fiber: 2g

Cheeze Sprinkle

Prep time: 5 minutes | Cook time: 0 minutes | Serves 4

½ cup raw almonds	½ teaspoon sea salt (optional)
½ cup raw cashews	¼ teaspoon garlic powder
¼ cup nutritional yeast	

1. In a food processor, combine the nuts, nutritional yeast, salt (if using), and garlic powder and pulse until finely chopped. The mixture should look like bread crumbs. 2. Transfer to an airtight container and store in a cool, dry place or the refrigerator for up to several weeks.

Per Serving:
calories: 164 | fat: 11g | protein: 8g | carbs: 9g | fiber: 4g

BBQ Sauce

Prep time: 5 minutes | Cook time: 0 minutes | Serves 16

2 cups canned or fresh tomato cubes	3 tablespoons smoked paprika
5 pitted dates	2 tablespoons garlic powder
	2 tablespoons onion powder

1. Add all the ingredients to a blender or food processor and blend to form a smooth sauce. 2. Store the BBQ sauce in the fridge, using an airtight container, and consume within 3 days. Alternatively, store it in the freezer for a maximum of 60 days and thaw at room temperature.

Per Serving:
calories: 11 | fat: 0g | protein: 0g | carbs: 2g | fiber: 0g

Peanut Sauce

Prep time: 5 minutes | Cook time: 0 minutes | Makes ¾ cup

⅓ cup natural peanut butter, or almond, cashew, or sunflower seed butter	3 tablespoons brown rice vinegar or apple cider vinegar
	2 tablespoons freshly squeezed
lime juice	1 tablespoon maple syrup (optional)
2 tablespoons tamari or soy sauce	Pinch red pepper flakes
1 tablespoon toasted sesame oil (optional)	¼ cup water

1. Put the peanut butter, vinegar, and lime juice in a medium mixing bowl and whisk to combine until thickened. 2. Add the tamari, sesame oil, maple syrup (if using), and red pepper flakes and stir to mix. Add the water a little at a time and whisk until you get a thick, creamy sauce, slightly thinner for a dressing and slightly thicker for a dip. Or you could purée everything in a blender or food processor until smooth and creamy.

Per Serving: (1 tablespoon)
calories: 223 | fat: 14g | protein: 9g | carbs: 17g | fiber: 1g

Mild Harissa Sauce

Prep time: 10 minutes | Cook time: 20 minutes | Makes 3 to 4 cups

1 large red bell pepper, seeded, cored, and cut into chunks	2 tablespoons tomato paste
1 yellow onion, cut into thick rings	1 tablespoon low-sodium soy sauce or tamari
4 garlic cloves, peeled	1 tablespoon Hungarian paprika
1 cup no-sodium vegetable broth or water	1 teaspoon ground cumin

1. Preheat the oven to 450°F (235°C). Line a baking sheet with parchment paper or aluminum foil. 2. Place the bell pepper on the prepared baking sheet, flesh-side up, and space out the onion and garlic around the pepper. 3. Roast on the middle rack for 20 minutes. Transfer to a blender. 4. Add the vegetable broth, tomato paste, soy sauce, paprika, and cumin. Purée until smooth. Served cold or warm. 5. Refrigerate in an airtight container for up to 2 weeks or freeze for up to 6 months.

Per Serving: (¼ cup)
calories: 15 | fat: 0g | protein: 1g | carbs: 3g | fiber: 1g

Flavorful Vegetable Broth

Prep time: 5 minutes | Cook time: 50 minutes | Makes 4 quarts

4½ quarts water	2 teaspoons dried thyme
2 medium onions, quartered	½ teaspoon black peppercorns
3 cups chopped celery	4 bay leaves
3 cups chopped carrots	1 cup chopped fennel bulb (optional)
4 large garlic cloves, minced	1 ounce (28 g) dried wild mushrooms (optional)
1 tablespoon chopped fresh rosemary	

1. Combine the water, onions, celery, carrots, garlic, rosemary, thyme, peppercorns, bay leaves, fennel (if using), and mushrooms (if using) in a large pot. Cover and bring to a boil. 2. Reduce the heat to low and cook for 45 minutes. 3. Line a strainer with a coffee filter or cheesecloth, and strain the mixture over a large bowl. 4. Transfer to glass jars, seal, and refrigerate for up to 7 days or freeze for up to 6 months.

Per Serving:
calories: 15 | fat: 0g | protein: 1g | carbs: 3g | fiber: 1g

Spicy Avocado Crema

Prep time: 10 minutes | Cook time: 0 minutes | Makes about ¾ cup

1 ripe avocado, halved and pitted	½ seranno chile pepper, seeds and ribs removed
¼ cup canned full-fat coconut milk	¼ cup fresh cilantro, chopped
2 tablespoons fresh lime juice	¼ teaspoon sea salt (optional)

1. In a blender or food processor, combine the avocado, coconut milk, lime juice, chile pepper, cilantro, and salt (if using). 2. Blend or process until smooth. Taste and add more salt or lime juice if needed. Transfer to an airtight container and refrigerate until ready to use.

Per Serving:

calories: 80 | fat: 7g | protein: 1g | carbs: 4g | fiber: 2g

Quick Bean Sauce

Prep time: 15 minutes | Cook time: 30 minutes | Makes 3 cups

2 tablespoons extra-virgin coconut or olive oil (optional)	thyme
1 medium onion, diced	2 (15½-ounce / 439-g) cans black beans, drained and rinsed well
½ teaspoon fine sea salt, plus more to taste (optional)	
3 large garlic cloves, finely chopped	1 cup filtered water
2 teaspoons chopped fresh	2 teaspoons raw apple cider vinegar

1. Warm the oil in a large skillet over medium-high heat. Add the onion and salt, if using, and cook for 5 minutes, or until the onion is light golden. Cover the pan, reduce the heat to low, and cook the onion for another 5 minutes, or until soft and beginning to brown. Stir in the garlic and cook, uncovered, for 3 to 4 minutes, until fragrant. Add the thyme and cook for 2 minutes. Stir in the beans and the water, raise the heat, and bring the mixture to a boil, then cover the pan, reduce the heat to low, and simmer for 5 minutes. Remove the lid and cook for another 5 minutes, or until the mixture is creamy and the beans are very soft. (If you would like a thicker sauce, continue cooking, uncovered, until the sauce reaches the desired consistency.) You can crush some of the beans with the back of a spoon to create a creamier, smoother sauce if you like. Stir in the vinegar and season with more salt to taste. 2. Serve immediately, or let cool and store in an airtight container in the fridge for up to 4 days.

Per Serving: (½ cup)

calories: 299 | fat: 6g | protein: 16g | carbs: 48g | fiber: 12g

Sunflower Parmesan "Cheese"

Prep time: 5 minutes | Cook time: 0 minutes | Makes ½ cup

½ cup sunflower seeds	½ teaspoon garlic powder
2 tablespoons nutritional yeast	

1. In a food processor or blender, combine the sunflower seeds, nutritional yeast, and garlic powder. Process on low for 30 to 45 seconds, or until the sunflower seeds have been broken down to the size of coarse sea salt. 2. Store in a refrigerator-safe container for up

to 2 months.

Per Serving:(1 tablespoon)

calories: 56 | fat: 4g | protein: 3g | carbs: 3g | fiber: 1g

Veggie Chow Mein

Prep time: 10 minutes | Cook time: 15 minutes | Serves 6

1 (8-ounce / 227-g) package Asian-style noodles	½ cup grated carrots
3 tablespoons water	1 teaspoon minced garlic
1 cup thinly sliced celery	½ cup vegetable broth
½ cup diced red, white, or yellow onion	2 tablespoons soy sauce
	1 cup bean sprouts

1. In a large pot over medium-high heat, boil water and cook the noodles according to the directions on the package. 2. While the noodles are cooking, prepare the vegetables. In a large pan or wok, heat the water. Add the celery, onion, carrots, and garlic and sauté for 3 to 4 minutes or until the celery and onion are tender and the onion is translucent. 3. Add the broth and soy sauce. Bring to a boil, then turn down the heat and simmer for 5 minutes. 4. Add the cooked noodles and bean sprouts and mix thoroughly. Cook for 5 minutes, stirring occasionally.

Per Serving:

calories: 86 | fat: 1g | protein: 4g | carbs: 16g | fiber: 1g

Perfect Baked Tofu

Prep time: 5 minutes | Cook time: 40 minutes | Serves 8

2 (14-ounce / 397-g) packages firm tofu, drained	Freshly ground black pepper

1. Preheat the oven to 450°F (235°C). 2. Cut each package of tofu into 8 equal slabs about ½ inch thick. 3. Arrange the tofu in a single layer on a parchment-lined baking sheet. Season with pepper. 4. Bake for 20 minutes, or until the tofu is starting to dry and slightly firm to the touch. 5. Carefully flip the tofu over. Season with pepper. Bake for 15 to 20 minutes, or until the tofu is dry and firm and the edges are slightly crispy. Remove from the oven. Store in an airtight container in the refrigerator until ready to use.

Per Serving:

calories: 49 | fat: 4g | protein: 8g | carbs: 2g | fiber: 1g

Plant-Powered "Sour Cream"

Prep time: 5 minutes | Cook time: 0 minutes | Makes 1 cup

8 ounces (227 g) silken tofu	1 teaspoon apple cider vinegar
2 tablespoons freshly squeezed lemon juice	1 teaspoon onion powder

1. In a blender, combine the tofu, lemon juice, vinegar, and onion powder. Blend for 1 minute, or until the mixture reaches a creamy consistency. 2. Store in a refrigerator-safe container for up to 5 days.

Per Serving: (1 tablespoon)

calories: 10 | fat: 0g | protein: 1g | carbs: 0g | fiber: 0g

Spicy Tahini Dressing

Prep time: 10 minutes | Cook time: 0 minutes | Serves 8

½ cup tahini
2 tablespoons lemon juice
1 clove garlic, minced

1 tablespoon paprika powder
½ cup water

1. Add all of the ingredients to a small bowl or a jar and whisk or shake until smooth. 2. Serve the tahini dressing chilled and enjoy as a topping or a side! 3. Store the tahini dressing in the fridge, using an airtight container, and consume within 4 days. Alternatively, store the tahini dressing in the freezer for a maximum of 60 days and thaw at room temperature

Per Serving:
calories: 102 | fat: 8g | protein: 4g | carbs: 2g | fiber: 1g

Refrigerator Pickles

Prep time: 20 minutes | Cook time: 10 minutes | Makes 2 pints

1 pound (454 g) small
cucumbers, preferably pickling
cucumbers, washed and dried
1 small yellow onion, chopped
or cut into rings
1 cup apple cider vinegar

1 cup water
¼ cup beet sugar (optional)
1 tablespoon kosher salt
(optional)
1 tablespoon pickling spice

1. Using a sharp knife or mandoline, cut the unpeeled cucumbers into ¼-inch-thick rounds. 2. In a large bowl, toss together the cucumbers and onion to evenly mix. Divide the mixture between 2 widemouthed 1-pint canning jars with lids, leaving ½ inch of headspace at the top where the lid rings begin, and pack them in using your clean hand or a heavy spoon. Be careful not to break the cucumbers. 3. In a small pot over high heat, combine the vinegar, water, beet sugar, salt (if using), and pickling spice. Bring to a boil, stirring, and cook until the sugar and salt dissolve. Pour the brine over the vegetables, leaving ½ inch of headspace at the top. You might not use all the brine. Loosely screw on the lids and gently tap the jars on the counter a couple of times to remove any air bubbles. If necessary, add more brine to fill the jars to the ½-inch line, then secure the lids tightly. Let the jars cool to room temperature. 4. Refrigerate for at least 24 hours before serving. These pickles will have even more flavor over time and they will retain a crisper texture than their grocery store cousins. 5. Due to the high acid content in the brine, you can keep these pickles refrigerated for 1 month or longer; however, because they did not go through a canning process, they are not shelf-stable.

Per Serving: (4 pickles)
calories: 218 | fat: 1g | protein: 4g | carbs: 50g | fiber: 7g

Cauliflower Bake Topping

Prep time: 10 minutes | Cook time: 15 minutes | Serves 6

1 large head cauliflower, cut
into 1½-inch florets
½ cup raw pine nuts, cashews,
or macadamia nuts
½ cup filtered water if using a
food processor

2 tablespoons extra-virgin olive
oil (optional)
3 tablespoons nutritional yeast,
plus more to taste
½ teaspoon fine sea salt, plus
more to taste (optional)

1. Set up a steamer pot with about 2 inches of filtered water in the bottom (the water shouldn't touch the bottom of the basket) and bring to a boil over high heat. Arrange the cauliflower florets in the steamer basket, cover, and steam for 10 to 12 minutes, until the cauliflower is cooked through but not falling apart. Remove from the heat and set aside. 2. High-Powered-Blender Method: Put the nuts, olive oil, yeast, and salt, if using, in a high-powered blender and add the steamed cauliflower. Starting on low speed and using the tamper stick to help press the cauliflower down, blend, gradually increasing the speed to high, until completely smooth and thick; use the tamper stick to keep the mixture moving and to scrape down the sides as you go. This will take a couple of minutes. Season with more nutritional yeast and salt to taste and blend to combine. 3. Food-Processor Method: Put the steamed cauliflower in a food processor. Combine the nuts, water, olive oil, yeast, and salt in a regular upright blender and blend until completely smooth. Pour into the food processor with the cauliflower and process until completely smooth, scraping down the sides as necessary. Season with more yeast and salt to taste. 4. The topping is ready to be baked on a filling of your choice, or it can be stored in an airtight container in the fridge for up to 3 days or frozen for up to 3 months.

Per Serving:
calories: 167 | fat: 13g | protein: 6g | carbs: 10g | fiber: 4g

Nutty Plant-Based Parmesan

Prep time: 10 minutes | Cook time: 0 minutes | Makes 1½ cups

1 cup raw cashews
½ cup nutritional yeast

½ teaspoon salt (optional)

1. In a blender, pulse the cashews until they become a fine dust. Transfer the cashew dust to a small bowl and add the nutritional yeast and salt (if using). Mix well with a spoon. Transfer any leftovers to an airtight container and refrigerate for up to 10 days or freeze for up to 3 months.

Per Serving:
calories: 79 | fat: 5g | protein: 3g | carbs: 5g | fiber: 0g

Sweet Corn Dressing

Prep time: 10 minutes | Cook time: 0 minutes | Makes 2 cups

2 large ears sweet corn, husked
and kernels cut off
6 tablespoons extra-virgin olive
oil (optional)
¼ cup freshly squeezed lime
juice, plus more to taste
2 (3-inch) pieces scallion,

white and light green parts
only, coarsely chopped
1 (½-inch) slice of a large
garlic clove
¾ teaspoon fine sea salt, plus
more to taste (optional)

1. Combine the corn kernels, olive oil, lime juice, scallion, garlic, and salt, if using, in an upright blender and blend until completely smooth and velvety. Scrape down the sides with a rubber spatula. Adjust the seasoning and lime juice to taste and blend again. 2. Serve immediately, or store in a glass jar in the fridge for up to 3 days. Shake well before using.

Per Serving: (¼ cup)
calories: 125 | fat: 10g | protein: 1g | carbs: 8g | fiber: 1g

Cilantro and Lime Chutney

Prep time: 10 minutes | Cook time: 0 minutes | Makes 1 cup

2 green chiles, stemmed
1 tablespoon grated peeled fresh ginger
1 teaspoon lime zest
Juice of 1 large lime
2 tablespoons water, plus more as needed

2 cups fresh cilantro, washed and shaken dry
1 tablespoon agave syrup, or pure maple syrup (optional)
½ teaspoon ground cumin
¼ teaspoon ground coriander

1. In a blender, combine the green chiles, ginger, lime zest and juice, and 2 tablespoons of water. Purée until smooth. 2. Add the cilantro, agave syrup (if using), cumin, and coriander. Purée again until smooth. Scrape down the sides, as needed, and add up to 2 tablespoons more water to reach your desired consistency. 3. Refrigerate in an airtight container for up to 2 weeks or freeze for up to 6 months.
Per Serving: (1 tablespoon)
calories: 8 | fat: 0g | protein: 0g | carbs: 2g | fiber: 0g

Pomegranate Ginger Sauce

Prep time: 5 minutes | Cook time: 0 minutes | Serves 8

2 cups fresh or frozen pomegranate seeds
10 dried pitted plums

1 (2-inch) piece ginger
1 tablespoon black pepper

1. Add all the ingredients to a blender or food processor and blend to form a smooth sauce. 2. Store the pomegranate sauce in the fridge, using an airtight container and consume within 3 days. Alternatively, store it in the freezer for a maximum of 60 days and thaw at room temperature.
Per Serving:
calories: 65 | fat: 0g | protein: 1g | carbs: 15g | fiber: 3g

Whipped Lentil Chipotle Dip

Prep time: 10 minutes | Cook time: 10 minutes | Makes 2 cups

1 cup split red lentils, rinsed
3 cloves garlic, peeled
2 chipotle peppers in adobo
1 tablespoon adobo sauce from the can (optional)
3 tablespoons raw cashew butter
1 tablespoon fresh lemon juice

1 teaspoon tomato paste
1½ teaspoons ground cumin
Salt and pepper, to taste (optional)
Garnishes (optional):
Virgin olive oil (optional)
Ground cumin
Sweet paprika

1. Place the lentils in a medium saucepan and cover them with 3 cups of filtered water. Bring to a boil over medium-high heat. Lower to a simmer and cook until the lentils are mushy and falling apart, about 8 minutes. 2. While the lentils are cooking, combine the garlic, chipotles, adobo, if using, cashew butter, lemon juice, tomato paste, and cumin in a blender. 3. Drain the cooked lentils, and scrape them into the blender with the garlic and chipotle mixture. Season with salt and pepper, if using. Whiz everything on high until the dip is completely smooth. You may have to stop the blender and scrape

down the sides a couple of times. 4. The dip will be quite warm. For optimal serving, scrape the dip into a container and cover it with plastic wrap, pressing it onto the surface of the dip. Refrigerate the dip for at least 1 hour before serving. 5. You can garnish the top with a drizzle of olive oil, some extra ground cumin, and a sprinkle of paprika if you like.
Per Serving: (½ cup)
calories: 261 | fat: 7g | protein: 14g | carbs: 38g | fiber: 6g

Strawberry Chia Jam

Prep time: 2 min Green Goddess Dressing

Prep time: 10 minutes | Cook time: 0 minutes | Makes 1 cup

½ cup tahini
2 tablespoons apple cider vinegar
Juice of 1 lemon
¼ cup tamari or soy sauce
2 garlic cloves, minced or pressed
½ cup water
½ cup fresh basil, minced

½ cup fresh parsley, minced
½ cup scallions or chives, minced
¼ teaspoon sea salt (optional)
Pinch freshly ground black pepper (optional)
1 tablespoon maple syrup (optional)

1. Put all the ingredients in a blender or food processor and blend until smooth, 30 to 45 seconds. Add more water if needed to get a thick, creamy dressing.
Per Serving: (1 tablespoon)
calories: 211 | fat: 16g | protein: 7g | carbs: 12g | fiber: 1g

High Protein Black Bean Dip

Prep time: 10 minutes | Cook time: 0 minutes | Serves 3

4 cups black beans, cooked, rinsed, and drained
2 tablespoons minced garlic
2 tablespoons Italian seasoning
2 tablespoons onion powder

1 tablespoon olive oil (optional)
1 tablespoon lemon juice
¼ teaspoon salt, to taste (optional)

1. Place black beans in a large bowl and mash them with a fork until everything is mostly smooth. Stir in the remaining ingredients and incorporate thoroughly. The mixture should be smooth and creamy. Add some additional salt (if desired) and lemon juice to taste and serve at room temperature.
Per Serving:
calories: 398 | fat: 7g | protein: 21g | carbs: 63g | fiber: 16g

Chimichurri

Prep time: 5 minutes | Cook time: 0 minutes | Serves 6

1 cup flat-leaf parsley leaves
Grated zest and juice of 2 lemons

4 garlic cloves
1 teaspoon dried oregano
¼ cup water

1. Pulse the parsley, lemon zest and juice, garlic, and oregano in a food processor until combined. With the food processor running, stream in the water, stopping when it reaches the desired consistency. 2. The chimichurri can be refrigerated in an airtight container for up

to 5 days. It can also be frozen in single portions for up to 6 months: Scoop into ice cube trays, freeze, then transfer to an airtight container.
Per Serving:
calories: 11 | fat: 0g | protein: 1g | carbs: 3g | fiber: 1g

Chapter 8   Snacks and Appetizers

Peanut Butter Balls

Prep time: 0 minutes | Cook time: 30 minutes | Makes 12 balls

1 cup old-fashioned rolled oats
½ cup creamy peanut butter
¼ cup raisins

1. Add all the ingredients to a large bowl. Using your hands, mix together thoroughly. 2. Roll the mixture into small balls with your hands, making each about the size of a tablespoon. Place the balls on a baking sheet. 3. Put the baking sheet into the freezer for 30 minutes. 4. Remove from the freezer and eat immediately, or store in an airtight container or plastic bag in your refrigerator for up to 5 days.

Per Serving: (2 balls)
calories: 168 | fat: 13g | protein: 8g | carbs: 14g | fiber: 4g

High-Protein Peanut Butter Cookie Dough

Prep time: 15 minutes | Cook time: 0 minutes | Makes 45 balls

1 cup crunchy peanut butter
1 cup maple syrup (optional)
½ teaspoon salt (optional)
1 cup chickpea flour
¾ cup almond meal flour
½ cup chopped peanuts
½ cup chopped cashews
½ cup old-fashioned oats
Finely ground peanuts, for coating (optional)

1. Mix the peanut butter and the syrup in a large bowl. Add the remaining ingredients and mix well. Shape into balls and eat. 2. If you'd like a little bit more of a refined look for serving, roll the balls into finely ground peanuts. For easier handling, store in the refrigerator between snacking.

Per Serving: (2 balls)
calories: 183 | fat: 7g | protein: 10g | carbs: 19g | fiber: 3g

Crispy Baked Chickpeas

Prep time: 5 minutes | Cook time: 25 minutes | Makes 1½ cups

1 (15-ounce / 425-g) can chickpeas, drained and rinsed
1 tablespoon extra-virgin olive oil (optional)
½ teaspoon smoked paprika
½ teaspoon salt
¼ teaspoon garlic powder

1. Preheat the oven to 425°F (220°C). 2. In a medium bowl, combine the chickpeas, olive oil, smoked paprika, salt, and garlic powder and toss until combined. Spread out the seasoned chickpeas on a sheet pan and bake for 15 minutes. Using a spatula, turn the chickpeas and continue to bake for another 10 minutes, or until crispy.

Per Serving:
calories: 147 | fat: 6g | protein: 5g | carbs: 18g | fiber: 5g

Holy Guacamole

Prep time: 15 minutes | Cook time: 0 minutes | Serves 8

4 ripe avocados, halved and pitted
1 ripe tomato, diced and seeds removed
½ cup fresh cilantro, roughly chopped
1 jalapeño chile pepper, minced, seeds and ribs removed
2 garlic cloves, minced
2 tablespoons fresh lime juice
½ teaspoon sea salt (optional)

1. In a medium bowl, mash the avocados well with a fork. Stir in the tomato, cilantro, chile pepper, garlic, lime juice, and salt (if using). 2. Serve immediately, or cover tightly and refrigerate until ready to eat. It will keep several days refrigerated. To prevent browning, press plastic wrap or waxed paper directly on the surface of the guacamole and/or place an avocado pit in the center.

Per Serving:
calories: 166 | fat: 14g | protein: 2g | carbs: 9g | fiber: 7g

Coco-Mango Performance Bars

Prep time: 2 minutes | Cook time: 0 minutes | Makes 6 bars

1 cup soft Medjool dates (about 10), pitted
1 cup shredded unsweetened coconut
½ cup raw macadamia nuts or cashews
¼ cup fresh or frozen mango
1 tablespoon chia seeds
2 teaspoons maca powder
2 tablespoons cacao nibs
2 tablespoons raw nuts/seeds (your favorite kind)

1. In a food processor, grind together all the ingredients, except the 2 tablespoons of nuts/seeds, until a coarse dough has formed (this process may take a couple of minutes). 2. Stop the machine and check the consistency—pinch the dough between 2 fingers and make sure it sticks together easily, so that your bars don't end up crumbly. If the dough is too dry, add a small amount of water—about ½ teaspoon at a time—and blend again until your desired stickiness is achieved. Then, add the 2 tablespoons of nuts/seeds and pulse several times until coarsely chopped, to give the bars a nice texture. 3. To shape into bars: Turn out the mixture onto a clean work surface. Flatten with your hands. Place a sheet of parchment paper on top, then roll out with a rolling pin to your desired thickness. Cut into bars. 4. Alternatively, form the mixture into a brick, then cut into slices. Or press the mixture into a parchment paper-lined baking dish or brownie pan, refrigerate for about 5 hours, then slice into bars. 5. As the bars dry in the fridge, they become easier to handle and slice. 6. Store in an airtight glass container for 1 week or in the freezer for up to 1 month.

Per Serving:
calories: 282 | fat: 16g | protein: 3g | carbs: 37g | fiber: 6g

Spiced Glazed Carrots

Prep time: 10 minutes | Cook time: 2 to 3 hours | Serves 4 to 6

2 pounds (907 g) fresh baby carrots or frozen cut carrots	(optional)
⅓ cup no-sugar-added apricot preserves, such as Polaner All Fruit brand	¼ teaspoon ground cinnamon
	¼ teaspoon ground nutmeg
	¼ teaspoon ground turmeric
	½ teaspoon ground ginger
2 tablespoons orange juice	1 teaspoon dried thyme
1 tablespoon balsamic vinegar	1 tablespoon cornstarch
1 tablespoon maple syrup	2 tablespoons water

1. Place the carrots into the slow cooker. In a measuring cup or medium bowl, stir together the apricot preserves, orange juice, vinegar, maple syrup (if using), cinnamon, nutmeg, turmeric, ginger, and thyme. Pour the sauce into the slow cooker and stir to coat the carrots. Cover and cook on High for 2 to 3 hours or on Low for 4 to 6 hours. 2. During the last 30 minutes of cooking, add the cornstarch and water to a small lidded jar. Cover and shake the jar well to form a slurry and pour it into the slow cooker, stirring occasionally to thicken the sauce and form a glaze.

Per Serving:
calories: 175 | fat: 0g | protein: 2g | carbs: 43g | fiber: 7g

Steamed Seitan Chipotle Links

Prep time: 15 minutes | Cook time: 40 minutes | Makes 4 links

⅓ cup plus 2 tablespoons vital wheat gluten	1 teaspoon onion powder
2 tablespoons chickpea flour	1 teaspoon taco seasoning
1 teaspoon garlic powder	2 tablespoons tomato sauce
	1 teaspoon chipotle hot sauce

1. Add the gluten, flour, garlic and onion powders, and taco seasoning to a large bowl. 2. Mix ¼ cup water, the tomato sauce, and hot sauce in a small bowl and mix well. Pour the liquid mixture into the dry ingredients and mix. Knead for 2 minutes until elastic. You will see it pull back into a rounder shape as you knead. This is a firm dough and will not double in size as cooking. 3. Cut into four equal pieces and roll each one into a log shape. 4. Add 5 cups water to a saucepan. Bring to a boil. Place a steamer basket inside the pan and turn down the heat. Add seitan links to the steamer basket and cover. Steam for 40 minutes. 5. Remove the seitan to cool and store in the refrigerator for up to 5 days or in the freezer for up to 4 months.

Per Serving: (1 links)
calories: 120 | fat: 1g | protein: 30g | carbs: 8g | fiber: 1g

Tempeh Stuffed Cremini Mushrooms

Prep time: 15 minutes | Cook time: 40 minutes | Serves 6

18 cremini mushrooms	Pinch of onion powder
2 tablespoons diced red onion, small dice	Pinch of cayenne pepper
	¼ cup rice, cooked
3 ounces (85 g) tempeh, diced very small, or pulsed small	1 tablespoon tamari

1. Remove stems from the mushrooms and set the caps aside. Finely chop the stems and set aside. 2. Heat 3 tablespoons of water in a medium skillet. Add the chopped mushroom stems and onion. Sauté 10 to 15 minutes or until onion is translucent. Add the tempeh and cook another 5 minutes. Add onion powder, cayenne pepper, rice, and tamari. Cook 2 minutes, stirring occasionally. 3. Preheat the oven to 350ºF (180ºC). 4. Stuff mushroom caps and place on baking sheet. Bake for 20 minutes.

Per Serving: (3 mushrooms)
calories: 58 | fat: 3g | protein: 6g | carbs: 6g | fiber: 2g

Protein Power Pistachio Bites

Prep time: 15 minutes | Cook time: 0 minutes | Makes 18 balls

½ cup old-fashioned oats	⅓ cup flaxseed meal
½ cup almond butter	⅓ cup pistachios, ground
¼ cup maple syrup (optional)	1 tablespoon raw shelled
⅓ cup oat bran	hempseed

1. Add all the ingredients to a large bowl and mix well. 2. Roll into eighteen balls.

Per Serving: (2 balls)
calories: 188 | fat: 12g | protein: 7g | carbs: 17g | fiber: 5g

Pressure Cooker Thai Nuggets

Prep time: 10 minutes | Cook time: 5 minutes | Serves 4

¾ cup plus 3 tablespoons vital wheat gluten	¾ cup vegetable broth
	2 teaspoons tamari, divided
¼ cup chickpea flour	4 teaspoons red curry paste, divided
½ teaspoon ground ginger	
½ teaspoon salt (optional)	1½ cups vegetable broth, divided
¼ teaspoon garlic powder	
¼ teaspoon paprika	

1. Add the gluten, flour, ginger, salt (if desired), garlic powder, and paprika to a large bowl. 2. Mix ¾ cup vegetable broth, 1 teaspoon tamari, and 2 teaspoons red curry paste in a small bowl. Pour the wet mixture into the dry ingredients. 3. Mix and then knead for about 2 to 3 minutes or until elastic. It's a very wet dough but you will see it is still elastic. It should be mildly stretchy and pull back but still pliable. Pinch off pieces of seitan dough into very small balls, about 1 to 1½ inches in diameter. They will fatten up when cooking. 4. Place in an electric pressure cooker. 5. Add 1½ cups vegetable broth, 1½ cups water, and 2 teaspoons red curry paste to a bowl and stir well. Pour over the nuggets in the pressure cooker. Close the lid, make sure the top knob is turned to sealing. Press Manual on the front of the pot. Push button to 4 (meaning 4 minutes). The pressure cooker will make a click and start to build pressure. It will take about 15 minutes to build pressure and cook. Leave the nuggets in the pot to set. They will cook more as the pressure is naturally releasing. Don't vent. 6. After about an hour, go ahead and vent. It may already have cooled completely, but vent to make sure the pressure has released and then open the lid. 7. Remove the nuggets from the liquid and set aside to cool. You can eat them right away, add to a recipe, or keep in the fridge overnight. They are great the next day. You can also freeze them.

Per Serving:
calories: 155 | fat: 2g | protein: 26g | carbs: 11g | fiber: 2g

Sunshine Everything Crackers

Prep time: 15 minutes | Cook time: 20 minutes | Makes 60 crackers

1 cup chickpea flour
1 cup certified gluten-free oat flour
2 teaspoons nutritional yeast
1 teaspoon fine sea salt (optional)
2 teaspoons garlic powder
1 teaspoon ground turmeric

Pinch of cayenne pepper (optional)
¼ cup plus 2 tablespoons coconut oil (optional)
¼ cup filtered water, plus extra if necessary
¼ cup mixed raw seeds

1. Preheat the oven to 350ºF (180ºC). 2. In the bowl of a food processor, combine the chickpea flour, oat flour, nutritional yeast, sea salt, garlic powder, ground turmeric, cayenne pepper, and coconut oil, if using. Pulse the machine to get everything lightly mixed. Mix on high until you have a wet and uniform crumbly mixture. 3. With the food processor on low, slowly pour the filtered water through the feed tube of the food processor. The cracker dough should start to form a large ball. If the ball isn't forming, add more water by the teaspoon through the feed tube. 4. Open the lid of the food processor and add the mixed seeds. Pulse the dough a couple of times to distribute the seeds. 5. Lay a sheet of parchment paper, about the size of a large baking sheet, on the counter. Dump the cracker dough onto the parchment and flatten it a bit with your hands. Lay another sheet of parchment paper on top of the dough. 6. With a rolling pin, evenly roll the cracker dough out to roughly an ⅛ inch thickness. Remove the top sheet of parchment paper. Carefully transfer the parchment with the rolled-out cracker dough to a large baking sheet. With a knife, score the cracker dough into a grid, forming 1-inch square crackers. Slide the baking sheet into the oven and bake until the edges of the crackers have browned slightly, about 20 minutes. Let the crackers cool completely before storing in a sealed container. The crackers will keep for about 5 days.

Per Serving: (6 crackers)
calories: 150 | fat: 9g | protein: 5g | carbs: 14g | fiber: 2g

Homemade Popcorn with Magic Dust

Prep time: 10 minutes | Cook time: 10 minutes | Serves 8

⅓ cup raw cashews
2 tablespoons nutritional yeast
1 tablespoon arrowroot powder
2 teaspoons fine sea salt (optional)
½ teaspoon ground turmeric

½ teaspoon garlic powder
Freshly ground black pepper, to taste
¼ cup refined coconut oil (optional)
⅔ cup organic popping corn

1. Place the raw cashews in the bowl of a food processor. Run the motor on high speed until the cashews have a mealy texture. To the ground cashews, add the nutritional yeast, arrowroot powder, sea salt, if using, turmeric, garlic powder, and black pepper. Run the food processor on high again until you have an even, slightly coarse powder. This is your magic dust. Set aside. 2. Place a large bowl on your counter before you start popping the kernels. 3. In a large pot with a well-fitting lid (preferably a Dutch oven or something similar), heat the coconut oil and 3 popcorn kernels over medium-high heat. Cover. 4. Once the 3 kernels have popped, remove the lid and carefully remove the popped corn. Pour in the remaining

popcorn kernels. Cover and remove the pot from the heat for 30 seconds. 5. Put the pot back on the heat and, with pot holders or kitchen towels in each hand, grab the handles of the pot and shake it with equal measures of vigor and control. I usually ball up a couple of thin kitchen towels in my hands and grab the handles while simultaneously holding the lid firmly down with my thumbs. 6. Shake the pot for roughly 2 minutes. The popcorn should be popping vigorously. Once the popping starts to slow, with about 3 seconds of silence between pops, remove the pot from the heat and take off the lid immediately. 7. As quickly and safely as you can, dump all the popcorn into the large bowl. Shake ¾ of the magic dust over top, and quickly mix it in with your hands. After the popcorn is evenly coated, garnish the top with the remaining magic dust and serve immediately.

Per Serving:
calories: 144 | fat: 12g | protein: 3g | carbs: 7g | fiber: 1g

Peanut Butter Granola Bars

Prep time: 10 minutes | Cook time: 0 minutes | Makes 12 bars

1 cup packed pitted dates
¼ cup pure maple syrup (optional)
¼ cup creamy natural peanut

butter or almond butter
1 cup coarsely chopped roasted unsalted almonds
1½ cups old-fashioned oats

1. In a food processor, combine the dates, maple syrup (if using), and peanut butter. Process for 1 to 2 minutes, or until the mixture starts to come together and feels slightly sticky. Stop right before or as it starts to turn into a ball of loose dough. 2. Add the almonds and oats and process for 1 minute. Press the dough into an 8-by-8-inch baking dish and cover with plastic wrap. Refrigerate for 20 minutes. 3. Remove the dough and cut into 12 pieces. Refrigerate in a sealable bag or airtight container for 1 to 2 weeks, or freeze for up to 6 months.

Per Serving: (1 bar)
calories: 181 | fat: 9g | protein: 5g | carbs: 24g | fiber: 4g

Maple-Glazed Mixed Nuts

Prep time: 5 minutes | Cook time: 15 minutes | Serves 6

1 cup walnuts
1 cup pecans

1 cup cashews
1½ cups maple syrup (optional)

1. Preheat the oven to 325ºF (165ºC). 2. Mix the nuts and maple syrup (if desired) together in a medium bowl. Make sure that each nut has been coated well. Spread out on a baking sheet so they are in one layer but still close to each other. Touching is okay. Bake for 7 minutes. 3. Remove from oven and flip with a spatula. They can overlap some at this point. Put back in the oven and bake another 6 minutes or so. Watch closely. If they're in too long, they start to burn quickly. 4. Take the baking sheet out of the oven, flip the nuts again, and let cool completely. Eat right away or pack in an airtight container. These nuts will keep in your pantry for quite a few weeks and will keep in the fridge about 2 to 3 months. The freezer will store them for 6 months.

Per Serving: (½ cup)
calories: 452 | fat: 24g | protein: 10g | carbs: 59g | fiber: 3g

Protein Power Grilled Veggie and Fruit Skewers

Prep time: 15 minutes | Cook time: 25 minutes | Serves 4

8 ounces (227 g) extra-firm tofu, drained, pressed, and cut into 1-inch cubes	4 ounces (113 g) cremini mushrooms
2 tablespoons tamari	1 pineapple, chopped into chunks
1 tablespoon rice vinegar	1 red bell pepper, chopped into large pieces
1 tablespoon maple syrup (optional)	1 yellow bell pepper, chopped into large pieces
¼ teaspoon chili powder	Extra virgin olive oil, for grilling (optional)
1 large sweet potato, peeled and chopped into bite-size chunks	

1. Cut off the stem end of the peppers. Slice lengthwise. Remove any seeds that are inside. Set aside. 2. Place all the remaining ingredients in a food processor. Pulse four or five times. The chickpeas should be chunky. Remove the blade and stir to make sure the mixture is blended well. 3. Stuff each pepper half full with about 2 tablespoons of the chickpea mixture. Set on a plate to serve.

Per Serving: (2 skewers)
calories: 236 | fat: 4g | protein: 16g | carbs: 45g | fiber: 6g

Mocha Chocolate Brownie Bars

Prep time: 15 minutes | Cook time: 0 minutes | Serves 3

2½ cups chocolate or vanilla vegan protein powder	1 teaspoon pure vanilla extract
½ cup cocoa powder	¼ teaspoon nutmeg
½ cup old-fashioned or quick oats	2 tablespoons agave nectar (optional)
	1 cup cold brewed coffee

1. Line a square baking dish with parchment paper and set it aside. 2. Mix the dry ingredients together in a large bowl. Slowly incorporate the agave nectar (if desired), vanilla extract, and cold coffee while stirring constantly until all the lumps in the mixture have disappeared. Pour the batter into the dish, while making sure to press it into the corners. Place the dish into the refrigerator until firm, or for about 4 hours. Alternatively use the freezer for just 1 hour. 3. Slice the chunk into 6 even squares, and enjoy, share, or store!

Per Serving:
calories: 213 | fat: 4g | protein: 27g | carbs: 17g | fiber: 4g

No-Bake Chocolate Peanut Butter Cookies

Prep time: 20 minutes | Cook time: 5 minutes | Makes 24 cookies

½ cup unsweetened dairy-free milk	chocolate chips
3 tablespoons dairy-free butter	1 teaspoon vanilla extract
⅓ cup coconut sugar (optional)	⅓ cup creamy peanut butter
1 tablespoon unsweetened cocoa powder	Pinch of salt (optional)
⅓ cup dairy-free semi-sweet	2½ cups old-fashioned oats or quick-cooking oats
	¼ cup raw shelled hempseed

1. Line a baking sheet with wax paper. 2. Place the milk, butter, sugar (if desired), cocoa powder, and chocolate chips in a large saucepan. Bring to a rolling boil and then look at the timer. Let boil for 2 minutes. Stir occasionally so that the chocolate chips don't stick to the bottom of the pan before they melt. Remove from the heat and add the vanilla, peanut butter, and salt (if desired) and mix until the peanut butter melts. Stir in the oats and hempseed. 3. With a spoon, drop dollops of the batter onto the prepared baking sheet. Within a minute or less you can handle them and shape into cookies. Let the cookies set for an hour or so. You can speed up the cooling and hardening process by placing them in the refrigerator.

Per Serving: (2 cookies)
calories: 220 | fat: 77g | protein: 7g | carbs: 29g | fiber: 5g

Gingerbread Protein Bars

Prep time: 20 minutes | Cook time: 15 minutes | Makes 8 bars

2 cups raw and unsalted almonds	chocolate flavor
10 pitted dates	1 (4-inch) piece ginger, minced
4 tablespoons five-spice powder	Optional Toppings:
2 scoops soy protein isolate,	Cocoa powder
	Shredded coconut

1. Preheat the oven to 257°F (125°C) and line a baking sheet with parchment paper. 2. Put the almonds on the baking sheet and roast them for about 10 to 15 minutes or until they're fragrant. 3. Meanwhile, cover the dates with water in a small bowl and let them sit for about 10 minutes. Drain the dates after soaking and make sure no water is left. 4. Add the almonds, dates, 5-spice powder, protein powder and ginger to a food processor and blend into a smooth mixture. Alternatively, add all ingredients to a medium bowl, cover it, and process using a handheld blender. 5. Line a loaf pan with parchment paper. Add the almond mixture to the loaf pan, spread it out and press it down firmly until it is 1 inch thick all over. 6. Put the loaf pan in the fridge for about 45 minutes, until it has firmed up. 7. Divide into 8 bars, serve cold with optional toppings and enjoy! 8. Store the bars in an airtight container in the fridge, and consume within 6 days. Alternatively, store in the freezer for a maximum of 90 days and thaw at room temperature.

Per Serving:
calories: 263 | fat: 18g | protein: 16g | carbs: 9g | fiber: 4g

Protein Peanut Butter Balls

Prep time: 20 minutes | Cook time: 0 minutes | Makes 24 balls

½ cup creamy peanut butter	¼ cup flaxseed meal
½ cup maple syrup (optional)	½ cup coconut flour
½ cup powdered soy milk, non-GMO	¼ cup peanuts, chopped fine

1. Place the peanut butter and maple syrup (if desired) in a medium bowl. Mix well. Add the powdered soy milk, flaxseed meal, and coconut flour. Mix well and roll into 24 balls. Lightly roll each ball in the chopped peanuts. 2. Store in the refrigerator for up to 2 weeks.

Per Serving: (2 balls)
calories: 133 | fat: 8g | protein: 10g | carbs: 12g | fiber: 2g

Crispy Chickpea Snackers

Prep time: 10 minutes | Cook time: 4 to 6 hours | Makes 7 to 8 cups

4 (14½-ounce / 411-g) cans chickpeas, drained and rinsed
Juice of 2 lemons
1 tablespoon garlic powder
1 tablespoon onion powder
2 teaspoons paprika
Salt (optional)

1. Put the chickpeas into the slow cooker. Add the lemon juice, garlic powder, onion powder, and paprika. Season with salt (if using). Toss gently to thoroughly coat every chickpea with the seasoning. 2. Cover the slow cooker and, using a wooden spoon or a chopstick, prop open the lid to allow the steam to escape. Cook on High for 4 to 6 hours or on Low for 8 to 10 hours, stirring every 30 to 45 minutes to keep the chickpeas from burning.
Per Serving:
calories: 56 | fat: 1g | protein: 3g | carbs: 9g | fiber: 3g

Chocolate Sunflower Protein Cookies

Prep time: 15 minutes | Cook time: 10 minutes | Serves 12

1 cup dairy-free butter
¾ cup plus 2 tablespoons coconut sugar (optional)
2 tablespoons ground chia seeds
2¼ cups whole wheat pastry flour
¼ cup protein powder
1 teaspoon baking soda
½ teaspoon baking powder
¼ teaspoon salt (optional)
1 teaspoon vanilla extract
1 cup dairy-free chocolate chips
¼ cup sunflower seed kernels

1. Preheat the oven to 375ºF (190ºC). Cut parchment paper to fit on a baking sheet. Set aside. 2. Add the butter and sugar (if desired) to the bowl of stand mixer and mix together on medium-low speed for 5 minutes. 3. Meanwhile, mix ground chia seeds with 6 tablespoons water and set aside. 4. Mix together the flour, protein powder, baking soda, baking powder, and salt (if desired) in a medium bowl. 5. Add the vanilla and chia mixture to the butter mixture. Mix until well blended. Mix in the flour mixture a little at a time. On low speed, mix in the chocolate chips and sunflower seeds. 6. Form into round balls and set on the prepared baking sheet about 2 inches apart. Flatten to about ½ inch thick. Bake for 8 to 9 minutes. 7. Cool on a wire rack.
Per Serving: (2 cookies)
calories: 281 | fat: g | protein: 7g | carbs: 16g | fiber: 3g

Cacao Crush Smoothie

Prep time: 5 minutes | Cook time: 0 minutes | Serves 1

1½ cups unsweetened almond milk
½ cup frozen cauliflower
¼ avocado, peeled
1 tablespoon cacao powder
½ teaspoon ground cinnamon
½ teaspoon pure vanilla extract

1. In a high-powered blender, combine the almond milk, cauliflower, avocado, cacao powder, cinnamon, and vanilla until smooth and creamy. 2. Serve immediately over a glass of ice.
Per Serving:
calories: 254 | fat: 7g | protein: 15g | carbs: 32g | fiber: 6g

Strawberry-Pistachio Date Balls

Prep time: 10 minutes | Cook time: 0 minutes | Makes 24 balls

¾ cup pitted dates
¾ cup rolled oats, divided
½ cup strawberries
1 tablespoon ground flaxseed
½ teaspoon vanilla extract
½ cup no-salt roasted pistachios

1. Line a plate with parchment paper. 2. In a food processor, combine the dates, ½ cup of oats, the strawberries, flaxseed, vanilla, and pistachios. Process until a paste forms. 3. Stir in the remaining ¼ cup of oats. 4. Using a 1-tablespoon scoop, form the paste into balls. 5. Place the balls in a single layer on the prepared plate. Serve immediately, or refrigerate in an airtight container for up to 5 days.
Per Serving:
calories: 36 | fat: 1g | protein: 1g | carbs: 7g | fiber: 1g

Greens and Beans Dip

Prep time: 10 minutes | Cook time: 0 minutes | Makes about 2 cups

1 (14-ounce / 397-g) can white beans, drained and rinsed, or 1½ cups cooked
Zest and juice of 1 lemon
1 tablespoon almond butter, tahini, or other mild nut or seed butter
1 to 2 leaves kale, rinsed and stemmed
1 tablespoon nutritional yeast (optional)
1 to 2 teaspoons curry powder
1 to 2 teaspoons ground cumin
1 teaspoon smoked paprika
¼ teaspoon sea salt (optional)

1. Put everything in a food processor and pulse until it comes together. If you don't have a food processor, mash the beans and chop the kale, then mix together. 2. Taste for seasoning, adding more spices, lemon juice, or salt (if using) as desired.
Per Serving:(1 cup)
calories: 112 | fat: 5g | protein: 6g | carbs: 13g | fiber: 6g

Cranberry Vanilla Protein Bars

Prep time: 15 minutes | Cook time: 0 minutes | Serves 4

1 cup old-fashioned oats
2 cups vanilla flavor vegan protein powder
⅓ cup shredded coconut
½ cup cashew butter
½ cup dried cranberries
¼ cup maple syrup (optional)
¼ cup chia seeds
1 tablespoon almond or soy milk
1 tablespoon pure vanilla extract

1. Line a square 8x8" baking dish with parchment paper and set it aside. 2. Add the oats, protein powder, and shredded coconut to a food processor and blend until they resemble a fine powder. Transfer the blended ingredients to a large mixing bowl and add the remaining ingredients; mix with a spoon until everything is thoroughly combined. Move the dough to the baking dish and press it down evenly until flattened as much as possible. Place the dish into the freezer until set and firm, around 1½ hours. 3. To serve, slice the chunk into 8 even bars, and enjoy, share, or store!
Per Serving:
calories: 243 | fat: 10g | protein: 16g | carbs: 23g | fiber: 3g

Gluten-Free Energy Crackers

Prep time: 25 minutes | Cook time: 40 minutes | Serves 6

¼ cup flax seeds	¼ cup peanuts, crushed
¼ cup chia seeds	¼ cup cashews, crushed
¾ cup water	¼ cup sesame seeds
1 tablespoon garlic, minced	¼ teaspoon paprika powder
½ tablespoon onion flakes	Salt and pepper to taste
½ cup pumpkin seeds, chopped	(optional)

1. Preheat the oven to 350ºF (180ºC). 2. Take a large bowl and combine the water, garlic, onion flakes, and paprika. Whisk until everything is combined thoroughly. Add the flax seeds, chia seeds, pumpkin seeds, peanuts, cashews, and sesame seeds to the bowl. Stir everything well, while adding pinches of salt (if desired) and pepper to taste, until it is thoroughly combined. 3. Line a baking sheet with parchment paper and spread out the mixture in a thin and even layer across the parchment paper. Bake for 20 to 25 minutes. Remove the pan from the oven and flip over the flat chunk so that the other side can crisp. Cut the chunk into squares or triangles, depending on preference and put the pan back into the oven and bake until the bars have turned golden brown, around 30 minutes. 4. Allow the crackers to cool before serving or storing.

Per Serving:

calories: 209 | fat: 16g | protein: 7g | carbs: 10g | fiber: 6g

Showtime Popcorn

Prep time: 5 minutes | Cook time: 1 minute | Serves 2

¼ cup popcorn kernels	¼ teaspoon garlic powder
1 tablespoon nutritional yeast	¼ teaspoon onion powder

1. Put the popcorn kernels in a paper lunch bag, folding over the top of the bag so the kernels won't spill out. 2. Microwave on high for 2 to 3 minutes, or until you hear a pause of 2 seconds in between kernels popping. 3. Remove the bag from the microwave, and add the nutritional yeast, garlic powder, and onion powder. Fold the top of the bag back over, and shake to thoroughly coat. 4. Pour into a bowl and enjoy.

Per Serving:

calories: 48 | fat: 1g | protein: 4g | carbs: 6g | fiber: 2g

Spirulina-Golden Berry Power Bars

Prep time: 2 minutes | Cook time: 0 minutes | Makes 8 bars

1 cup mixed raw seeds (pumpkin, sunflower, sesame, hemp)	2 tablespoons chopped fresh mint
1 tablespoon chia seeds	2 teaspoons spirulina powder
1 cup Medjool dates (about 10 large), pitted	1 tablespoon fresh lime juice
	½ cup golden berries

1. In a food processor fitted with the S blade, combine all the ingredients, except the golden berries. 2. Process until a coarse dough has formed (this may take a couple of minutes). Stop the machine and check the consistency—pinch the dough between 2 fingers and make sure it sticks together easily so that your bars don't end up crumbly. If the dough is too dry, add a small amount of water—about ½ teaspoon at a time—and blend again until the desired stickiness is achieved. 3. Add the golden berries and pulse several times until they're just coarsely chopped, to give the bars a nice texture. 4. Place a large sheet of parchment paper on a flat surface and tip out the dough on top. Gather into a solid mass in the center, then fold the parchment paper over the top and, using a rolling pin, roll flat until about ¼ inch (6 mm) thick. 5. Place in the freezer for a few hours, then carefully use a knife or cookie cutter to cut the bars into your desired shapes. 6. Store in an airtight glass container for 2 to 3 weeks or in the freezer for up to 3 months.

Per Serving:

calories: 186 | fat: 8g | protein: 6g | carbs: 26g | fiber: 3g

Herbed Smashed Potatoes with Lemon Aioli

Prep time: 5 minutes | Cook time: 1 hour | Serves 4

Potatoes:	2 tablespoons finely chopped
12 small red potatoes	fresh parsley
2 tablespoons extra-virgin olive	Lemon Aioli:
oil (optional)	½ cup store-bought plant-based
1 teaspoon garlic powder	mayonnaise
½ teaspoon salt (optional)	Juice of 1 lemon
1 teaspoon Italian seasoning	1 garlic clove, minced

1. Preheat the oven to 400ºF (205ºC). 2. Make the Potatoes: Put the potatoes in a large pot over high heat, add enough water to cover, and bring to a boil. Cook for 15 minutes. Drain well and pat the potatoes dry with a clean kitchen towel. Transfer the potatoes to a large bowl. 3. Add the olive oil, garlic powder, and salt and gently toss until all the potatoes are coated in the seasonings. Spread out the seasoned potatoes in one layer on a sheet pan. 4. Bake for 15 minutes. Using tongs, turn the potatoes and continue to bake for another 15 minutes. Using the back of a fork, smash the potatoes flat. Sprinkle them with the Italian seasoning and bake for an additional 10 minutes, or until crispy and golden. 5. Make the lemon Aioli: While the potatoes finish baking, in a small bowl, mix together the mayo, lemon juice, and garlic. 6. Transfer the potatoes to a platter, sprinkle with parsley, and serve with the lemon aioli on the side for dipping.

Per Serving:

calories: 520 | fat: 17g | protein: 12g | carbs: 84g | fiber: 9g

Slow-Cooker Applesauce

Prep time: 10 minutes | Cook time: 4 to 5 hours | Makes about 4½ cups

5 pounds (2.3 kg) apples, peeled, cored, and roughly chopped	3 tablespoons fresh lemon juice (from 1 lemon)
1 cup water	2 cinnamon sticks
	Pure maple syrup (optional)

1. In a slow cooker, combine the apples, water, lemon juice, and cinnamon sticks. Cook on low heat for 8 to 10 hours or on high for 4 to 5 hours, until the apples are cooked through. 2. Remove and discard the cinnamon sticks. Using an immersion blender, purée the applesauce to the desired consistency. Alternatively, mash the apples by hand. 3. Taste the applesauce. If it's not sweet enough, add maple syrup to taste.

Per Serving:

calories: 132 | fat: 0g | protein: 0g | carbs: 35g | fiber: 6g

Legit Salsa

Prep time: 10 minutes | Cook time: 0 minutes | Makes 5 cups

2 jalapeño chile peppers, diced
1 yellow onion, quartered
1 small bunch fresh cilantro, leaves and tender stems
2 garlic cloves, halved

1 (28-ounce / 794-g) can diced tomatoes, undrained
¼ cup fresh lime juice
1 teaspoon sea salt (optional)

1. In a blender, combine all the ingredients and pulse until the desired texture is reached. Taste and add more salt (if using), if needed. Store in an airtight container in the refrigerator for up to 1 week.
Per Serving:
calories: 43 | fat: 0g | protein: 2g | carbs: 9g | fiber: 4g

Calorie Bomb Cookies

Prep time: 15 minutes | Cook time: 30 minutes | Makes 24 cookies

4 cups old-fashioned rolled oats
1½ cups whole wheat flour
1 teaspoon baking powder
½ teaspoon salt (optional)
3 ripe bananas
1 cup coconut sugar (optional)
⅓ cup coconut oil (optional)
¼ cup plus 2 tablespoons water
2 tablespoons chia seeds or

ground flaxseeds
2 teaspoons vanilla extract
1 cup dark chocolate chips
1 cup raw walnut pieces
½ cup raw sunflower seeds
½ cup unsweetened shredded coconut (optional)

1. Preheat the oven to 350°F (180°C). Line two baking sheets with parchment paper. 2. Place 2 cups of the oats in a food processor or blender and pulse until they are finely ground. Transfer to a large bowl and add the flour, baking powder, salt (if desired), and remaining oats. 3. Combine the bananas, sugar, oil (if desired), water, chia seeds, and vanilla in the blender or food processor. Add to the oat mixture and stir with a sturdy wooden spoon until combined. Add the chocolate chips, walnuts, sunflower seeds, and coconut. 4. With wet hands, form about ¼ cup dough. Flatten them to ¾ to 1 inch thick. 5. Bake for 30 minutes, or until golden brown. Allow to cool completely before removing from the baking sheets. Store in an airtight container for up to 1 week or freeze for up to 3 months. Wrap in parchment paper for on-the-go eating.
Per Serving: (2 cookies)
calories: 491 | fat: 24g | protein: 9g | carbs: 68g | fiber: 9g

Salsa with Mushrooms and Olives

Prep time: 30 minutes | Cook time: 0 minutes | Serves 3

½ cup finely chopped white button mushrooms
1 tablespoon chopped fresh parsley
1 tablespoon chopped fresh basil
2 Roma tomatoes, finely chopped

1 tablespoon finely chopped scallions
⅓ cup chopped marinated artichoke hearts
½ cup chopped olives
1 tablespoon balsamic vinegar
3 slices sourdough toast

1. Combine the mushrooms, parsley, basil, tomatoes, scallions, artichoke hearts, and olives in a medium mixing bowl. 2. Dress with the balsamic vinegar. Let marinate at room temperature about 20 minutes to blend flavors. Alternatively, refrigerate until serving time. 3. Serve the salsa with the slices of sourdough toast.
Per Serving:
calories: 205 | fat: 3g | protein: 9g | carbs: 41g | fiber: 4g

Avomame Spread

Prep time: 10 minutes | Cook time: 0 minutes | Makes 1½ cups

1 cup frozen shelled edamame beans, thawed
1 tablespoon apple cider vinegar, or lemon juice, or lime juice
1 tablespoon tamari or soy

sauce
1 teaspoon grated fresh ginger
1 avocado, coarsely chopped
¼ cup fresh cilantro, basil, mint, or parsley, chopped
½ cup alfalfa sprouts (optional)

1. Pulse the beans in a food processor with a bit of water and the apple cider vinegar until they're roughly chopped. If you don't have a food processor, thaw and then chop the beans. 2. Add the tamari, ginger, and avocado, and purée. Add the cilantro and sprouts (if using), and purée again until everything is smooth. If you don't have a food processor, mash the avocado and finely chop the rest to mix together.
Per Serving:
calories: 265 | fat: 18g | protein: 11g | carbs: 17g | fiber: 11g

Artichoke Quinoa Dip

Prep time: 20 minutes | Cook time: 25 minutes | Serves 4

½ cup quinoa
1 tablespoon extra virgin olive oil (optional)
½ cup diced onion
4 ounces (113 g) baby spinach, with stems chopped off
¼ cup raw shelled hempseed
½ teaspoon onion powder

½ teaspoon garlic powder
1 teaspoon salt (optional)
¼ teaspoon ground black pepper
8 ounces (227 g) artichoke hearts in water, drained
1 tablespoon lemon juice

1. Place quinoa in a sieve and rinse well. Combine quinoa and 1 cup water in a small saucepan. Bring to a boil, cover, and reduce to a simmer. Cook for 10 to 15 minutes or until the liquid is absorbed. Remove from the heat and let set with the cover on for 5 minutes. Remove lid and fluff. 2. Heat the oil (if desired) in a large skillet over medium-high heat. Add the onion and sauté over medium heat for 10 minutes. Stir in the spinach and cook until wilted, about a minute or so. Add the hempseed and spices and stir in quickly. Remove from the heat. 3. Cut off the top of the artichoke hearts. Discard the toughest of the outside leaves. 4. Add everything to a food processor. Process until well combined and chopped very small. 5. Serve with homemade pita chips (see note). Note: Making homemade pita chips is a very simple process: Buy a bag of pita pockets or flatbread. Brush pita pockets with oil and cut into triangles. Lay on a baking sheet. Bake at 400°F (205°C) for about 5 to 7 minutes. Watch very closely to make sure they do not burn.
Per Serving:
calories: 155 | fat: 5g | protein: 10g | carbs: 23g | fiber: 6g

Olive-Chickpea Waffles

Prep time: 10 minutes | Cook time: 30 minutes | Makes 6 waffles

2 cups chickpea flour
1 tablespoon chopped rosemary or thyme
1 teaspoon gluten-free baking powder
¼ teaspoon salt (optional)
⅛ teaspoon black pepper

½ cup pitted Kalamata olives, chopped
¼ cup sun-dried tomatoes, thinly sliced
1½ cups hot water
Hummus

1. Preheat a waffle iron. 2. Combine the flour, rosemary, baking powder, salt (if desired), and pepper in a large bowl. Stir in the olives and sun-dried tomatoes, then whisk in the hot water. The batter should be thick but thoroughly combined. 3. Spread about ½ to ¾ cup batter onto the waffle iron, close the lid, and cook through, according to waffle iron directions, about 6 minutes. 4. Top with hummus and serve.

Per Serving: (1 waffle)
calories: 175 | fat: 5g | protein: 8g | carbs: 24g | fiber: 5g

Chocolate-Coconut-Pecan Chewy Bars

Prep time: 15 minutes | Cook time: 10 minutes | Makes 8 bars

1 cup pitted dates, soaked in hot water for 10 minutes and drained
¼ cup brown rice syrup
⅓ cup plus ¼ cup chopped pecans

1½ cups old-fashioned rolled oats
⅓ cup mini chocolate chips
⅓ cup unsweetened shredded coconut

1. Preheat the oven to 300ºF (150ºC). Line a 9-inch square baking dish with parchment paper. 2. Pulse, then process the dates in a food processor until smooth. Transfer to a large bowl, then stir in the brown rice syrup. 3. Process ¼ cup of the pecans and ½ cup of the oats in the now-empty food processor until finely ground. Add to the bowl with the dates, then fold in the remaining pecans, remaining oats, the chocolate chips, and coconut. (The dates and syrup make this thick so you'll need to use some muscle to fold the ingredients.) 4. Transfer to the dish. Bake for 10 minutes, or until fragrant and golden brown. Allow to cool completely, then slice into 8 bars using a sharp knife and serve. 5. Store in an airtight container for up to 1 week. Individual bars can be wrapped in parchment and taken on the go.

Per Serving: (1 bar)
calories: 293 | fat: g | protein: 3g | carbs: 51g | fiber: 4g

Lemon-Pepper Bean Dip with Rosemary

Prep time: 10 minutes | Cook time: 0 minutes | Serves 4 to 6

1 (15-ounce / 425-g) can reduced-sodium white beans, drained and rinsed
1 tablespoon lemon juice
1 tablespoon red-wine vinegar

1 teaspoon freshly ground black pepper
½ teaspoon garlic powder
½ teaspoon dried rosemary
Pinch red pepper flakes

1. In a medium bowl, combine the beans, lemon juice, vinegar, pepper, garlic powder, rosemary, and red pepper flakes. Gently mix until combined (although this dip can be mixed and slightly mashed to create a chunkier texture).

Per Serving:
calories: 88 | fat: 0g | protein: 5g | carbs: 16g | fiber: 4g

Oatmeal Granola Bar Bites

Prep time: 5 minutes | Cook time: 25 minutes | Serves 12

1½ cups rolled oats
⅓ cup unsweetened applesauce
¼ cup unsweetened natural peanut butter
2 tablespoons pure maple syrup
2 tablespoons ground flaxseed
1 tablespoon finely chopped

pecans
1 tablespoon sliced almonds
1 tablespoon unsweetened raisins
1 tablespoon mini vegan chocolate chips

1. Preheat the oven to 350ºF (180ºC). Line an 8-by-8-inch baking dish and a baking sheet with parchment paper. 2. In a large bowl, using a wooden spoon or rubber spatula, mix together the oats, applesauce, peanut butter, maple syrup, flaxseed, pecans, almonds, raisins, and chocolate chips. 3. Using the back of a measuring cup, firmly press the mixture into the prepared baking dish. 4. Lift the pressed mixture out, and cut into 12 equal pieces. 5. Place the cut pieces in single layer on the prepared baking sheet. 6. Transfer the baking sheet to the oven, and bake for 20 to 25 minutes, flipping halfway through, or until the bars are golden brown. Remove from the oven.

Per Serving:
calories: 98 | fat: 5g | protein: 3g | carbs: 12g | fiber: 2g

Popeye Protein Balls

Prep time: 5 minutes | Cook time: 0 minutes | Makes 20 to 26 balls

1 cup raw hazelnuts
¼ cup pumpkin seeds
Handful of fresh baby spinach
2 tablespoons raw cacao or carob powder
1 cup raisins, soaked in water for 15 minutes, rinsed and drained
2 tablespoons hemp protein

powder
1 teaspoon ground cinnamon
Pinch of Himalayan pink salt (optional)
2 to 4 tablespoons superfood powder (açai, maqui, maca, spirulina, matcha or moringa), depending on potency, for dusting (optional)

1. In a food processor fitted with the S blade, combine all the ingredients, except the superfood powder, and process until the mixture forms a ball. Do not overprocess! If you do, the dough will become too soft. (If that happens, add up to 2 tablespoons of pumpkin seeds and refrigerate for 30 minutes before forming into balls.) 2. To shape into balls, use a tablespoon or your hands to scoop the mixture (however much you like to make 1 ball) and roll between the palms of your hands. 3. Place on a plate and refrigerate for a minimum of 1 hour before serving. 4. If desired, before refrigerating, roll the balls in a plate of superfood powder to dust their exterior.

Per Serving:
calories: 167 | fat: 10g | protein: 5g | carbs: 15g | fiber: 2g

Tropical Lemon Protein Bites

Prep time: 20 minutes | Cook time: 0 minutes | Makes 24 balls

1¾ cups cashews	hempseed
¼ cup coconut flour	3 tablespoons maple syrup
¼ cup unsweetened shredded coconut	(optional)
3 tablespoons raw shelled	3 tablespoons fresh lemon juice

1. Place the cashews in a food processor and process until very fine. Add the rest of the ingredients and process until well blended. Dump the mixture into a large bowl. 2. Take a clump of the dough and squeeze it into a ball. Keep squeezing and working it a few times until a ball is formed and solid.

Per Serving: (2 balls)

calories: 165 | fat: 9g | protein: 8g | carbs: 13g | fiber: 1g

White Bean and Spinach Artichoke Dip

Prep time: 10 minutes | Cook time: 15 minutes | Serves 8

½ yellow onion, peeled and sliced	miso paste
3 garlic cloves, coarsely chopped	1 tablespoon tapioca starch
1 tablespoon water	1 cup unsweetened oat milk
1 (15-ounce /425-g) can cannellini beans, drained and rinsed	1 (15-ounce /425-g) can pumpkin
½ cup nutritional yeast	1 (1-pound / 454-g) package chopped frozen spinach
2 tablespoons yellow (mellow)	1 (14-ounce / 397-g) can quartered artichoke hearts, drained

1. In a medium nonstick sauté pan or skillet over high heat, combine the onion, garlic, and water. Cook for 3 minutes, or until the onion is translucent and just beginning to brown. Transfer to a blender and add the cannellini beans, nutritional yeast, miso paste, tapioca starch, oat milk, and pumpkin. Purée until smooth. Set aside. 2. Return the pan to medium heat and add the spinach. Cook for 4 to 7 minutes, stirring, to thaw the spinach. 3. Stir in the purée mixture. Cook for 3 to 5 minutes, stirring occasionally, until the dip begins to bubble and thicken. Add the artichoke hearts and stir to combine. Serve warm. 4. You can also put the pan, if it's heat-safe, under the broiler for 1 to 2 minutes to give the top layer a little crust and char.

Per Serving:

calories: 147 | fat: 2g | protein: 12g | carbs: 23g | fiber: 9g

Skillet Spinach and Artichoke Dip

Prep time: 10 minutes | Cook time: 15 minutes | Serves 6

8 ounces (227 g) silken tofu	1 (12-ounce / 340-g) jar plain
½ cup soy milk	artichoke hearts, chopped
2 tablespoons chickpea flour	¼ cup nutritional yeast
¼ cup vegetable broth	2 teaspoons liquid aminos
10 ounces (283 g) frozen spinach	1 teaspoon onion powder
	1 teaspoon garlic powder

1. In a blender, combine the tofu, soy milk, and flour. Blend until smooth. 2. In a sauté pan, heat the broth over medium heat. Add the spinach, and bring to a simmer. Cover, and cook for 4 to 5 minutes. 3. Add the tofu mixture, artichoke hearts, nutritional yeast, liquid aminos, onion powder, and garlic powder. Simmer, stirring occasionally, for 5 to 7 minutes, or until thickened. Remove from the heat.

Per Serving:

calories: 143 | fat: 2g | protein: 12g | carbs: 20g | fiber: 11g

Sweet Potato and Black Bean Quesadillas

Prep time: 10 minutes | Cook time: 20 minutes | Serves 4 to 6

Black Bean Spread:	¼ teaspoon red miso paste
1 (15-ounce / 425-g) can black beans, drained and rinsed	⅛ teaspoon garlic powder
	Quesadillas:
2 to 4 tablespoons chopped fresh cilantro stems and leaves	1 pound (454 g) sweet potatoes, peeled and shredded
1 scallion, green and white parts, thinly sliced	4 to 6 (8-inch) whole-grain tortillas
1 tablespoon lime juice	Hot sauce, for serving
1 teaspoon chipotle hot sauce	

Make the Black Bean Spread: 1. In a small bowl, using a fork, mash the beans to a creamy texture. 2. Mix in the cilantro, scallion, lime juice, hot sauce, miso, and garlic powder. Make the Quesadillas: 3. Heat a large nonstick skillet over medium heat. 4. Put the sweet potatoes in the skillet, and cook, stirring every few minutes, for about 10 minutes, or until tender and browned. Transfer to a plate. 5. Wipe out the skillet, and return to the stove. 6. Divide the bean spread (about ¼ cup to 6 tablespoons per tortilla) among the tortillas, and spread evenly. 7. Divide the sweet potatoes (about ¼ cup per tortilla) onto half of each tortilla, fold in half, and press gently. 8. Place the tortillas in the hot skillet, and cook for 2 to 5 minutes per side, or until the tortillas are golden brown. Remove from the heat. 9. Serve the quesadillas with hot sauce.

Per Serving:

calories: 201 | fat: 1g | protein: 6g | carbs: 7g | fiber: 41g

Pump Up the Power Energy Balls

Prep time: 20 minutes | Cook time: 0 minutes | Makes 32 balls

1 cup old-fashioned oats	1 teaspoon ground cinnamon
¾ cup almond meal	¼ teaspoon ground nutmeg
⅓ cup wheat germ	½ cup dried currants
¼ cup flaxseed meal	½ cup peanut butter
¼ cup pepitas	⅓ cup maple syrup (optional)
2 tablespoons raw shelled hempseed	1 teaspoon vanilla extract
	¼ teaspoon salt (optional)

1. Mix the oats, almond meal, wheat germ, flaxseed meal, pepitas, hempseed, cinnamon, nutmeg, and currants together in a medium bowl. 2. Add the peanut butter, maple syrup, vanilla, and salt (if desired) to the bowl of a stand mixer. Mix on medium speed until well combined. Pour the dry ingredients into the wet mixture. Mix on low until well combined. 3. Roll into thirty-two balls.

Per Serving:(3 balls)

calories: 168 | fat: 8g | protein: 10g | carbs: 22g | fiber: 4g

Rainbow Veggie Protein Pinwheels

Prep time: 20 minutes | Cook time: 0 minutes | Serves 6

¼ cup hummus
¼ cup tempeh, crumbled in a food processor
2 large spinach tortillas
¼ cup thinly sliced red bell pepper
¼ cup thinly sliced yellow bell pepper
1 thinly sliced carrot
¼ cup thinly sliced purple cabbage

1. Mix together the hummus and tempeh. 2. Lay out tortillas. Spread hummus mixture in a thin layer over the whole surface of each tortilla stopping 1 inch from the edges. Lay a thin strip of each of the four vegetables, next to each other, over the hummus mixture. 3. Roll each tortilla tightly and cut crosswise into pinwheels. You can use toothpicks if needed, but the hummus helps them stick together at the edges.

Per Serving: (2 pinwheels)
calories: 66 | fat: 2g | protein: 9g | carbs: 8g | fiber: 4g

Lemon-Oatmeal Cacao Cookies

Prep time: 30 minutes | Cook time: 35 minutes | Makes 14 cookies

12 pitted Medjool dates	as needed (optional)
Boiling water, for soaking the dates	1½ cups old-fashioned oats
1 cup unsweetened applesauce	1 cup oat flour
1 tablespoon freshly squeezed lemon juice	¾ cup coarsely chopped walnuts
1 teaspoon vanilla extract	2 tablespoons lemon zest
1 tablespoon water, plus more	1 tablespoon cacao powder
	½ teaspoon baking soda

1. In a small bowl, combine the dates with enough boiling water to cover. Let sit for 15 to 20 minutes to soften. 2. While the dates soak, preheat the oven to 300ºF (150ºC). Line 2 baking sheets with parchment paper or silicone mats. 3. Drain the excess liquid from the dates and put them in a blender, along with the applesauce, lemon juice, and vanilla. Purée until a thick paste forms. Add water, 1 tablespoon at a time, if the mixture isn't getting smooth. 4. In a large bowl, stir together the oats, oat flour, walnuts, lemon zest, cacao powder, and baking soda. Pour in the date mixture and stir to combine. One at a time, scoop ¼-cup portions of dough, gently roll into a ball, and press down lightly on the prepared baking sheets. The cookie should be about 1 inch thick and roughly 3 inches in diameter. 5. Bake for 30 to 35 minutes, or until the tops of the cookies look crispy and dry. Transfer to a wire rack to cool. 6. Store in an airtight container at room temperature for up to 1 week.

Per Serving: (1 cookie)
calories: 174 | fat: 6g | protein: 4g | carbs: 30g | fiber: 4g

Strawberry Shortcake Rice Bites

Prep time: 20 minutes | Cook time: 25 minutes | Makes 8 balls

3 cups water	3 tablespoons fresh lemon juice
3 cups white sushi rice	½ teaspoon vanilla extract
½ cup coconut sugar (optional)	2 cups strawberries, hulled and

quartered
3 tablespoons chia seeds

Salt (optional)

1. Bring the water to a boil in a large saucepan, then lower the heat to medium-low and stir in the rice. Cook, stirring often, until soft, about 15 to 20 minutes. You want it to be moist (but not soggy) and very sticky and tender. 2. Transfer the cooked rice to a large bowl. Working quickly, add the sugar, lemon juice, and vanilla. Stir thoroughly to combine and allow to cool slightly. 3. Spread out a sushi mat or silicone liner. Cover with plastic wrap and spread 1 cup rice on top of the plastic. With wet hands, press the rice into a uniform ½-inch thick layer. 4. Place a row of strawberries, end to end, about 1 inch from the bottom edge. Sprinkle with 1 teaspoon chia seeds. Starting with the edge closest to you, roll the rice tightly into a cylinder, using the plastic wrap and mat to assist. Be sure to pull the plastic and mat away from the rice as you roll. Repeat with the remaining ingredients. 5. Sprinkle the outside of the rolls with salt to taste, if desired. Let sit for 5 minutes, then slice each roll into 8 to 10 pieces using a very sharp knife. Wrap tightly in parchment paper and plastic wrap if eating on the go. Refrigerate for up to 2 days or freeze individual pieces for up to 3 months. (If frozen, allow to thaw overnight before eating.)

Per Serving:
calories: 385 | fat: 2g | protein: 9g | carbs: 87g | fiber: 5g

Baked Vegetable Chips

Prep time: 20 minutes | Cook time: 35 minutes | Serves 2

1 pound (454 g) starchy root vegetables, such as russet potato, sweet potato, rutabaga, parsnip, red or golden beet, or taro	moisture
	1 teaspoon garlic powder
	1 teaspoon paprika
	½ teaspoon onion powder
1 pound (454 g) high-water vegetables, such as zucchini or summer squash	½ teaspoon freshly ground black pepper
Kosher salt, for absorbing	1 teaspoon avocado oil or other oil (optional)

1. Preheat the oven to 300ºF (150ºC). Line 2 baking sheets with parchment paper. Set aside. 2. Scrub the root vegetables well to remove the dirt. Wash and dry the high-water vegetables. 3. Using a mandoline or sharp kitchen knife, cut all the vegetables into ⅛-inch-thick slices. The thinner you slice them, the crispier they will be. 4. Place the sliced high-water vegetables on a clean kitchen towel or paper towel. Sprinkle with a generous amount of kosher salt, which draws out moisture. If you skip this step, your high-water vegetables won't crisp and will remain soggy after baking. Let sit for 15 minutes. Use a paper towel to dab off excess moisture and salt. 5. In a small bowl, stir together the garlic powder, paprika, onion powder, and pepper. 6. Transfer all the vegetables to the prepared baking sheets and place them in a single layer. Brush with oil, if using. Evenly sprinkle the spice mix on the prepared vegetables. 7. Bake for 15 minutes. Switch the pans between the oven racks and bake for 20 minutes more, or until the vegetables are darker in color and crispy on the edges. 8. Using a spatula, transfer the chips to a wire rack to cool. The baked chips will crisp within a few minutes of cooling.

Per Serving:
calories: 250 | fat: 3g | protein: 8g | carbs: 51g | fiber: 6g

Over-the-Top Bars to Go

Prep time: 20 minutes | Cook time: 15 minutes | Makes 16 squares

1½ cups old-fashioned oats
½ cup pecans
½ cup pistachios
½ cup cashews
½ cup dried cranberries
¼ cup dates, pitted and chopped
¼ cup sunflower seed kernels
¼ cup pepitas
2 tablespoons raw shelled hempseed
½ cup peanut butter
½ cup brown rice syrup
3 tablespoons maple syrup (optional)

1. Line an 8-inch square baking dish with parchment paper and come up about 3 inches on opposite sides. This will act as a handle to remove the bars from the dish. 2. Mix all the ingredients except the peanut butter and the syrups together in a large bowl. Add the peanut butter and start to mix in with a wooden spoon, and then use your hands to mix and pinch so that the peanut butter is well incorporated into the dry ingredients. 3. Add the brown rice syrup and maple syrup (if desired) to a small saucepan. Bring to a boil and cook to hard ball stage, 260°F (127°C), on a candy thermometer. Pour the syrups over the oat mixture and stir well. Then quickly spread the mixture into the prepared dish. It will cool quickly, so you can use your fingertips to press down into the dish as evenly as possible. You can also use the bottom of a measuring cup to press down firmly. Refrigerate for at least 30 minutes. 4. Grab the "handles" of the parchment paper and lift out of the dish. Place on a cutting board and slice into sixteen squares.

Per Serving: (2 squares)
calories: 352 | fat: 22g | protein: 14g | carbs: 33g | fiber: 7g

Slow Cooker Versatile Seitan Balls

Prep time: 15 minutes | Cook time: 6 hours | Makes 34 balls

1½ cups vital wheat gluten
½ cup chickpea flour
1 tablespoon mushroom powder
½ teaspoon dried oregano
½ teaspoon onion powder
¼ teaspoon garlic powder
¼ teaspoon nutmeg
¼ teaspoon ground ginger
¼ teaspoon ground cloves
¼ teaspoon ground sage
½ teaspoon salt (optional)
½ cup tomato sauce, divided
1 teaspoon liquid smoke
1½ cups vegetable broth, divided

1. Mix the gluten, flour, mushroom powder, oregano, onion and garlic powders, nutmeg, ginger, cloves, sage, and salt (if desired) in a large bowl. 2. In a small bowl, add ¼ cup tomato sauce, ¼ cup water, liquid smoke, and ½ cup vegetable broth. Mix well. 3. Make a well in the center of the dry ingredients and pour in the tomato sauce mixture. Mix well and start to knead. Knead for 1 minute or until the dough becomes mildly elastic. You will see the dough slightly pull back as you are kneading and it will be a bit sticky. Pour remaining ¼ cup tomato sauce, 1 cup vegetable broth, and 3 cups water into the slow cooker. Stir. 4. Tear off small chunks of the dough, squeeze into a round shape, and drop into the liquid in the slow cooker. There will be forty-four balls. You can also make seventeen larger balls and cut them after cooking and cooling. Or make two logs and cut into desired shapes. Cover and cook on low for 4 to 6 hours. They will grow in size as they cook. Check at 4 hours and see if you like

the texture. They will become firmer as they sit in the refrigerator. 5. Remove from the pot and let cool. Store in the refrigerator for up to 5 days or freeze for up to 4 months.

Per Serving: (½ cup)
calories: 161 | fat: 1g | protein: 30g | carbs: 10g | fiber: 2g

Miso Nori Chips

Prep time: 10 minutes | Cook time: 15 minutes | Makes 48 chips

6 tablespoons almond or cashew butter
¼ cup unpasteurized chickpea miso or sweet white miso
4 teaspoons mirin
1 tablespoon melted extra-
virgin coconut oil (optional)
1 tablespoon filtered water
8 sheets nori
½ cup raw unhulled sesame seeds, toasted

1. Preheat the oven to 300°F (150°C). Line a rimmed baking sheet with parchment paper and set aside. 2. Combine the nut butter, miso, mirin, oil, and water in a small bowl and stir until smooth. Place one sheet of nori on a cutting board, top with 3 tablespoons of the miso mixture, and spread it evenly over the nori, all the way to the edges. Sprinkle with 2 tablespoons of the sesame seeds, top with another sheet of nori, and press to seal. Cut the stacked nori lengthwise in half and cut each half crosswise into 6 strips, to get 12 pieces. Arrange on the baking sheet and repeat with the remaining nori and miso mixture. 3. Bake for 10 to 15 minutes, until the nori is crinkled; the chips will crisp up as they cool. Remove from the oven and allow to cool. Store the chips in an airtight container for up to 2 weeks.

Per Serving: (2 chips)
calories: 50 | fat: 4g | protein: 1g | carbs: 3g | fiber: 1g

Pepita and Almond Squares

Prep time: 20 minutes | Cook time: 15 minutes | Makes 16 squares

1 cup almonds, coarsely chopped
1 cup old-fashioned oats
⅔ cup pepitas
⅔ cup dried cranberries
½ cup unsweetened shredded
coconut
¼ cup raw shelled hempseed
⅓ cup peanut butter
⅔ cup brown rice syrup
¼ cup maple syrup (optional)
2 teaspoons vanilla extract

1. Line an 8-inch square baking dish with parchment paper and come up about 3 inches on opposite sides. This will act as a handle to remove the squares from the dish. 2. In a large mixing bowl, add the almonds, oats, pepitas, cranberries, coconut, and hempseed. Mix well. Stir in the peanut butter and try to get it evenly combined. You can use your fingers when most of it is worked in. 3. Add the brown rice syrup, maple syrup (if desired), and vanilla to a small saucepan. Bring to a boil and continue boiling until it reaches the hard ball stage, 260°F (127°C), on a candy thermometer. When this temperature is reached, quickly pour over the almond mixture and stir well. It will start to harden up quickly. Pour into the prepared dish and press down firmly into the dish and as evenly as possible. Refrigerate for at least 30 minutes. 4. Grab the "handles" of the parchment paper and lift out of the dish. Place on a cutting sheet and slice into sixteen squares.

Per Serving: (2 squares)
calories: 198 | fat: 11g | protein: 12g | carbs: 22g | fiber: 4g

Steamed Seitan Smoky Nuggets

Prep time: 10 minutes | Cook time: 40 minutes | Serves 4

¾ cup vital wheat gluten
¼ cup plus 2 tablespoons chickpea flour
2 teaspoons garlic powder
2 teaspoons onion powder
½ cup vegetable broth

2 tablespoons tomato sauce
1 tablespoon tamari
1 teaspoon liquid smoke
½ teaspoon coconut oil (optional)

1. Add the gluten, flour, and garlic and onion powders to a large bowl. 2. Add the broth, tomato sauce, tamari, liquid smoke, and oil (if desired) to a small bowl and mix well. Pour the liquid into the dry ingredients and mix. Knead for 2 minutes until elastic. You will see it pull back into a rounder shape as you knead. This is a firm dough and will not double in size while cooking. 3. Add 5 cups water to a saucepan. Bring to a boil. Place a steamer basket inside the pan and turn down the heat to simmer. 4. Use a pastry cutter to slice off irregular pieces. You can squeeze them into a ball, as best you can, or leave chunky. You can also steam as one log and cut into chunks after steaming and cooling. 5. Steam for 40 minutes. 6. Remove the seitan to cool and store in the refrigerator for up to 5 days or in the freezer for up to 4 months.

Per Serving: (½ cup)
calories: 234 | fat: 2g | protein: 31g | carbs:12 g | fiber: 2g

Simple Hummus

Prep time: 5 minutes | Cook time: 0 minutes | Makes about 2 cups

1 (15-ounce / 425-g) can chickpeas, drained and rinsed
¼ cup extra-virgin olive oil, plus more for drizzling (optional)
3 tablespoons fresh lemon juice

(from 1 lemon)
½ cup tahini
3 garlic cloves
1 teaspoon ground cumin
½ teaspoon sea salt (optional)
Dash of paprika

1. In a food processor or blender, pulse the chickpeas until chopped. Add ¼ cup oil (if using), the lemon juice, tahini, garlic, cumin, and salt (if using) and process or blend until smooth. Stop to scrape down the sides as needed. 2. Transfer the hummus to a bowl, then drizzle with oil (if using) and throw on a dash of paprika.

Per Serving:
calories: 772 | fat: 59g | protein: 20g | carbs: 48g | fiber: 14g

Choco Almond Bars

Prep time: 10 minutes | Cook time: 15 minutes | Makes 4 bars

1 cup raw and unsalted almonds
5 pitted dates
1 scoop soy protein isolate,

chocolate flavor
Optional Toppings:
Shredded coconut
Cocoa powder

1. Preheat the oven to 257ºF (125ºC) and line a baking sheet with parchment paper. 2. Put the almonds on the baking sheet and roast them for about 10 to 15 minutes or until they're fragrant. 3. Meanwhile, cover the dates with water in a small bowl and let them sit for about 10 minutes. Drain the dates after soaking and make sure no water is left. 4. Take the almonds out of the oven and let them cool down for about 5 minutes. 5. Add all the ingredients to a food processor and blend into a chunky mixture. 6. Alternatively, add all ingredients to a medium bowl, cover it, and process using a handheld blender. 7. Line a loaf pan with parchment paper. Add the almond mixture to the loaf pan, spread it out and press it down firmly until it is 1 inch (2.5 cm) thick all over. 8. Divide into 4 bars, serve cold with the optional toppings and enjoy! 9. Store the bars in an airtight container in the fridge and consume within 4 days. Alternatively, store in the freezer for a maximum of 90 days and thaw at room temperature.

Per Serving:
calories: 254 | fat: 18g | protein: 16g | carbs: 8g | fiber: 4g

White Bean Caponata

Prep time: 10 minutes | Cook time: 0 minutes | Serves 4 to 6

¼ cup dry-packed, oil-free sun-dried tomatoes
1 (15-ounce / 425-g) can reduced-sodium white beans, drained and rinsed
½ cup unsweetened raisins
¼ cup grated carrot

¼ cup water-packed roasted red pepper
¼ cup green olives with pimentos
3 tablespoon red-wine vinegar
2 tablespoons pine nuts, toasted
2 tablespoons capers, drained

1. In a small bowl, cover the sun-dried tomatoes with water, and let sit for 5 to 7 minutes, or until soft. Drain, and chop the tomatoes. 2. In a medium bowl, combine the sun-dried tomatoes, beans, raisins, carrot, roasted red pepper, olives, vinegar, pine nuts, and capers. Using a wooden spoon or spatula, mix gently.

Per Serving:
calories: 182 | fat: 4g | protein: 8g | carbs: 32g | fiber: 7g

Peanut Butter Snack Squares

Prep time: 10 minutes | Cook time: 20 minutes | Serves 8

½ cup coconut sugar (optional)
1 cup creamy peanut butter
1 teaspoon vanilla extract
¾ cup whole wheat flour
¼ cup garbanzo flour
1 teaspoon baking soda

½ teaspoon baking powder
1 cup old-fashioned oats
½ cup dairy-free milk
½ cup peanuts
½ cup dates, pitted and chopped small

1. Preheat the oven to 350ºF (180ºC). Lightly grease an 8-inch square baking dish. 2. Mix the sugar (if desired) and peanut butter with a hand or stand mixer on medium speed for 5 minutes. Mix in the vanilla. Add the flours, baking soda, and baking powder and mix on medium speed. Add the oats and mix for a few seconds. This will be stiff. Add the milk and mix on medium until just combined. 3. Fold in the peanuts and dates and make sure everything is well incorporated. 4. You can use your hands to press the dough lightly into the prepared dish. Bake for 15 to 20 minutes or until lightly golden brown. 5. Place on a wire rack to cool. Cut into sixteen squares and store in the refrigerator.

Per Serving: (2 squares)
calories: 366 | fat: 17g | protein: 14g | carbs: 44g | fiber: 7g

Basic Oil-Free Hummus

Prep time: 10 minutes | Cook time: 0 minutes | Makes 1½ cups

1 (15-ounce / 425-g) can chickpeas, drained and rinsed
1 tablespoon tahini
¼ teaspoon garlic powder
¼ teaspoon ground cumin

¼ cup lemon juice
1/16 teaspoon cayenne
¼ teaspoon za'atar

1. In a food processor, combine the chickpeas, tahini, garlic powder, cumin, lemon juice, cayenne, and za'atar. Process until smooth and creamy.
Per Serving:
calories: 136 | fat: 6g | protein: 3g | carbs: 21g | fiber: 3g

Homemade Hummus

Prep time: 10 minutes | Cook time: 0 minutes | Makes 2 cups

1 (15-ounce / 425-g) can chickpeas, drained and rinsed
2 cloves garlic
¼ cup tahini
2 tablespoons lemon juice

3 tablespoons water
1 teaspoon ground cumin
Salt, to taste (optional)

1. In a food processor or blender, blend all the ingredients on high until completely smooth.
Per Serving: (½ cup)
calories: 183 | fat: 10g | protein: 8g | carbs: 19g | fiber: 6g

Chapter 9 Stews and Soups

Coconut Curry Soup

Prep time: 25 minutes | Cook time: 20 minutes | Serves 6

3 tablespoons water
¾ cup diced red, white, or yellow onion
1½ teaspoons minced garlic
1 cup diced green or red bell pepper
1 (14½-ounce / 411-g) can diced tomatoes with their juices
1 (15-ounce / 425-g) can chickpeas, drained and rinsed
4 cups vegetable broth

1½ teaspoons ground cumin
2½ teaspoons curry powder
1 (13½-ounce / 383-g) can full-fat coconut milk
½ cup cooked brown rice
Salt and pepper, to taste (optional)
Optional Toppings:
Red chili flakes
Minced cilantro

1. In a large pot, heat the water over medium heat. 2. Add the onion, garlic, and bell pepper. Cook, stirring occasionally, for 5 minutes or until the veggies are tender. 3. Add the tomatoes, chickpeas, broth, cumin, and curry powder. Bring to a boil. Reduce the heat to low and simmer gently, stirring occasionally, for 10 minutes. 4. Add the coconut milk and brown rice and cook for 5 minutes, stirring occasionally. 5. Add salt (if desired) and pepper.
Per Serving:
calories: 126 | fat: 2g | protein: 5g | carbs: 24g | fiber: 6g

Vegetable Goulash

Prep time: 5 minutes | Cook time: 25 minutes | Serves 4 to 6

4 cups vegetable broth
4 cups diced (½-inch) yellow potatoes
2 cups frozen carrots
2 tablespoons tomato paste
½ cup chopped water-packed roasted red pepper
¼ cup sweet paprika
1 teaspoon whole caraway

seeds
3 strips dried porcini mushrooms, chopped (about 2 tablespoons)
1 tablespoon onion powder
½ teaspoon garlic powder
2 teaspoons dried parsley
½ teaspoon smoked paprika
1 bay leaf

1. In a large Dutch oven or saucepan, combine the broth, potatoes, carrots, tomato paste, roasted red pepper, sweet paprika, caraway, mushrooms, onion powder, garlic powder, parsley, smoked paprika, and bay leaf. Bring to a boil over high heat. 2. Reduce the heat to low. Cover, and simmer for 15 to 20 minutes, or until the potatoes are tender and a knife slides in easily. Remove from the heat. 3. Remove the bay leaf, and serve.
Per Serving:
calories: 295 | fat: 2g | protein: 14g | carbs: 55g | fiber: 10g

Minty Beet and Sweet Potato Soup

Prep time: 10 minutes | Cook time: 40 minutes | Makes 6 bowls

5 cups water, or salt-free vegetable broth (if salted, omit the sea salt below)
1 to 2 teaspoons olive oil or vegetable broth
1 cup chopped onion
3 garlic cloves, minced
1 tablespoon thyme, fresh or dried
1 to 2 teaspoons paprika
2 cups peeled and chopped beets

2 cups peeled and chopped sweet potato
2 cups peeled and chopped parsnips
½ teaspoon sea salt (optional)
1 cup fresh mint, chopped
½ avocado, or 2 tablespoons nut or seed butter (optional)
2 tablespoons balsamic vinegar (optional)
2 tablespoons pumpkin seeds

1. In large pot, boil the water. 2. In another large pot, warm the olive oil (if using) and sauté the onion and garlic until softened, about 5 minutes. 3. Add the thyme, paprika, beets, sweet potato, and parsnips, along with the boiling water and salt (if using). Cover and leave to gently boil for about 30 minutes, or until the vegetables are soft. 4. Set aside a little mint for a garnish and add the rest, along with the avocado (if using). Stir until well combined. 5. Transfer the soup to a blender or use an immersion blender to purée, adding the balsamic vinegar (if using). 6. Serve topped with fresh mint and pumpkin seeds, and maybe chunks of the other half of the avocado, if you used it.
Per Serving:(1 bowl)
calories: 157 | fat: 5g | protein: 3g | carbs: 26g | fiber: 6g

Four-Can Chili

Prep time: 5 minutes | Cook time: 30 minutes | Serves 6

1 (28-ounce / 794-g) can crushed tomatoes
1 (15-ounce / 425-g) can low-sodium black beans
1 (15-ounce / 425-g) can low-sodium cannellini beans
1 (15-ounce / 425-g) can low-

sodium chickpeas
1 tablespoon chili powder
1 teaspoon garlic powder
1 teaspoon onion powder
½ teaspoon ground cumin
½ teaspoon red pepper flakes (optional)

1. In a large stockpot, combine the tomatoes, black beans, cannellini beans, and chickpeas and their liquids with the chili powder, garlic powder, onion powder, cumin, and red pepper flakes, if using. Bring the chili to a boil over medium-high heat. 2. Cover, reduce the heat to medium-low, simmer for 25 minutes, and serve.
Per Serving:
calories: 185 | fat: 1g | protein: 11g | carbs: 33g | fiber: 13g

Root Vegetable Soup

Prep time: 15 minutes | Cook time: 30 minutes | Makes 3 quarts

2 tablespoons extra-virgin coconut oil (optional)
1 medium yellow onion, diced
3 large garlic cloves, finely chopped
2 teaspoons fine sea salt, plus more to taste (optional)
4½ pounds (2 kg) parsnips,

sweet potatoes, or other root vegetables, peeled and cut into 1-inch dice
6 bay leaves
6 cups filtered water, or as needed
Freshly ground black pepper
Tamari (optional)

1. Warm the oil in a large pot over medium-high heat. Add the onion and cook for 6 to 8 minutes, until beginning to brown. Stir in the garlic and salt, if using, and cook for 3 to 4 minutes, until the garlic is golden and fragrant. Add the root vegetables, bay leaves, and water (the water should almost cover the vegetables), raise the heat, and bring to a boil; then cover the pot, reduce the heat to low, and simmer for 15 minutes, or until the vegetables are cooked through. Test by inserting a fork into a vegetable cube; it should glide in easily. Remove the bay leaves (compost them). Stir in pepper to taste and let the soup cool slightly. 2. Working in batches, scoop the soup into an upright blender (filling it no more than two-thirds full). Puree on high speed until smooth and velvety, adding water if necessary to get the desired consistency, then pour into a large bowl or another large pot. Season to taste with more salt and pepper, and with tamari, if using, and serve warm. Store leftover soup in jars in the fridge for up to 5 days, or freeze for up to 3 months.
Per Serving: (1 quart)
calories: 304 | fat: 6g | protein: 4g | carbs: 63g | fiber: 17g

Zucchini Soup

Prep time: 10 minutes | Cook time: 25 minutes | Makes 2 quarts

2 tablespoons extra-virgin coconut oil (optional)
1 medium yellow onion, diced
2 large garlic cloves, finely chopped
1½ teaspoons fine sea salt, plus

more to taste (optional)
8 medium-large zucchini, cut into 1-inch pieces
3¼ cups filtered water
Freshly ground black pepper
Tamari (optional)

1. Warm the oil in a large pot over medium-high heat. Add the onion and cook for 6 to 8 minutes, until beginning to brown. Stir in the garlic and salt, if using, and cook for 3 to 4 minutes, until the garlic is golden and fragrant. Add the zucchini and water, raise the heat, and bring a boil. Cover the pot, reduce the heat to low, and simmer for 8 to 10 minutes, until the zucchini is tender, pressing it down into the liquid a couple of times during cooking to ensure that it cooks evenly. Test by pressing a piece of zucchini against the side of the pot; it should crush easily. Remove from the heat and set aside to cool slightly. 2. Scoop out 2 cups of the liquid and set aside. Season the soup with pepper. Working in batches, scoop the soup into an upright blender (filling it no more than two-thirds full) and puree on high speed until smooth and velvety, adding some of the reserved cooking liquid if necessary to reach the desired consistency, then pour into a large bowl or another large pot. Season to taste with more salt and pepper, and with tamari, if using, and serve warm. Store leftover soup in jars in the fridge for up to 4 days or freeze for up to

3 months.
Per Serving: (1 quart)
calories: 153 | fat: 14g | protein: 2g | carbs: 8g | fiber: 2g

Lentil Soup with Cauliflower, Potatoes and Spinach

Prep time: 25 minutes | Cook time: 1 hour | Serves 8 to 10

1 large onion, peeled and chopped
6 cloves garlic, peeled and minced
2 bay leaves
2 teaspoons curry powder, or to taste
½ teaspoon turmeric
Pinch ground nutmeg
1 (15-ounce / 425-g) can diced tomatoes
1 cup green lentils, rinsed

2 large waxy potatoes, scrubbed and cut into ½-inch dice
1 small head cauliflower, cut into florets
6 cups finely chopped spinach leaves
2 tablespoons minced cilantro
Zest and juice of 1 lemon
Salt and freshly ground black pepper, to taste

1. Place the onions in a large pot and sauté over medium for 10 minutes. Add water 1 to 2 tablespoons at a time to keep the onion from sticking to the pot. Add the garlic and cook for 1 minute. Add the bay leaves, curry powder, turmeric, and nutmeg and cook for 1 minute. Stir in the tomatoes and cook for 3 minutes. Add the lentils and 6 cups of water and bring to a boil over high heat. Reduce the heat to medium and cook, covered, for 30 minutes. Add the potatoes and cauliflower and cook until the lentils are tender, about 15 more minutes. 2. Stir in the spinach, cilantro, and lemon zest and juice. Season with salt and pepper.
Per Serving:
calories: 130 | fat: 0g | protein: 7g | carbs: 25g | fiber: 5g

Curried Cauliflower Bisque

Prep time: 15 minutes | Cook time: 1 hour | Serves 4

1 large onion, peeled and diced
2 teaspoons grated ginger
1 jalapeño pepper, minced (for less heat, remove the seeds)
2 cloves garlic, peeled and minced
1½ teaspoons curry powder

1 large head cauliflower, cut into florets
4 cups vegetable stock, or low-sodium vegetable broth
¼ cup chopped cilantro
4 green onions (white and green parts), thinly sliced

1. Place the onion in a large saucepan and sauté over medium heat for 10 minutes. Add water 1 to 2 tablespoons at a time to keep the onion from sticking to the pan. Add the ginger, jalapeño pepper, garlic, and curry powder and cook for 30 seconds. Add the cauliflower and vegetable stock and bring the pot to a boil over high heat. Reduce the heat to medium and cook, covered, for 20 to 25 minutes, or until the cauliflower is tender. 2. Purée the soup using an immersion blender or in batches in a blender with a tight-fitting lid, covered with a towel to avoid splatter. Return to the pot and season with salt and pepper. Serve garnished with the cilantro and green onions.
Per Serving:
calories: 58 | fat: 0g | protein: 2g | carbs: 13g | fiber: 3g

Broccoli and "Cheddar" Soup

Prep time: 10 minutes | Cook time: 30 minutes | Serves 4

4 cups peeled and diced butternut squash
2 sweet potatoes, peeled and diced (about 2 cups)
1 small yellow onion, peeled and halved
2 garlic cloves, peeled
4 cups water

2 teaspoons salt (optional)
1 (13-ounce / 369-g) can light unsweetened coconut milk
1 tablespoon red miso paste
3 tablespoons nutritional yeast
1 tablespoon tapioca flour
3 cups frozen broccoli

1. In a large pot, combine the butternut squash, sweet potatoes, onion, garlic, and water and bring to a boil over high heat. Lower the heat to medium-low and cook until fork-tender, about 20 minutes. 2. Transfer the mixture (including the liquid) to a blender and purée until smooth. You may need to do this in batches. 3. Return the soup to the pot and add the salt (if using), coconut milk, red miso, nutritional yeast, tapioca flour, and broccoli and cook over medium heat, stirring often, until heated through, about 10 minutes.

Per Serving:
calories: 353 | fat: 20g | protein: 8g | carbs: 42g | fiber: 9g

Moroccan-Inspired Chickpea Stew

Prep time: 20 minutes | Cook time: 30 minutes | Serves 4

1 tablespoon Hungarian paprika
1 teaspoon smoked paprika
1 teaspoon ground cumin
1 teaspoon onion powder
1 large yellow onion, coarsely chopped
4 garlic cloves, diced
1 tablespoon water, plus more as needed
2 carrots, diced
1 tablespoon pure maple syrup (optional)
1 (28-ounce / 794-g) can crushed tomatoes
½ cup packed chopped fresh cilantro
1 (15-ounce /425-g) can chickpeas, drained and rinsed
1 (15-ounce /425-g) dark red kidney beans, drained and rinsed
Juice of ½ lime

1. In a small bowl, stir together the Hungarian paprika, smoked paprika, cumin, and onion powder. Set aside. 2. In an 8-quart pot over high heat, combine the onion, garlic, and 1 tablespoon of water. Turn the heat to medium-low. Cook for at least 10 minutes, stirring occasionally. Add more water, 1 tablespoon at a time, to prevent burning, until the onion is deeply browned. 3. Stir in the carrots. Turn the heat to high. 4. Stir in the paprika mixture and cook for 30 seconds, stirring continuously to prevent burning. Pour in the maple syrup (if using) and cook for 30 seconds more, stirring. 5. Carefully pour in the tomatoes with their juices. To avoid splatter, pour the tomatoes onto a spoon and not directly into the hot pot. Bring to a simmer, stirring, then turn the heat to low, cover the pot, and cook for 10 minutes. 6. Stir in the cilantro, chickpeas, and kidney beans. Cover the pot and cook for 5 minutes more to warm. 7. Sprinkle with lime juice before serving. 8. Enjoy this stew as is or top as desired. I like coarsely chopped cilantro leaves, scallion greens, and jalapeño pepper.

Per Serving:
calories: 331 | fat: 3g | protein: 17g | carbs: 65g | fiber: 15g

Lentil Soup

Prep time: 5 minutes | Cook time: 25 minutes | Serves 2 to 4

4 cups vegetable broth
1 cup dried green or brown lentils, rinsed
2 teaspoon onion powder
1 teaspoon dried parsley

½ teaspoon ground cumin
½ teaspoon smoked paprika
¼ teaspoon garlic powder
¼ teaspoon ground coriander
1 bay leaf

1. In a Dutch oven or saucepan, combine the broth, lentils, onion powder, parsley, cumin, paprika, garlic powder, coriander, and bay leaf. Bring to a boil over high heat. 2. Reduce the heat to medium-low. Cover, and simmer for 20 minutes, or until the lentils are tender. Remove from the heat. 3. Remove the bay leaf, and serve immediately.

Per Serving:
calories: 100 | fat: 3g | protein: 11g | carbs: 7g | fiber: 1g

Creamy Jalapeño Corn Chowder

Prep time: 15 minutes | Cook time: 35 minutes | Serves 4

2 teaspoons virgin olive oil (optional)
1 medium yellow onion, small diced
1 stalk celery, small diced
1 small red bell pepper, small diced
2 teaspoons minced fresh thyme leaves
½ teaspoon smoked paprika
½ teaspoon Old Bay seasoning or celery salt
1 jalapeño pepper, seeded and

minced
1 clove garlic, minced
1 pound (454 g) new potatoes, diced
3 cups fresh or frozen corn kernels
Salt and pepper, to taste (optional)
4 cups low-sodium vegetable stock
2 teaspoons white wine vinegar
Chopped chives, for garnish

1. Heat the olive oil in a large soup pot over medium heat. Add the onions, and sauté until soft and translucent, about 4 minutes. 2. Add the celery and red pepper and stir. Add the thyme, paprika, Old Bay, and jalapeño. Sauté the vegetables and spices until the celery is soft and the spices are fragrant, about 1 minute. Add the garlic and cook until fragrant, 30 seconds. 3. Add the potatoes and corn, and stir to coat in the spices and oil, if using. Season everything generously with salt and pepper, if using. Pour the vegetable stock over the vegetables. Cover and bring to a boil. Lower the heat and simmer until the potatoes are quite tender, about 25 minutes. 4. Carefully ladle half of the soup into a blender. Place the lid on top and slowly bring the speed up to high. Blend until you have a smooth and creamy purée. Add the puréed soup back to the pot and stir to combine into one unified chowder. Add the white wine vinegar and stir once more. 5. Check the soup for seasoning and adjust if necessary. Serve the chowder hot with the chopped chives on top.

Per Serving:
calories: 333 | fat: 5g | protein: 10g | carbs: 69g | fiber: 10g

Chipotle Pumpkin Chili with Tempeh and Beer

Prep time: 15 minutes | Cook time: 35 minutes | Serves 6

1 tablespoon virgin olive oil (optional)	pumpkin or butternut squash or sweet potatoes
1 large onion, chopped	2 cups cooked black beans
3 cloves garlic, minced	1 block (8 ounces / 227 g)
3 to 5 canned chipotles in adobo, chopped	tempeh, finely chopped or crumbled
2 teaspoons ground cumin	1 can (28 ounces / 794 g)
2 teaspoons chili powder	crushed tomatoes
1 teaspoon ground coriander	Salt and pepper, to taste
1 tablespoon unsweetened cocoa powder	(optional)
1 cup beer or vegetable stock or water	Serve:
	Chopped fresh cilantro leaves
2 cups peeled and chopped	Diced ripe avocado

1. Heat the olive oil in a large pot over medium heat. Add the onions and sauté until translucent, about 3 minutes. 2. Add the garlic, chipotles, cumin, chili powder, coriander, and cocoa powder to the pot and stir. Keep stirring until the garlic is very fragrant, about 30 seconds. The pot should look quite dry. 3. Pour the beer into the pot, and start scraping up any bits from the bottom. Add the chopped pumpkin, black beans, tempeh, and tomatoes. Stir to combine. Season the chili liberally with salt and pepper, if using. Stir one more time. 4. Cover and bring to a boil. Lower the heat to a simmer. Cook the chili, covered, for 30 to 35 minutes or until the pieces of pumpkin are tender. Stir the chili occasionally. 5. Serve the chili hot with chopped cilantro and diced avocado

Per Serving:
calories: 233 | fat: 7g | protein: 14g | carbs: 32g | fiber: 8g

Bean and Bulgur Chili

Prep time: 10 minutes | Cook time: 25 minutes | Serves 4 to 6

1 (28-ounce / 794-g) can crushed fire-roasted tomatoes	½ cup vegetable broth or water
1 (15-ounce / 425-g) can kidney beans, drained and rinsed	2 tablespoons chili powder
	1 tablespoon onion powder
1 (15-ounce / 425-g) can pinto beans, drained and rinsed	1 teaspoon paprika
	1 teaspoon ground cumin
1 (14-ounce / 397-g) can diced fire-roasted tomatoes	½ teaspoon garlic powder
	½ teaspoon dried oregano
1 (4-ounce / 113-g) can green chiles	¼ teaspoon freshly ground black pepper
½ cup medium-grind red bulgur	⅛ teaspoon cayenne
	¼ cup lime juice
	½ cup packed fresh cilantro, chopped

1. In a large Dutch oven or saucepan, combine the crushed tomatoes, kidney beans, pinto beans, diced tomatoes, chiles, bulgur, broth, chili powder, onion powder, paprika, cumin, garlic powder, oregano, pepper, and cayenne. Bring to a boil over high heat. 2. Reduce the heat to low. Cover, and simmer, stirring occasionally, for 20 to 25 minutes, or until the chili is fragrant and cooked through. Remove from the heat. 3. Stir in the lime juice and cilantro. Serve immediately.

Per Serving:
calories: 254 | fat: 2g | protein: 10g | carbs: 54g | fiber: 16g

Sick Day Soup

Prep time: 15 minutes | Cook time: 25 minutes | Serves 6

3 tablespoons water	5 cups vegetable broth
½ cup diced red, white, or yellow onion	4 to 5 tablespoons lemon juice
	1 (14-ounce / 397-g) block
2 carrots, thinly sliced	extra-firm tofu, pressed and cut into ½-inch cubes
2 ribs celery, thinly sliced	
⅓ cup grated or finely chopped ginger	⅓ cup hot sauce
	1 (8-ounce / 227-g) package
8 cloves garlic, peeled and halved	rice noodles

1. In a large pot over medium-high heat, heat the water. 2. Add the onion, carrots, celery, ginger, and garlic and cook for 10 minutes or until the onion is tender and translucent. 3. Add the broth, lemon juice, tofu, and hot sauce. 4. Add the noodles and cook for the amount of time suggested on the package.

Per Serving:
calories: 131 | fat: 5g | protein: 9g | carbs: 16g | fiber: 1g

Indian Red Split Lentil Soup

Prep time: 5 minutes | Cook time: 50 minutes | Makes 4 bowls

1 cup red split lentils	potato
2 cups water	1 cup sliced zucchini
1 teaspoon curry powder plus 1 tablespoon, divided, or 5 coriander seeds (optional)	Freshly ground black pepper, to taste
	Sea salt, to taste (optional)
1 teaspoon coconut oil, or 1 tablespoon water or vegetable broth	3 to 4 cups vegetable stock or water
1 red onion, diced	1 to 2 teaspoons toasted sesame oil (optional)
1 tablespoon minced fresh ginger	1 bunch spinach, chopped
2 cups peeled and cubed sweet	Toasted sesame seeds

1. Put the lentils in a large pot with 2 cups water, and 1 teaspoon of the curry powder. Bring the lentils to a boil, then reduce the heat and simmer, covered, for about 10 minutes, until the lentils are soft. 2. Meanwhile, heat a large pot over medium heat. Add the coconut oil (if using) and sauté the onion and ginger until soft, about 5 minutes. Add the sweet potato and leave it on the heat about 10 minutes to soften slightly, then add the zucchini and cook until it starts to look shiny, about 5 minutes. Add the remaining 1 tablespoon curry powder, pepper, and salt (if using), and stir the vegetables to coat. 3. Add the vegetable stock, bring to a boil, then turn down to simmer and cover. Let the vegetables slowly cook for 20 to 30 minutes, or until the sweet potato is tender. 4. Add the fully cooked lentils to the soup. Add another pinch salt, the toasted sesame oil (if using), and the spinach. Stir, allowing the spinach to wilt before removing the pot from the heat. 5. Serve garnished with toasted sesame seeds.

Per Serving: (1 bowl)
calories: 238 | fat: 3g | protein: 15g | carbs: 38g | fiber: 9g

Cauliflower, Chickpea, Quinoa, and Coconut Curry

Prep time: 15 minutes | Cook time: 3 to 4 hours | Serves 5 to 7

1 head cauliflower, cut into bite-size pieces (about 4 cups)
1 medium onion, diced
3 garlic cloves, minced
1 medium sweet potato (about ⅓ pound / 136 g), peeled and diced
1 (14½-ounce / 411-g) can chickpeas, drained and rinsed
1 (28-ounce / 794-g) can no-salt-added diced tomatoes
¼ cup store-bought low-sodium vegetable broth
¼ cup quinoa, rinsed
2 (15-ounce / 425-g) cans full-fat coconut milk
1 (1-inch) piece fresh ginger, peeled and minced
2 teaspoons ground turmeric
2 teaspoons garam masala
1 teaspoon ground cumin
1 teaspoon curry powder
Ground black pepper
Salt (optional)
½ bunch cilantro, coarsely chopped (optional)

1. Put the cauliflower, onion, garlic, sweet potato, chickpeas, tomatoes, broth, quinoa, coconut milk, ginger, turmeric, garam masala, cumin, curry powder, pepper, and salt (if using) in the slow cooker. 2. Cover and cook on High for 3 to 4 hours or on Low for 7 to 8 hours. At the end of cooking, stir in the cilantro (if using), reserving a couple of tablespoons to garnish each dish.
Per Serving:
calories: 503 | fat: 32g | protein: 11g | carbs: 48g | fiber: 12g

Savory Split Pea Soup

Prep time: 15 minutes | Cook time: 1 hour 30 minutes | Makes 6 bowls

¼ cup white wine, or vegetable stock, or water
1 onion, chopped
1 to 2 garlic cloves, minced
1 cup split peas
2 bay leaves
1 tablespoon dried thyme
1 tablespoon dried oregano
3 to 4 cups water or salt-free vegetable stock
1 large carrot or zucchini, chopped (optional)
1 tablespoon miso, or tamari, or ¼ teaspoon sea salt
Pinch freshly ground black pepper
2 tablespoons nutritional yeast (optional)
¼ cup sun-dried tomatoes or olives, chopped
¼ cup cherry tomatoes, chopped
2 tablespoons chopped scallions

1. In a large pot over medium-high heat add the wine, onion, and garlic. Stir them every so often until they're lightly cooked, about 5 minutes. Add the peas and the bay leaves, thyme, and oregano. Pour in the water and bring to a boil. (If you want a thick soup, use 3 cups liquid and add more if needed when you purée the soup.) 2. Cover and turn down to simmer. The peas will take about an hour to cook, but if you leave them to cook longer they'll get even softer. 3. Add the carrot (if using), about 20 minutes before you finish cooking the soup. This will allow it to soften but not overcook. 4. Once the peas are soft, take the bay leaves out and purée the soup in the blender or with an immersion blender. Return to the pot. 5. Stir in the miso, pepper, and nutritional yeast (if using), and then add the sun-dried tomatoes. They can be soaked before you add them to the soup, or let them soften in the soup for a few minutes. 6. Serve topped with cherry tomatoes and some scallions.

Per Serving:(1 bowl)
calories: 151 | fat: 0g | protein: 10g | carbs: 27g | fiber: 10g

Quick Creamy Herbed Tomato Soup

Prep time: 5 minutes | Cook time: 15 minutes | Serves 4

2 teaspoons extra-virgin olive oil (optional)
4 garlic cloves, roughly chopped
2 (15-ounce / 425-g) cans crushed tomatoes
½ teaspoon maple syrup (optional)
2 cups plain unsweetened plant-based milk
1 teaspoon Italian seasoning
2 tablespoons roughly chopped fresh mint
½ teaspoon salt (optional)
Black pepper

1. In a medium saucepan, heat the oil over medium heat. Add the garlic and cook it until it is fragrant and beginning to turn golden, about 2 minutes. Remove from the heat and let cool. 2. In a blender or food processor, combine the tomatoes, maple syrup, plant-based milk, Italian seasoning, mint, salt (if using), and cooled garlic and blend until smooth. 3. Return the mixture to the saucepan and bring to a boil over high heat. Lower the heat to medium-low and simmer, stirring occasionally, for 5 minutes. Ladle into bowls, sprinkle with black pepper, and serve.
Per Serving:
calories: 126 | fat: 5g | protein: 6g | carbs: 17g | fiber: 5g

Creamy Tomato Soup

Prep time: 10 minutes | Cook time: 35 minutes | Serves 4

2 carrots, coarsely chopped
½ cup water, plus 1 tablespoon and more as needed
1 yellow onion, coarsely chopped
2 to 4 garlic cloves, coarsely chopped
1 (6-ounce / 170-g) can tomato paste
1 tablespoon Hungarian paprika
1 (28-ounce / 794-g) can diced tomatoes
1 (14-ounce / 397-g) can full-fat coconut milk
1 teaspoon dried thyme
No-sodium vegetable broth or water, for thinning (optional)

1. In an 8-quart pot over medium-high heat, combine the carrots and ½ cup of water. Cover the pot and cook for 10 minutes, or until the carrots can be easily pierced with a fork. Add more water, ¼ cup at a time, if the water evaporates while cooking. Drain and transfer the cooked carrots to a bowl. Set aside. 2. Place the same pot over medium-low heat and combine the onion and garlic. Sauté for 5 to 7 minutes, adding water, 1 tablespoon at a time, to prevent burning, until the onion is fully browned. 3. Turn the heat to medium-high. Add the tomato paste and paprika. Cook, stirring continuously, for 30 seconds to 1 minute. 4. Add the diced tomatoes, coconut milk, thyme, and cooked carrots. Bring the liquid to a simmer. Cover the pot and reduce the heat to medium-low. Cook for 10 minutes, stirring occasionally. 5. Using an immersion blender, blend the soup until smooth. Alternatively, transfer the soup to a standard blender, working in batches as needed, and blend until smooth. 6. Add vegetable broth or water to thin as needed.
Per Serving:
calories: 292 | fat: 19g | protein: 6g | carbs: 28g | fiber: 7g

Lentil Pepper Pot

Prep time: 15 minutes | Cook time: 35 minutes | Serves 4

⅔ cup dried green lentils
1 cup canned or fresh tomato cubes
1 red bell pepper
4 cups vegetable stock

¼ cup chopped fresh mint
Optional Toppings:
Tahini
Sun-dried tomatoes

1. Put a large pot over medium-high heat and add the vegetable stock along with the green lentils. 2. Bring the stock to a boil then turn the heat down to medium. 3. Cook the lentils for about 15 minutes, without cover the pot, remove any foam produced by the lentils and stir occasionally. 4. Add the chopped mint leaves, bring the heat down to a simmer, cover the pot with a lid and let it simmer for another 10 minutes. 5. Remove the stem, seeds and placenta of the bell pepper and dice the flesh. 6. Add the tomato cubes and bell pepper to the pot, stir well and let it simmer for another 10 minutes. 7. Turn the heat off and let the soup cool down for 5 minutes. 8. Divide between two bowls, serve with the optional toppings and enjoy! 9. Store the soup in an airtight container in the fridge, and consume within 2 days. Alternatively, store in the freezer for a maximum of 60 days and thaw at room temperature. The soup can be reheated in a pot or the microwave.

Per Serving:
calories: 127 | fat: 0g | protein: 9g | carbs: 24g | fiber: 6g

Chickpea Vegetable Soup

Prep time: 15 minutes | Cook time: 30 minutes | Serves 4

1 yellow onion, coarsely chopped
2 carrots, coarsely chopped
2 celery stalks, coarsely chopped
1 red bell pepper, coarsely chopped
3 garlic cloves, minced
1 tablespoon water, plus more as needed
2 teaspoons grated peeled fresh ginger
1 small cauliflower head, cut

into small florets
1 teaspoon ground turmeric
1 teaspoon Hungarian sweet paprika
6 cups no-sodium vegetable broth
2 cups chopped kale
1 (15-ounce /425-g) can chickpeas, rinsed and drained
Freshly ground black pepper, to taste
Chopped scallions, green parts only, for garnish

1. In a large pot over medium-high heat, combine the onion, carrots, celery, bell pepper, and garlic. Cook, stirring occasionally, for 5 minutes, or until the onion is translucent but not browned. Add water, 1 tablespoon at a time, if it seems like the onion and garlic are cooking too quickly. 2. Add the ginger and cook, stirring, for 30 seconds. 3. Stir in the cauliflower, turmeric, and paprika to coat the cauliflower evenly with the spices. 4. Pour in the vegetable broth and bring the liquid to a simmer. Reduce the heat to medium-low, cover the pot, and cook for 10 minutes. 5. Add the kale and chickpeas and cook for 5 minutes to soften the kale leaves. Season with pepper and garnish with scallions. 6. Refrigerate leftovers in an airtight container for up to 1 week or freeze for up to 1 month.

Per Serving:
calories: 173 | fat: 3g | protein: 8g | carbs: 32g | fiber: 9g

Spanish Chickpea Stew

Prep time: 30 minutes | Cook time: 40 minutes | Serves 4

1 medium onion, peeled and diced small
1 green bell pepper, seeded and diced small
2 cloves garlic, peeled and minced
1 teaspoon cumin seeds, toasted and ground
1 teaspoon sweet paprika
½ teaspoon smoked paprika
1 bay leaf
1 large tomato, diced small

3 medium Yukon Gold potatoes (about 1 pound / 454 g), cut into ½-inch dice
5 cups vegetable stock, or low-sodium vegetable broth
2 cups cooked chickpeas, or 1 (15-ounce / 425-g) can, drained and rinsed
1 medium bunch Swiss chard, ribs removed, chopped
Salt and freshly ground black pepper, to taste

1. Place the onion and pepper in a large pot and sauté over medium heat for 10 minutes. Add water 1 to 2 tablespoons at a time to keep the vegetables from sticking to the pot. 2. Add the garlic, cumin, both kinds of paprika, and bay leaf and cook for 1 minute. Stir in the tomato and cook for 3 minutes. Add the potatoes, vegetable stock, and chickpeas and bring the pot to a boil over high heat. 3. Reduce the heat to medium and cook, covered, for 20 minutes, or until the potatoes are tender. Add the Swiss chard, season with salt and pepper, and cook, covered, until the chard wilts, about 5 minutes.

Per Serving:
calories: 304 | fat: 2g | protein: 12g | carbs: 60g | fiber: 11g

Lotsa Vegetable Chowder

Prep time: 30 minutes | Cook time: 30 minutes | Serves 4 to 6

8 small Yukon Gold, white, or russet potatoes (about 2 pounds / 907 g), cut into ½-inch chunks
½ small onion, peeled and chopped
3 ears fresh corn, kernels removed (about 1¾ cups), cobs reserved
2 medium carrots, peeled and diced
2 celery stalks, chopped
¼ cup chopped red bell pepper

1 cup chopped broccoli and cauliflower stalks, outer fibrous parts removed and discarded (about ½ pound / 227 g)
1 clove garlic, peeled and minced
2 tablespoons chopped thyme
⅛ teaspoon white pepper
2 teaspoons ground cumin
3 tablespoons chopped dill
Salt, to taste (optional)

1. In a large pot, combine the potatoes, onion, corn kernels and cobs, carrots, celery, red pepper, broccoli and cauliflower, garlic, thyme, white pepper, cumin, and 6 cups of water. Bring to a boil over high heat. Reduce the heat to medium-low and simmer for 30 minutes, or until the vegetables are tender. 2. Remove the corn cobs and let cool. Remove 1 cup of the soup and purée in a blender with a tight-fitting lid, covered with a towel. (If you like a thicker soup, purée 2 cups.) Return the puréed soup to the pot and add the dill. Scrape corn cobs with back of a knife to remove the creamy corn "milk" left over from the kernels, and add it to the pot. Stir well and season with salt, if using.

Per Serving:
calories: 262 | fat: 0g | protein: 8g | carbs: 60g | fiber: 6g

Corn Chowder

Prep time: 25 minutes | Cook time: 40 minutes | Serves 6

2 medium yellow onions, peeled and diced small
2 red bell peppers, seeded and finely chopped
3 ears corn, kernels removed (about 2 cups)
3 cloves garlic, peeled and minced
2 large russet potatoes, peeled

and diced
1½ pounds (680 g) tomatoes (4 to 5 medium), diced
6 cups vegetable stock, or low-sodium vegetable broth
¾ cup finely chopped basil
Salt and freshly ground black pepper, to taste

1. Place the onions and peppers in a large saucepan and sauté over medium heat for 10 minutes. Add water 1 to 2 tablespoons at a time to keep the vegetables from sticking to the pan. Add the corn and garlic, and sauté for 5 more minutes. Add the potatoes, tomatoes, peppers, and vegetable stock. Bring the mixture to a boil over high heat. Reduce the heat to medium and cook, uncovered, for 25 minutes, or until the potatoes are tender. 2. Purée half of the soup in batches in a blender with a tight-fitting lid, covered with a towel. Return the puréed soup to the pot. Add the basil and season with salt and pepper.

Per Serving:
calories: 209 | fat: 0g | protein: 6g | carbs: 48g | fiber: 5g

Autumn Vegetable Stew with North African Spices

Prep time: 35 minutes | Cook time: 50 minutes | Serves 6 to 8

1 large onion, peeled and chopped
2 large carrots, peeled and chopped
2 celery stalks, cut into ½-inch slices
3 cloves garlic, peeled and minced
1 tablespoon grated ginger
1½ tablespoons sweet paprika
2 teaspoons ground cumin
1 tablespoon ground coriander
2 (1-inch) pieces cinnamon stick
8 cups vegetable stock, or low-sodium vegetable broth
1 medium butternut squash (about 1 pound / 454 g), peeled, halved, seeded, and cut

into ¾-inch pieces
1 turnip, peeled and cut into ½-inch pieces
1 russet potato, peeled and cut into ½-inch pieces
1 (15-ounce / 425-g) can crushed tomatoes
2 cups cooked chickpeas, or 1 (15-ounce / 425-g) can, drained and rinsed
2 large pinches saffron, soaked for 15 minutes in ¼ cup warm water
2 tablespoons finely chopped mint
Salt and freshly ground black pepper, to taste
½ cup finely chopped cilantro

1. Place the onion, carrots, and celery in a large pot and sauté for 10 minutes. Add water 1 to 2 tablespoons at a time to keep the vegetables from sticking to the pot. Add the garlic, ginger, paprika, cumin, coriander, and cinnamon sticks and cook for 3 minutes. 2. Add the vegetable stock, squash, turnip, potato, tomatoes, and chickpeas and bring to a boil over high heat. Reduce the heat to medium-low and cook, uncovered, for 25 minutes. Add the mint and the saffron with its soaking water and season the stew with salt and

pepper. Cook for 10 minutes more, or until the vegetables are tender.
3. Serve garnished with the cilantro.

Per Serving:
calories: 156 | fat: 1g | protein: 6g | carbs: 31g | fiber: 6g

Lemony Herbed Lentil Soup

Prep time: 10 minutes | Cook time: 35 minutes | Serves 2

1 cup dried brown or green lentils, rinsed
4 cups water
1 teaspoon extra-virgin olive oil (optional)
½ small yellow onion, chopped
2 garlic cloves, minced
1 celery stalk, minced
2 carrots, sliced
1 potato, peeled and diced

1 zucchini, diced
1 (15-ounce / 425-g) can crushed tomatoes
1 teaspoon Italian seasoning
½ teaspoon smoked paprika
2 cups baby spinach
Juice of 1 lemon
1 teaspoon salt, plus more as needed (optional)

1. In a large saucepan, combine the lentils and water and bring to a boil over high heat. Lower the heat to medium and cook until soft, about 25 minutes. 2. Meanwhile, in a large skillet, heat the olive oil over medium heat. Add the onion and garlic and cook until fragrant, about 5 minutes. Add the celery, carrots, and potato and cook for 5 minutes. Add the mixture to the cooked lentils and stir until combined. 3. Add the zucchini, tomatoes, Italian seasoning, and smoked paprika and bring to a boil over medium-high heat. Lower the heat to medium and simmer until the flavors meld, about 10 minutes. 4. Add the spinach, stir, and cook until wilted. Add the lemon juice and salt (if using) and stir until combined. Taste and add more salt if needed.

Per Serving:
calories: 546 | fat: 5g | protein: 31g | carbs: 102g | fiber: 21g

Potato-Leek Soup

Prep time: 15 minutes | Cook time: 3 to 4 hours | Serves 6 to 8

6 yellow potatoes (about 2 pounds / 907 g), unpeeled and cut into 1½-inch cubes
3 leeks, light green and white parts, sliced and rinsed
2 celery stalks, chopped
2 garlic cloves, crushed
½ cup raw cashews
6 cups store-bought low-

sodium vegetable broth
2 teaspoons chopped fresh thyme, or 1 teaspoon dried thyme
1 bay leaf
Ground black pepper
Salt (optional)
¼ to 1 cup unsweetened plant-based milk, for thinning

1. Put the potatoes, leeks, celery, garlic, cashews, broth, thyme, bay leaf, pepper, and salt (if using) in the slow cooker. Cover and cook on High for 3 to 4 hours or on Low for 7 to 8 hours. 2. After cooking, remove and discard the bay leaf. Using an immersion blender or a countertop blender, purée the soup until rich and creamy. If the soup is too thick, add the milk, ¼ cup at a time, until it reaches your preferred consistency.

Per Serving:
calories: 221 | fat: 5g | protein: 7g | carbs: 40g | fiber: 4g

Black-Eyed Pea and Collard Stew with Spicy Tahini

Prep time: 20 minutes | Cook time: 40 minutes | Serves 6

Stew:
2 tablespoons olive oil (optional)
1 large yellow onion, chopped
1 large green bell pepper, chopped
2 small carrots, chopped
1 large celery rib, chopped
1 teaspoon dried thyme
1 bay leaf
¼ teaspoon cayenne pepper or crushed red pepper
3 garlic cloves, minced
1 (14½-ounce / 411-g) can fire-roasted tomatoes with juice
1 cup pearled barley, soaked
1 teaspoon reduced-sodium tamari
2 cups water

1 cup vegetable broth
1 bunch collard greens, stemmed and chopped
2 cups cooked black-eyed peas
1 tablespoon fresh lemon juice
Salt and black pepper (optional)

Spicy Tahini:
2 tablespoons nutritional yeast
1 to 2 tablespoons Sriracha sauce
1 teaspoon fresh lemon juice
1 teaspoon maple syrup (optional)
¼ teaspoon liquid smoke
¼ cup tahini
¼ to ½ cup water
Sliced scallions

1. To make the stew, heat the oil (if desired) in a Dutch oven over medium- high heat. Add the onion, bell pepper, carrots, and celery and stir to thoroughly coat. Cook for 2 minutes, reduce the heat to medium, and cover. Gently cook the vegetables for 5 minutes, stirring every minute or so. 2. Add the thyme, bay leaf, and cayenne, then the garlic. Stir and cook for 2 minutes. 3. Add the tomatoes with their juice, barley, and tamari. Cook, stirring often, until the moisture has evaporated, about 3 minutes. 4. Add the water, broth, and collards. Increase the heat to high, bring to a boil, then reduce the heat to medium-low. Cover and cook for 15 minutes. 5. Stir in the black-eyed peas. Remove from the heat and let sit for 15 minutes. Discard the bay leaf. Stir in the lemon juice and season with salt (if desired) and pepper to taste. 6. While the stew is resting, make the sauce. Combine the nutritional yeast, Sriracha, lemon juice, maple syrup (if desired), liquid smoke, and tahini in a jar with a tight-fitting lid. Add the water, 1 tablespoon at a time, shaking to mix, until the sauce is pourable but will stick to a spoon. Refrigerate until ready to serve. 7. Top the stew with the sauce and scallions and serve.
Per Serving:
calories: 354 | fat: 11g | protein: 14g | carbs: 54g | fiber: 15g

Wild Rice Mushroom Soup

Prep time: 15 minutes | Cook time: 45 minutes | Serves 4

4 cups no-sodium vegetable broth
½ cup walnuts
9 ounces (255 g) baby portabella mushrooms, coarsely chopped
4 ounces (113 g) shiitake mushrooms, coarsely chopped
1 tablespoon balsamic vinegar, plus more for drizzling

4 garlic cloves, minced
½ celery stalk, minced
3 thyme sprigs, divided
3 tablespoons whole wheat flour
4 cups unsweetened nondairy milk
½ cup wild rice
½ cup brown rice
1 rosemary sprig

Freshly ground black pepper, to taste

1. In a high-speed blender, combine the vegetable broth and walnuts. Let sit for 1 hour to soften the walnuts. You can also soak the walnuts overnight in an airtight glass container. 2. In an 8-quart pot over medium-high heat, combine the portabella and shiitake mushrooms. Cook for 5 minutes to expel most of the liquid from the mushrooms. Pour on the vinegar and cook for 1 minute more. Turn off the heat. Transfer the mushrooms to a non-plastic bowl. 3. Transfer ¼ cup of the mushroom mixture to the blender with the vegetable broth and walnuts. Blend until the mushrooms and walnuts are fully incorporated. Set aside. 4. Place the empty pot over medium-high heat and combine the garlic, celery, and 1 thyme sprig. Sauté for 1 minute. 5. Add the mushrooms back to the pot. Add the flour and stir to coat the mushrooms. 6. Pour in the blended stock and add the milk, wild and brown rice, rosemary sprig, and remaining 2 thyme sprigs. Bring the mixture to a simmer, turn the heat to medium-low, cover the pot, and cook for 25 to 30 minutes, or until the rice is tender but chewy. 7. Season with pepper and a drizzle of vinegar.
Per Serving:
calories: 337 | fat: 12g | protein: 12g | carbs: 51g | fiber: 6g

Lentil Rice Soup

Prep time: 10 minutes | Cook time: 30 minutes | Serves 4

⅓ cup dry quick-cooking brown rice
⅔ cup dried green lentils
1 cup canned or fresh tomato cubes
3 cups vegetable stock

¼ cup tahini
Optional Toppings:
Fresh chili slices
Fresh cilantro
Green peppercorns

1. Put a large pot over medium-high heat and add the vegetable stock along with the green lentils. 2. Bring the stock to a boil and turn the heat down to medium. 3. Cook the lentils for about 15 minutes, without covering the pot. From time to time, remove any foam produced by the lentils and give the pot a stir. 4. Add the brown rice and bring the heat down to a simmer, then cover the pot with a lid and let it simmer for another 10 minutes. 5. Add the tomato cubes and tahini, stir well and let it simmer for another 5 minutes. 6. Turn the heat off and let the soup cool down for 5 minutes. 7. Divide between two bowls, serve with the optional toppings and enjoy! 8. Store the soup in an airtight container in the fridge, and consume within 2 days. Alternatively, store in the freezer for a maximum of 60 days and thaw at room temperature. The soup can be reheated in a pot or the microwave.
Per Serving:
calories: 284 | fat: 10g | protein: 15g | carbs: 33g | fiber: 12g

Kale White Bean Soup

Prep time: 20 minutes | Cook time: 2 hours | Serves 6

1 pound (454 g) navy beans
1 tablespoon coconut oil (optional)
½ cup coarsely chopped onions
1 clove garlic, minced
¼ cup nutritional yeast
1 diced red bell pepper

4 chopped Roma tomatoes
2 cups sliced carrots
5 cups vegetable broth
1 teaspoon Italian seasoning
2 teaspoons salt (optional)
½ teaspoon ground black pepper

1 pound (454 g) kale, de-   stemmed and coarsely chopped

1. Place the beans in a large stockpot and cover with water by about 3 inches. Let it sit overnight to let the beans expand. If you want to do the quick method for preparing the beans—instead of soaking overnight—then cover beans with water by 2 inches in the stockpot. Cover with a lid and bring to a boil. Remove from the heat and let stand, uncovered, 1 hour. Drain beans in a colander and set aside. 2. Put the oil (if desired) in the same stockpot and heat over medium heat. Add the onions and sauté for about 10 to 15 minutes until soft and translucent. Add the garlic and cook, stirring, for 1 minute. Add 4 cups water, the beans, nutritional yeast, bell pepper, tomatoes, carrots, broth, Italian seasoning, salt (if desired), and pepper. Cover and bring to a boil. Uncover and turn down to a simmer. Cook until beans are tender, about 1 to 1½ hours. 3. Stir in kale and 2 cups water and simmer, uncovered, until kale is tender, about 12 to 15 minutes.

Per Serving:
calories: 131 | fat: 4g | protein: 14g | carbs: 20g | fiber: 7g

Carrot Ginger Soup

Prep time: 15 minutes | Cook time: 25 minutes | Serves 6

3 tablespoons water	3 cups chopped carrots
1 cup diced red, white, or yellow onion	2 cups chopped russet potatoes
1 teaspoon minced garlic	4 cups vegetable broth
2 tablespoons minced ginger	Salt and pepper, to taste (optional)

1. In a large pot, heat the water over medium-high heat. 2. Add the onion, garlic, and ginger and sauté for 2 to 3 minutes or until the onion becomes translucent and tender. 3. Add the carrots, potatoes, and broth, and cook for 20 minutes or until the carrots and potatoes are tender. 4. Remove from the heat. Purée the soup using an immersion blender (or with a regular blender, working in batches). Add salt and pepper.

Per Serving:
calories: 80 | fat: 0g | protein: 2g | carbs: 18g | fiber: 3g

Masoor Dal Stew

Prep time: 10 minutes | Cook time: 30 minutes | Serves 8

2 cups dried red lentils (masoor dal)	1 large yellow onion, finely diced
1 tablespoon yellow curry powder	6 garlic cloves, minced
1 teaspoon whole mustard seeds	1 tablespoon minced peeled fresh ginger
1 teaspoon ground coriander	1 celery stalk, finely chopped
1 teaspoon ground cumin	2 green chiles, minced (and seeded if you want less heat)
8 cups water, plus 3 tablespoons and more as needed	1 (15-ounce /425-g) can diced tomatoes
	Fresh cilantro, for garnish

1. Place the lentils in a fine-mesh sieve. Sift through them to look for stones or other debris. Rinse under cold water for a few minutes. 2. In a small dish, combine the curry powder, mustard seeds, coriander, and cumin. Set aside. 3. In an 8-quart pot over high heat, combine the lentils and 8 cups of water. Bring to a boil. Turn the heat to medium-

low, partially cover the pot, and cook for 20 minutes. The lentils should be very tender. 4. While the lentils cook, make the tadka or tempered spices. In a skillet over medium heat, combine the onion, garlic, ginger, celery, and green chiles. Cook for 5 minutes, adding water, 1 tablespoon of at a time, to prevent burning. The onion should be deeply browned and soft. 5. Spread the mixture out in the pan so that there is a small well or opening in the center. Pour the spices into the well and add 2 tablespoons of water. Cook for 1 minute, stirring continuously, slowly mixing the spices into the cooked vegetables. 6. Carefully add the tomatoes and stir to combine. Cook over medium-low heat for 7 minutes, stirring frequently. 7. Add the tadka to the cooked lentils, stir well, and cook for 5 minutes over medium heat. Serve immediately, garnished with cilantro, or refrigerate and serve the following day. Dal gets more flavorful with a day or two of resting in the refrigerator.

Per Serving:
calories: 206 | fat: 1g | protein: 13g | carbs: 37g | fiber: 7g

Bloody Caesar Gazpacho

Prep time: 20 minutes | Cook time: 0 minutes | Serves 6

6 cups chopped ripe tomatoes	(optional)
1 small red onion, chopped	Vegan gluten-free worcestershire sauce or gluten-free tamari soy sauce, to taste
1 English cucumber, chopped	
2 stalks celery, chopped	
2 cloves garlic, chopped	Hot sauce, to taste
Fresh chili pepper, chopped, to taste (optional)	Freshly ground black pepper, to taste
2 teaspoons celery salt (optional)	Garnishes:
	Thinly sliced celery
⅓ cup raw almonds, soaked for at least 6 hours	Thinly sliced red onion
	Lime wedges
2 tablespoons red wine vinegar	Pitted green olives
⅓ cup virgin olive oil	Additional hot sauce

1. In a large bowl, toss together the chopped tomatoes, red onions, cucumber, celery, garlic, chili, if using, and celery salt, if using. Cover the bowl with plastic wrap, and let it sit at room temperature for 1 hour. 2. Uncover the vegetables and transfer them to the bowl of a food processor. Pour all the marinating liquid from the bowl into the food processor as well. Drain the almonds and add them to the food processor. Run the motor on high until the vegetables and almonds are puréed. Reduce the speed to low, and drizzle in the red wine vinegar and olive oil, if using. Stop the machine when you have a smooth mixture. 3. Run the gazpacho through a fine strainer into a large bowl. Season with vegan Worcestershire sauce, hot sauce, and black pepper. 4. Store the gazpacho, covered, in the refrigerator until ready to serve with the garnishes. The gazpacho will keep in the refrigerator for up to 5 days.

Per Serving:
calories: 140 | fat: 10g | protein: 4g | carbs: 12g | fiber: 4g

Basic Dal

Prep time: 10 minutes | Cook time: 1 hour | Serves 6

1 tablespoon full-fat coconut milk solids, plus more for serving	4 garlic cloves, minced
	1 jalapeño, minced, seeds and ribs removed for less heat
1 tablespoon minced or grated fresh ginger	½ teaspoon ground cumin
	½ teaspoon ground turmeric

1 cup yellow split peas or brown lentils, soaked overnight and drained
½ cup brown basmati rice
4 cups vegetable broth or
water, plus extra as needed
Salt and pepper (optional)
Fresh lime juice
Chopped cilantro

1. Place a large stockpot over medium heat. Melt the milk solids and add the ginger, garlic, jalapeño, cumin, and turmeric. Cook until the spices are fragrant, about 2 minutes. 2. Add the split peas and rice. Stir to combine, then add the broth. Increase the heat to medium-high, bring to a boil, then reduce the heat to low. Cook with the lid slightly ajar until the lentils and rice are tender, about 1 hour. (Add additional broth if you prefer a soup-like consistency.) 3. Season with salt (if desired) and pepper, drizzle with lime juice, sprinkle with cilantro, and serve. (The dal can be refrigerated for up to 5 days.)
Per Serving:
calories: 120 | fat: 1g | protein: 4g | carbs: 23g | fiber: 4g

Pumpkin and Anasazi Bean Stew

Prep time: 30 minutes | Cook time: 35 minutes | Serves 6 to 8

1 large yellow onion, peeled and diced
2 large carrots, peeled and diced
2 celery stalks, diced
2 cloves garlic, peeled and minced
2 tablespoons cumin seeds, toasted and ground
2 tablespoons tomato paste
1 small pumpkin (about 1
pound / 454 g), peeled, seeded, and cut into 1-inch cubes
4 cups cooked anasazi beans, or 2 (15-ounce / 425-g) cans, drained and rinsed
6 cups vegetable stock, or low-sodium vegetable broth
Salt and freshly ground black pepper, to taste
6 green onions (white and green parts), thinly sliced

1. Place the onion, carrots, and celery in a large saucepan and sauté over medium heat for 10 minutes. Add water 1 to 2 tablespoons at a time to keep the vegetables from sticking to the pan. 2. Add the garlic and cook for another minute. Add the cumin, tomato paste, pumpkin, beans, and vegetable stock and bring to a boil over high heat. Reduce the heat to medium and cook, covered, for 25 minutes, or until the pumpkin is tender. 3. Season with salt and pepper and serve garnished with the green onions.
Per Serving:
calories: 70 | fat: 0g | protein: 2g | carbs: 15g | fiber: 3g

White Bean Gazpacho

Prep time: 20 minutes | Cook time: 0 minutes | Serves 4

6 large ripe tomatoes (about 4 pounds / 1.8 kg)
2 large cucumbers, peeled, halved, seeded, and diced
1 large red bell pepper, seeded and diced small
1 medium Vidalia onion, peeled and diced small
¼ cup red wine vinegar
Zest of 1 lemon
½ cup chopped basil
Salt and freshly ground black pepper, to taste
2 cups cooked cannellini beans, or 1 (15-ounce / 425-g) can, drained and rinsed

1. Coarsely chop 2 of the tomatoes and purée them in a blender. Transfer to a large bowl. Chop the remaining 4 tomatoes and add

them to the bowl. Add the cucumbers, red pepper, onion, red wine vinegar, lemon zest, basil, salt and pepper, and beans and mix well. Chill for 1 hour before serving.
Per Serving:
calories: 100 | fat: 1g | protein: 4g | carbs: 20g | fiber: 6g

Spinach Vichyssoise

Prep time: 20 minutes | Cook time: 30 minutes | Serves 6 to 8

2 large leeks (white and light green parts), rinsed and diced
1 tablespoon chopped dill, or to taste
1 bay leaf
5 cups vegetable stock, or low-sodium vegetable broth
1½ pounds (680 g) russet potatoes (4 to 5 medium),
peeled and diced
½ pound (227 g) spinach, chopped
Zest of 1 lemon
Salt and freshly ground black pepper, to taste
1 cup unsweetened plain almond milk

1. Place the leeks in a large pot and sauté over medium heat until tender, about 5 minutes. Add water 1 to 2 tablespoons at a time to keep the leeks from sticking to the pot. Add the dill and bay leaf and cook for another minute. Add the vegetable stock and potatoes and bring to a boil. Cook for 15 to 20 minutes, or until the potatoes are tender. 2. Add the spinach and lemon zest and season with salt and pepper. Cook for another 5 minutes, or until the spinach is wilted. Purée the soup using an immersion blender or in batches in a blender with a tight-fitting lid, covered with a towel. Return the soup to a pot and add the almond milk. Let cool completely, then chill until ready to serve.
Per Serving:
calories: 109 | fat: 0g | protein: 4g | carbs: 23g | fiber: 2g

Miso Noodle Soup with Shiitake Mushrooms

Prep time: 5 minutes | Cook time: 25 minutes | Serves 4 to 6

1 (8-ounce / 227-g) package brown rice noodles
4 cups vegetable broth
2 cups water
1 (5-ounce / 142-g) package shiitake mushrooms, cut into ¼-inch-thick slices
3 scallions, green and white
parts, thinly sliced on a bias (about ½ cup)
3 garlic cloves, sliced
3 or 4 (¼-inch) slices unpeeled fresh ginger
8 ounces (227 g) bok choy
2 tablespoons red miso paste
1 tablespoon soy sauce

1. Cook the noodles for about 5 minutes. 2. Meanwhile, in a large Dutch oven or saucepan, combine the broth, water, mushrooms, scallions, garlic, and ginger. Cover, and bring to a boil over high heat. 3. Reduce the heat to low. Cover, and simmer for 15 minutes. 4. Uncover, and increase the heat to medium. Add the bok choy, and simmer for 3 minutes, or until the bok choy is crisp-tender. 5. Add the noodles, and heat through. Remove from the heat. 6. Add the miso and soy sauce. Stir until the miso has dissolved. 7. Remove the ginger, and serve.
Per Serving:
calories: 396 | fat: 3g | protein: 13g | carbs: 80g | fiber: 8g

Sweet Potato Bisque

Prep time: 20 minutes | Cook time: 40 minutes | Serves 6

1 large onion, peeled and diced
2 cloves garlic, peeled and minced
1 tablespoon grated ginger
1 tablespoon thyme
½ teaspoon ground nutmeg
1 teaspoon ground cinnamon
3 large sweet potatoes, peeled
and diced
6 cups vegetable stock, or low-sodium vegetable broth
Zest and juice of 1 orange
1½ cups unsweetened plain almond milk
Salt and freshly ground black pepper, to taste

1. Place the onion in a large saucepan and sauté over medium heat for 10 minutes. Add water 1 to 2 tablespoons at a time to keep the onion from sticking to the pan. Add the garlic, ginger, thyme, nutmeg, and cinnamon and cook for 1 minute. Add the sweet potatoes, vegetable stock, and orange zest and juice and bring the pot to a boil over high heat. Reduce the heat to medium and cook, covered, for 25 minutes, or until the sweet potatoes are tender. 2. Purée the soup using an immersion blender or in batches in a blender with a tight-fitting lid, covered with a towel. Return the soup to the pot and add the almond milk. Cook for an additional 5 minutes, or until heated through, and season with salt and pepper.
Per Serving:
calories: 110 | fat: 0g | protein: 3g | carbs: 24g | fiber: 3g

Bean and Mushroom Chili

Prep time: 20 minutes | Cook time: 38 minutes | Serves 6

1 large onion, peeled and chopped
1 pound (454 g) button mushrooms, chopped
6 cloves garlic, peeled and minced
1 tablespoon ground cumin
1 tablespoon ancho chile powder
4 teaspoons ground fennel
½ teaspoon cayenne pepper, or to taste
1 tablespoon unsweetened cocoa powder
1 (28-ounce / 794-g) can diced tomatoes
4 cups cooked pinto beans, or 2 (15-ounce / 425-g) cans, drained and rinsed
Salt, to taste (optional)

1. Place the onion and mushrooms in a large saucepan and sauté over medium heat for 10 minutes. Add water 1 to 2 tablespoons at a time to keep the vegetables from sticking to the pan. 2. Add the garlic, cumin, chile powder, fennel, cayenne pepper, and cocoa powder and cook for 3 minutes. Add the tomatoes, beans, and 2 cups of water and simmer, covered, for 25 minutes. Season with salt, if using.
Per Serving:
calories: 229 | fat: 1g | protein: 14g | carbs: 42g | fiber: 15g

Broccoli Potato Soup

Prep time: 15 minutes | Cook time: 20 minutes | Serves 8

3 tablespoons water
1 cup diced red, white, or yellow onion
1 teaspoon minced garlic
5 cups vegetable broth
6 cups chopped russet or red potatoes
1 (10-ounce / 283-g) bag frozen
broccoli
Juice of 1 small lemon
Pinch of pepper

1. In a medium pan over medium-low heat, heat the water. Add the onion and garlic and sauté for 5 minutes or until the onion becomes tender and translucent. 2. Add the broth, potatoes, broccoli, lemon juice, and pepper. 3. Bring to a boil. 4. Boil until the potatoes are cooked all the way through, 10 to 15 minutes. 5. Remove from the heat. Purée half of the soup using an immersion blender (or with a regular blender, working in batches). Return the puréed soup to the pot and combine with the remaining soup.
Per Serving:
calories: 116 | fat: 0g | protein: 4g | carbs: 26g | fiber: 3g

Hearty Potato, Tomato, and Green Beans Stufato

Prep time: 10 minutes | Cook time: 3 to 4 hours | Serves 4 to 6

1 large onion, chopped
4 garlic cloves, minced
3 red or yellow potatoes (about 1 pound / 454 g), unpeeled and cut into 1- to 2-inch chunks
1 pound (454 g) fresh or frozen green beans, cut into bite-size pieces
1 (28-ounce / 794-g) can no-salt-added crushed tomatoes
2 teaspoons dried oregano
2 teaspoons dried basil
1 teaspoon dried rosemary
½ teaspoon red pepper flakes (optional)
Ground black pepper
Salt (optional)
Chopped fresh parsley, for garnish (optional)

1. Put the onion, garlic, potatoes, green beans, tomatoes, oregano, basil, rosemary, red pepper flakes (if using), pepper, and salt (if using) in the slow cooker. 2. Cover and cook on High for 3 to 4 hours or on Low for 6 to 7 hours, until the potatoes are fork tender. Serve garnished with parsley (if using).
Per Serving:
calories: 197 | fat: 1g | protein: 8g | carbs: 40g | fiber: 9g

Cream of Broccoli Soup

Prep time: 10 minutes | Cook time: 20 minutes | Serves 6

3 large leeks (white parts only), sliced and rinsed
1 teaspoon thyme leaves
4 cups broccoli florets (from about 2 large heads)
4½ cups vegetable stock, or
low-sodium vegetable broth, plus more as needed
3 tablespoons nutritional yeast (optional)
Salt and freshly ground black pepper, to taste

1. Place the leeks in a large saucepan and sauté over medium heat for 10 minutes. Add water 1 to 2 tablespoons at a time to keep the leeks from sticking to the pan. Add the thyme and cook for another minute, then add the broccoli, vegetable stock, and nutritional yeast (if using). Bring to a boil over high heat, reduce the heat to medium, and cook, covered, until the broccoli is tender, about 10 minutes. 2. Purée the soup using an immersion blender or in batches in a blender with a tight-fitting lid, covered with a towel. Return the soup to the pot and season with salt and pepper.
Per Serving:
calories: 61 | fat: 0g | protein: 3g | carbs: 11g | fiber: 3g

Roasted Eggplant and Lentil Stew

Prep time: 20 minutes | Cook time: 1 hour 10 minutes | Serves 8

1 large eggplant
4 carrots, coarsely chopped
4 cups no-sodium vegetable broth
1 cup dried brown or green lentils
1 large yellow onion, diced
1 bunch chopped scallions, white and green parts, divided
3 garlic cloves, diced
1 tablespoon water, plus more as needed
1 (14-ounce / 397-g) can full-

fat coconut milk
1 tablespoon red miso paste
1 tablespoon low-sodium soy sauce
1 (28-ounce / 794-g) can diced tomatoes
4 teaspoons ground cumin
1 teaspoon adobo chili powder or smoked paprika
1 celery stalk, coarsely chopped
Fresh cilantro leaves, for serving

1. Preheat the oven to 350ºF (180ºC). 2. Halve the eggplant lengthwise and place it on a baking sheet, flesh-side up. Spread the carrots around the eggplant on the same baking sheet. 3. Roast for 30 minutes, or until the eggplant and carrots are lightly browned or caramel colored and the carrots are fork-tender. 4. Set the carrots aside. Let the eggplant cool before handling it. Scoop out as much flesh as possible without scooping into the skin and set aside in a bowl. 5. In an 8-quart pot over high heat, bring the vegetable broth to a boil. Lower the heat to maintain a simmer and add the lentils. Cover the pot and cook for 20 to 30 minutes, or until the lentils are soft yet retain their shape. 6. While the lentils cook, in a small sauté pan or skillet over medium heat, cook the onion, white parts of the scallion, and garlic for 7 to 10 minutes, adding water, 1 tablespoon at a time, to prevent burning, until darkly browned. 7. In a blender, combine the roasted eggplant and onion mixture with the coconut milk, miso paste, and soy sauce. Purée for 2 to 3 minutes until smooth. 8. Once the lentils are finished cooking, add the tomatoes, cumin, chili powder, and celery. Bring the mixture to a simmer. Pour in the eggplant sauce and add the roasted carrots. Cook until warmed to your liking. 9. This stew is best served with a few fresh cilantro leaves and scallion greens on top.

Per Serving:
calories: 259 | fat: 10g | protein: 10g | carbs: 35g | fiber: 9g

Summer Vegetable Minestrone

Prep time: 10 minutes | Cook time: 25 minutes | Serves 4 to 6

2 celery stalks, thinly sliced (about 1 cup)
1 shallot, thinly sliced (about 1 cup)
3 garlic cloves, sliced or minced
¼ cup water
3 cups vegetable broth
2 small zucchini, halved and cut into ¼-inch-thick slices (about 2 cups)
2 small yellow squash, halved

and cut into ¼-inch-thick slices (about 2 cups)
1 (28-ounce / 794-g) can crushed tomatoes with basil
1 (15-ounce / 425-g) can great northern beans
4 ounces (113 g) whole-grain rotini pasta (about 2 cups)
1 cup loosely packed fresh basil, chopped

1. In a Dutch oven or saucepan, combine the celery, shallot, garlic, and water. Sauté over medium heat for about 5 minutes, or until soft.

2. Add the broth, zucchini, squash, tomatoes, and beans with their liquid. Cover, and bring to a boil over high heat. 3. Reduce the heat to a medium-low. Simmer for about 5 minutes. 4. Stir in the pasta, cover, and simmer, stirring occasionally, for about 10 minutes, or until the pasta is tender. Remove from the heat. 5. Stir in the basil, and serve.

Per Serving:
calories: 265 | fat: 1g | protein: 13g | carbs: 55g | fiber: 10g

Comforting Tomato Soup

Prep time: 15 minutes | Cook time: 3 to 4 hours | Serves 6 to 8

1 medium onion, chopped
1 medium red bell pepper, chopped
4 garlic cloves, coarsely chopped
2 (28-ounce / 794-g) cans no-salt-added diced tomatoes
½ cup drained and rinsed canned white beans

2 cups store-bought low-sodium vegetable broth
2 teaspoons dried basil
1 teaspoon ground turmeric
Ground black pepper
Salt (optional)
5 to 6 fresh basil leaves, for garnish (optional)

1. In a medium skillet over medium-low heat, dry sauté the onion and bell pepper for about 5 minutes, or until the onion is translucent. 2. Transfer the onion and bell pepper to the slow cooker. Add the garlic, tomatoes, beans, broth, dried basil, turmeric, black pepper, and salt (if using). Cover and cook on High for 3 to 4 hours or on Low for 6 to 8 hours. 3. Using an immersion blender or a countertop blender, purée the soup until creamy. Some small foamy bubbles may form on the surface from blending. Use a slower blending speed, allow the bubbles to dissipate for a few minutes before serving, or simply serve it as is. Divide among bowls, top with the fresh basil (if using), and serve.

Per Serving:
calories: 113 | fat: 0g | protein: 4g | carbs: 23g | fiber: 7g

Sweet Potato, Red Beans, and Lentil Stew

Prep time: 15 minutes | Cook time: 3 to 4 hours | Serves 5 to 7

¼ cup chickpea flour
4 medium sweet potatoes (about 1½ pounds / 680 g), peeled and cut into 1½-inch cubes
1 medium onion, diced
1 garlic clove, minced
1 (14½-ounce / 411-g) can red kidney beans, drained and rinsed

1 cup dried brown or green lentils, rinsed and sorted
4½ cups store-bought low-sodium vegetable broth
1 cup orange juice (from 2 to 3 oranges)
1 teaspoon dried oregano
½ teaspoon celery seed
Ground black pepper
Salt (optional)

1. Place the chickpea flour and sweet potatoes in a gallon-size resealable bag and shake well to coat. 2. Transfer the floured potatoes to the slow cooker. Add the onion, garlic, beans, lentils, broth, orange juice, oregano, celery seed, and pepper. Season with salt (if using). 3. Cover and cook on High for 3 to 4 hours or on Low for 7 to 8 hours.

Per Serving:
calories: 396 | fat: 2g | protein: 18g | carbs: 78g | fiber: 24g

Prep time: 20 minutes | Cook time: 35 minutes | Serves 4

2 cups cooked or canned pinto beans
1 (7-ounce / 198-g) pack tempeh
2 cups canned or fresh tomato cubes
2 cups cooked or canned sweet corn
6 tablespoons Mexican chili spices

3 cups water
Optional Toppings:
Jalapeño slices
Fresh cilantro
Lime juice

1. When using dry beans, soak and cook ⅔ cup of dry pinto beans. 2. Cut the tempeh into small cubes, put them into an airtight container and add 2 tablespoons of the Mexican chili spices. 3. Close the airtight container, shake well and put it in the fridge, allowing the tempeh to marinate for at least 1 hour, and up to 12 hours. 4. Put a large pot over medium-high heat and add the water, tempeh cubes and the pinto beans. 5. Bring the stock to a boil, and let it cook for about 15 minutes. 6. Turn the heat down to a simmer and add the tomato cubes, corn and the remaining Mexican spices to the pot. 7. Make sure to stir well, then let it simmer for another 20 minutes. 8. Turn the heat off and let the soup cool down for 5 minutes. 9. Divide between two bowls, serve with the optional toppings and enjoy! 10. Store the soup in an airtight container in the fridge, and consume within 2 days. Alternatively, store in the freezer for a maximum of 60 days and thaw at room temperature. The soup can be reheated in a pot or the microwave.

Per Serving:
calories: 298 | fat: 4g | protein: 21g | carbs: 44g | fiber: 15g

Appendix 1: Measurement Conversion Chart

The Dirty Dozen and Clean Fifteen

The Environmental Working Group (EWG) is a nonprofit, nonpartisan organization dedicated to protecting human health and the environment Its mission is to empower people to live healthier lives in a healthier environment. This organization publishes an annual list of the twelve kinds of produce, in sequence, that have the highest amount of pesticide residue-the Dirty Dozen-as well as a list of the fifteen kinds ofproduce that have the least amount of pesticide residue-the Clean Fifteen.

THE DIRTY DOZEN

- The 2016 Dirty Dozen includes the following produce. These are considered among the year's most important produce to buy organic:

Strawberries	Spinach
Apples	Tomatoes
Nectarines	Bell peppers
Peaches	Cherry tomatoes
Celery	Cucumbers
Grapes	Kale/collard greens
Cherries	Hot peppers

- *The Dirty Dozen list contains two additional itemskale/collard greens and hot peppers-because they tend to contain trace levels of highly hazardous pesticides.*

THE CLEAN FIFTEEN

- The least critical to buy organically are the Clean Fifteen list. The following are on the 2016 list:

Avocados	Papayas
Corn	Kiw
Pineapples	Eggplant
Cabbage	Honeydew
Sweet peas	Grapefruit
Onions	Cantaloupe
Asparagus	Cauliflower
Mangos	

- *Some of the sweet corn sold in the United States are made from genetically engineered (GE) seedstock. Buy organic varieties of these crops to avoid GE produce.*

Appendix 2: The Dirty Dozen and Clean Fifteen

MEASUREMENT CONVERSION CHART

VOLUME EQUIVALENTS(DRY)

US STANDARD	METRIC (APPROXIMATE)
1/8 teaspoon	0.5 mL
1/4 teaspoon	1 mL
1/2 teaspoon	2 mL
3/4 teaspoon	4 mL
1 teaspoon	5 mL
1 tablespoon	15 mL
1/4 cup	59 mL
1/2 cup	118 mL
3/4 cup	177 mL
1 cup	235 mL
2 cups	475 mL
3 cups	700 mL
4 cups	1 L

VOLUME EQUIVALENTS(LIQUID)

US STANDARD	US STANDARD (OUNCES)	METRIC (APPROXIMATE)
2 tablespoons	1 fl.oz.	30 mL
1/4 cup	2 fl.oz.	60 mL
1/2 cup	4 fl.oz.	120 mL
1 cup	8 fl.oz.	240 mL
1 1/2 cup	12 fl.oz.	355 mL
2 cups or 1 pint	16 fl.oz.	475 mL
4 cups or 1 quart	32 fl.oz.	1 L
1 gallon	128 fl.oz.	4 L

TEMPERATURES EQUIVALENTS

FAHRENHEIT(F)	CELSIUS(C) (APPROXIMATE)
225 °F	107 °C
250 °F	120 °C
275 °F	135 °C
300 °F	150 °C
325 °F	160 °C
350 °F	180 °C
375 °F	190 °C
400 °F	205 °C
425 °F	220 °C
450 °F	235 °C
475 °F	245 °C
500 °F	260 °C

WEIGHT EQUIVALENTS

US STANDARD	METRIC (APPROXIMATE)
1 ounce	28 g
2 ounces	57 g
5 ounces	142 g
10 ounces	284 g
15 ounces	425 g
16 ounces (1 pound)	455 g
1.5 pounds	680 g
2 pounds	907 g

Appendix 3: Recipe Index

Printed in Great Britain
by Amazon

23933156R00057